DECIDING TO SEE

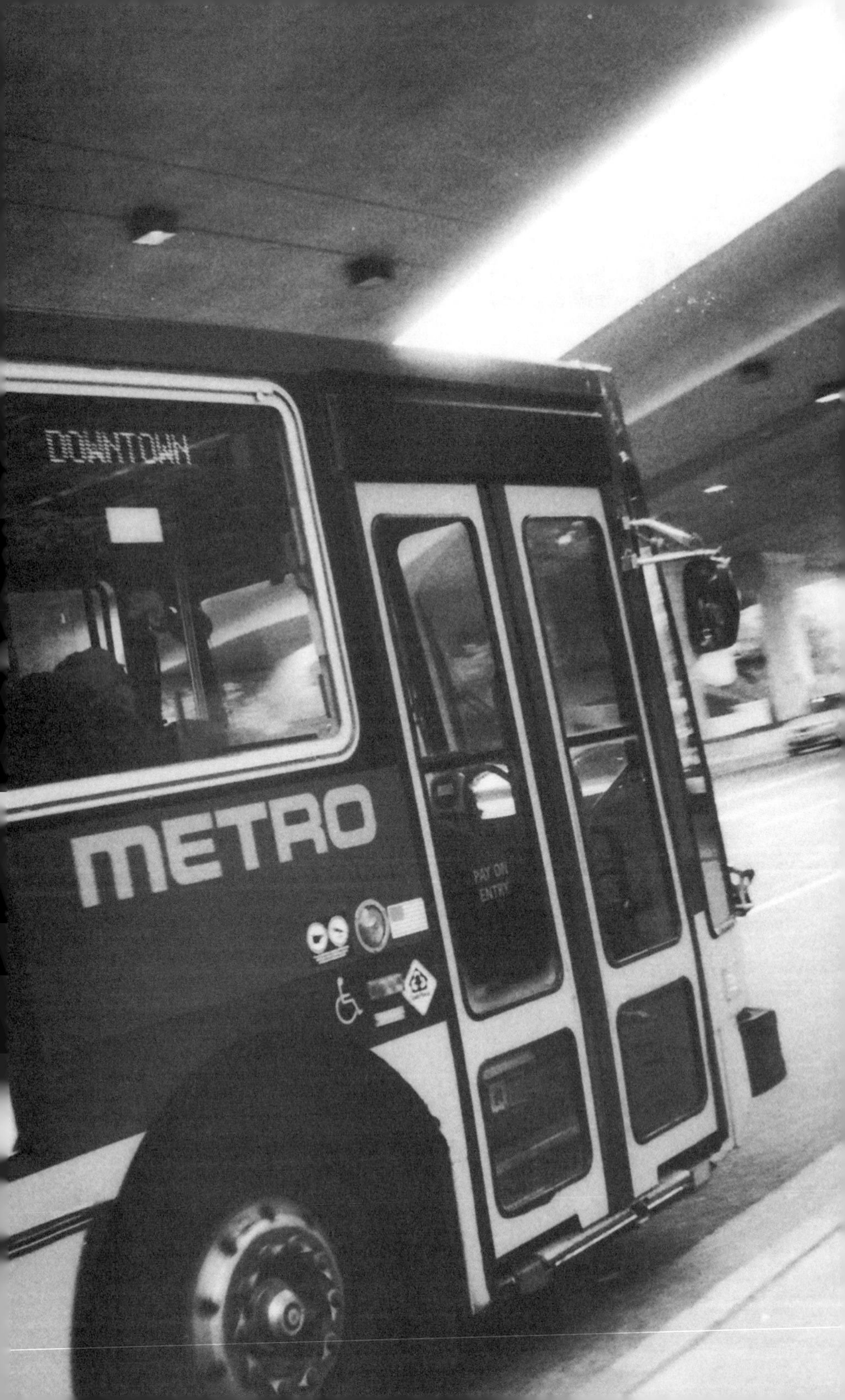

DOWNTOWN
METRO
PAY ON ENTRY

DECIDING TO SEE

The View from Nathan's Bus

Stories and photos by
Nathan Vass

Chin Music Press
Seattle, Washington

Library of Congress Control Number: 2024947128
ISBN 978-1-63405-077-7

Chin Music Press
Seattle, Washington
www.chinmusicpress.com

Design by Thomas Eykemans
Typeset in Georgia and Helvetica
Proofread by Katie Kahlenberg
Printed and bound in the USA by Kingery Printing

All photographs shot on 35mm by Nathan Vass.

Contents

Part V: Hard Times

Part VI: Softly, While We Still Can

ACKNOWLEDGMENTS

This book exists thanks to every designer, publisher, reader, buyer, critic, teacher, interviewer, and enthusiast who made my first book the springboard which allowed this work to follow it—Chin Music Press's Bruce Rutledge and Tome Press's Tom Eykemans being the giants leading this charge. In their talent and professionalism, these two are unmatched.

Equally essential are the laser-sharp proficiency of editor Katie Kahlenberg, whose skillful eye and commitment to form elevates everyone involved, and the focused enthusiasm of readers and advocates Alexandra, Brian, Laura, and Rebekah. No adverb can convey how thankful I am to Quinn for her unfailing support, and to Donald and Esther for their outlook, who with both their presence and absence teach me more than can be articulated in mere words.

Finally, I need to thank my friends on the street, who number in the unsung thousands. You, who are feared, hated, ignored, harassed, underestimated. You, who fill the air with your language and spirit, who extend your hand when you don't have to, enfolding me in your citywide embrace. What gift is larger? I did not know the world contained this much goodness. To me you are loved, honored, respected. To me you have a place in this world, not least because you help me feel like I belong.

Show this book to the ones who think you have no name.

For Q, M, & B

DECIDING TO SEE

INTRODUCTION

I remember the first second of the first moment it all began, nearly two years into my bus driving career. So far I'd been doing the expected: driving safely and being polite. But sometime in 2008, I pulled up outside the Airport Way methadone rehab clinic in South Seattle and gulped. The zone was populated by at least two dozen intending passengers matching descriptions I'd been taught to fear. These were the folks who—and I say this without judgment—you crossed the street to avoid.

I felt like a child then and looked it. I've always looked younger than I am, and back when I was twenty-two, I looked twelve. *In about two seconds I'm going to be out of my depth.* I'd never talked for more than an instant to such people before. How should I behave toward this ragtag crew? Something else I'd been taught came to mind: if you treat people kindly, they'll generally be kind in return. I wondered how far that rule went.

I decided to open the doors and gave it a whirl.

In hindsight, the outcome isn't surprising, but imagine the relief I felt in the moment, as anxiety turned to exhilaration. I treated each incoming passenger as if they were already a friend, and they glowed in response. "You're the first driver to actually *talk* to us, let alone be nice," one woman said. Respect, I would learn, is the ultimate currency of the street. It opens doors like you wouldn't believe. Those folks would become the friendliest passengers on that entire route.

From then on, I began greeting people from all life's stations with gusto, announcing stops myself with complete sentences, making eye contact with each incoming soul, nodding hello or asking how they're doing, yelling a thank you as they left through the back.

The more I put out there, the more I got in return. Has this strategy worked every single time? You know the answer. No strategy works every time. But being kind and respectful toward others has quite the batting average.

The hours began to fly by.

The more I was welcomed into communities I never thought I'd be part of, the more I felt accepted on a plane beyond the individual, experiencing that unique neurochemical reaction caused by positive encounters with strangers, that interactions with friends and family don't activate: a sense of belonging to the World, to Society at Large. This was a togetherness born not from clicks or advertising but from a thousand compounding moments of *direct contact*, extending across all classes and demographics . . . it's an intoxicating sensation.

On Getting It All Down

Too many beautiful moments were happening. This was when I began scribbling. I'm pretty sure I'm the only bus driver who loves red lights; they afford me the precious minutes needed to hurriedly write down what just happened. Over the years, my muscle for memorizing dialogue has improved beyond what I thought possible. Capturing speech with accuracy is the most crucial element for me. As you'll discover, actual transcribed conversation reads differently than fictional dialogue, involving more repetition, placeholder words, and rhythm. I find this exciting—and important to document. Describing truthfully the flavor of their word choice and tone, how they sound out their vowels, what slang they use; this is how I can respect the faces I meet. (Only the names have been changed, including some repeat characters from *Lines,* which occasionally used real names; pardon the confusion.)

It all started with this, the very first moment which ever got scribbled down, on a 4 × 4 napkin I still have tucked away somewhere:

On the bus—a Black American couple is getting off, twenties, she's got the empty stroller and he's got the requisite doo rag and flat-billed hat sideways, pants down around his knees. He leans in and says, "Hey man, all I got is a twenty," and shows me his wallet, which is only very large bills. I say, "That's okay—" hand gestures—"it ain't worth twenty dollars." Relief smiles across his face, and something else too. I say, "Oh yeah, you're fine. Guys have a good night." He says "thank you" in italics, and she says sincerely, "I appreciate it," and we exchange some more 'have-a-good-nights' and 'you-too's,' except they feel so big and real and what else, and they're almost gone when he turns back and yells out, "and Happy Father's day, if you have a son!" An hour later I saw them again, wandering into the street. He had taken off his shirt. I leaned out of the bus and waved, and we all recognized each other ("Heeeyyyy!"), and the excited goodness in them glowed. As though we three were all the same special species, the kind that sees new possibilities, and you felt the juice that makes one excited about humanity. Our generation. The size of these moments.

Thus, my blog was born, and later my first book, *The Lines That Make Us*, which blossomed into a Seattle bestseller, thriving academic textbook, and all-around critical success. But those weren't the achievements I was hoping for in taking on the project of creating these documents. They come from a deeper compulsion; it has somehow felt right, necessary, to record the things I've seen happen on the street corners, buses, and transit centers throughout these early years of the 21st century. Most human life is experienced on ground level. These stories are an attempt to capture the texture of those chaotic and multilayered quotidian hours, in all their color and uncelebrated light. Who is writing down the good things that happened, the small things, the interrupted moments of deep joy we forget all too soon?

On The Book's Structure

By the time you read these lines, I will have been driving city buses, mostly high-incident routes at night, for twenty years. What have I learned? This book is my best answer. In filmmaking we speak of the cut, from one image to another, as the essential unit for communicating substance; by juxtaposing two shots you allow the viewer to create a third thing, the meaning, out of thin air. That's the methodology behind the organization of stories here. They may seem like a series of unrelated moments, much like the crisscross patchwork of days we all live through, or the unconnected passengers who board through the doors on my bus, but they are all linked, and together they gradually reveal something hidden between the lines. I'll leave it to you to give that emerging shape a name.

Also, as you will discover, I underwent a traumatic event in 2015 which threads its way through these stories. What I didn't anticipate was how significant a role interactions with strangers would play in the recovery process. Counseling and other mental health interventions have their valuable place, but the arena for processing our troubles is the Everyday, the banal encounters where we grow, expand our perception, prove ourselves. The journey of recovery is a non-linear one, and the stories likewise have been arranged in a chronology that, although broadly linear (to preserve the evolution of recurring characters and other events), frequently doubles back on itself, jumping about as our minds do, finding meaning in contrast and steering a course toward gradual healing.

In keeping with my filmmaking training, I have mostly endeavored to show rather than didactically tell or instruct, and in the same manner have attempted to engage with today's social justice concerns without becoming political or otherwise issue-driven. Readers of *Lines* will be nodding their heads; this text takes a similar structural approach, albeit with subject matter both further-reaching and more personal.

Finally, a note on capitalization: In keeping with the Chicago Manual of Style, the APA Style Guide, the National Association of

Black Journalists, and the Center for the Study of Social Policy, we have capitalized White in addition to Black when referring to race. While debatable as a solution, I've chosen it because lowercasing White subconsciously reinforces Whiteness as an invisible default, a status quo that is neutral and standard. Capitalizing all other races, but not White, suggests they are anomalies which deviate from the starting norm of Whiteness, which is a framework I do not wish to perpetuate. Alongside maintaining the fiction that Whiteness is invisible, lowercasing the word also allows Whiteness to sidestep interrogations of privilege and accountability, and reinforces the idea that race is "other people's problem." Additionally, the White characters in this book are usually a minority race in the spaces described, and their race thus stands out, a fact that capitalizing helps illustrate. For myself, I can see compelling reasons for lowercasing White as well, but as a biracial person who can claim neither White nor Black as an identity, it feels odd to uppercase one racial group while lowercasing another. Make of this what you will.

A Quick Tutorial on Seattle

You've heard of the place, and know something of its consciousness, even if you've never been there. As a port city with rough-and-tumble origins, Seattle once epitomized our nation's frontier spirit; its capacity for rebuilding itself, as after its great 1889 fire; its proud heritage as an industrial and aerospace giant; and its name's complicated, problematic legacy, an imperfect homage to the land's original people. It represents in synecdoche an exaggeration of many of our nation's highlights and problems. Seattle is the country's epicenter for tech growth and is regularly listed as the fastest-growing city in the US, which to residents means suffocating gentrification, debilitating inequality, and a homelessness problem in outrageous proportion to its population, which goes unsolved by its government year after year. The increasing social stratification, combined with tech culture's tendency toward isolation, has led to a general sense of alienation and anxiety. If you've spent time in any major US city, these issues will not surprise you. They just exist in sharper relief in Seattle.

Human connection is the warmth and solution missing in all of the above-listed problems, and we in the modern world crave it as never before. Perhaps it is appropriate to use the Emerald City as a source for my writing, that city whose famous "Seattle Freeze" would have us declare it the least likely metropolis in which the following stories of compassion could take place.

What, precisely, is the Freeze comprised of?

Many Seattleites today are recent arrivals, eliminating the long-standing pride of solidarity found in places like Chicago or New York. Many of us came here to get away from others. The degree of diversity in language and culture creates divisions which, as in my hometown of Los Angeles, often remain as such. There has been an explosion of untreated mental health on the streets of Seattle's downtown core. And with the shadow of Amazon, Google, and others, there is a new class-conscious resentment against those companies' well-heeled young professionals and the accordingly elevated real-estate market. The pervasive presence of technology outpaces that of other cities, and like everywhere but more so, a disproportionate number of younger generations prefer communicating via a digital intermediary, rather than directly with people. This is what you've heard about, and it's all true.

But there's always more.

You can carve out a niche, and it becomes your understanding of the place, your very own personal city. All the other Seattles recede from view. You get to take part in giving it a name.

For me, Seattle is friendly. It's always been mostly ethnic: Asian and East Indian in my childhood, now generally Black, American or African, with a healthy smattering of East Asian and Latino backgrounds. The respect carried in smiles and nods are the common language here, a predominantly working-class town, earthy. We are vocal, sometimes too much, but who's counting; the White folks are artists, servicewomen and men; everyone stimulating to be around, with overlap for days. These are the people I spend my work nights with.

What a fine bunch.

Yes, mental health, drugs, and desperation bubble in the periphery. There are the problems of violence, new money, the downturn of politics and education. There are conversations. But mostly, we shake hands with our words and eyes, vibrant and accepting, living in the place where we have things in common.

I know my Seattle is small, and perhaps sounds ridiculous. A warm, welcoming Seattle? *What*?

But everyone's version of the city is authentic because their experiences are valid. How many thousands of smiling faces I see, night after night and years in and out, nameless or otherwise. Faces which respond to kindness, to me, the little boy acting like he still lives on a small-town neighborhood block.

If it can be found here, it can exist anywhere.

Part of this island of identity we build has to do with geography in the literal sense. I spend most of my time in the working-class and low-income neighborhoods of South Seattle (which, along with Downtown and North Seattle's notorious Aurora Avenue corridor, is where much of this book takes place). South Seattle is more than twice the land mass of North Seattle; its Rainier Valley is a vast floodplain famous for containing one of the country's most diverse zip codes (98118).

The 7/49, a combined route connecting the full length of Rainier Valley to Downtown and points further north, remained my favorite route for as long as it existed, and was for many years Metro's busiest, most storied, feared, celebrated, talked-about route (it's since been dismantled, in part because a light rail line now approximates its travel path). We'll be spending our time primarily there and on Aurora Avenue, a seven-lane, 200-block-long expanse known for its high-visibility sex work and longstanding drug distribution patterns. The route serving this corridor (the E Line) is, like "the 7," a name whispered with fear and awe. These are the spaces which often only get discussed in the context of crime. But those of us who've been there know there's more.

Join me.

Have you managed to preserve it,
in these days of loneliness and suffering?

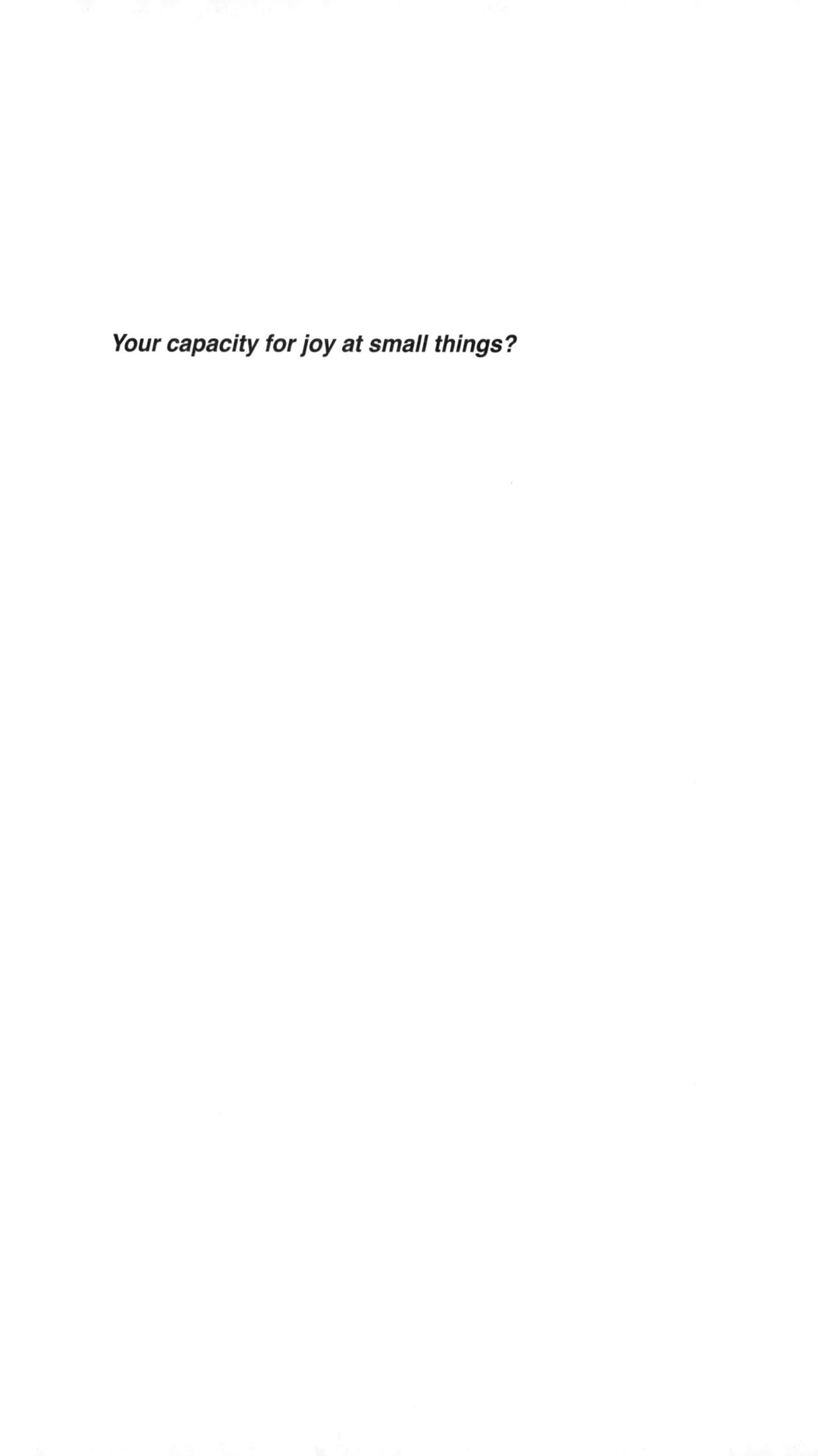

Your capacity for joy at small things?

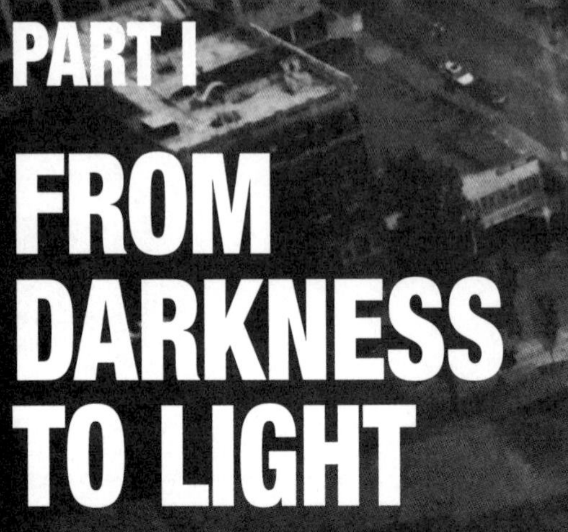

PART I

FROM DARKNESS TO LIGHT

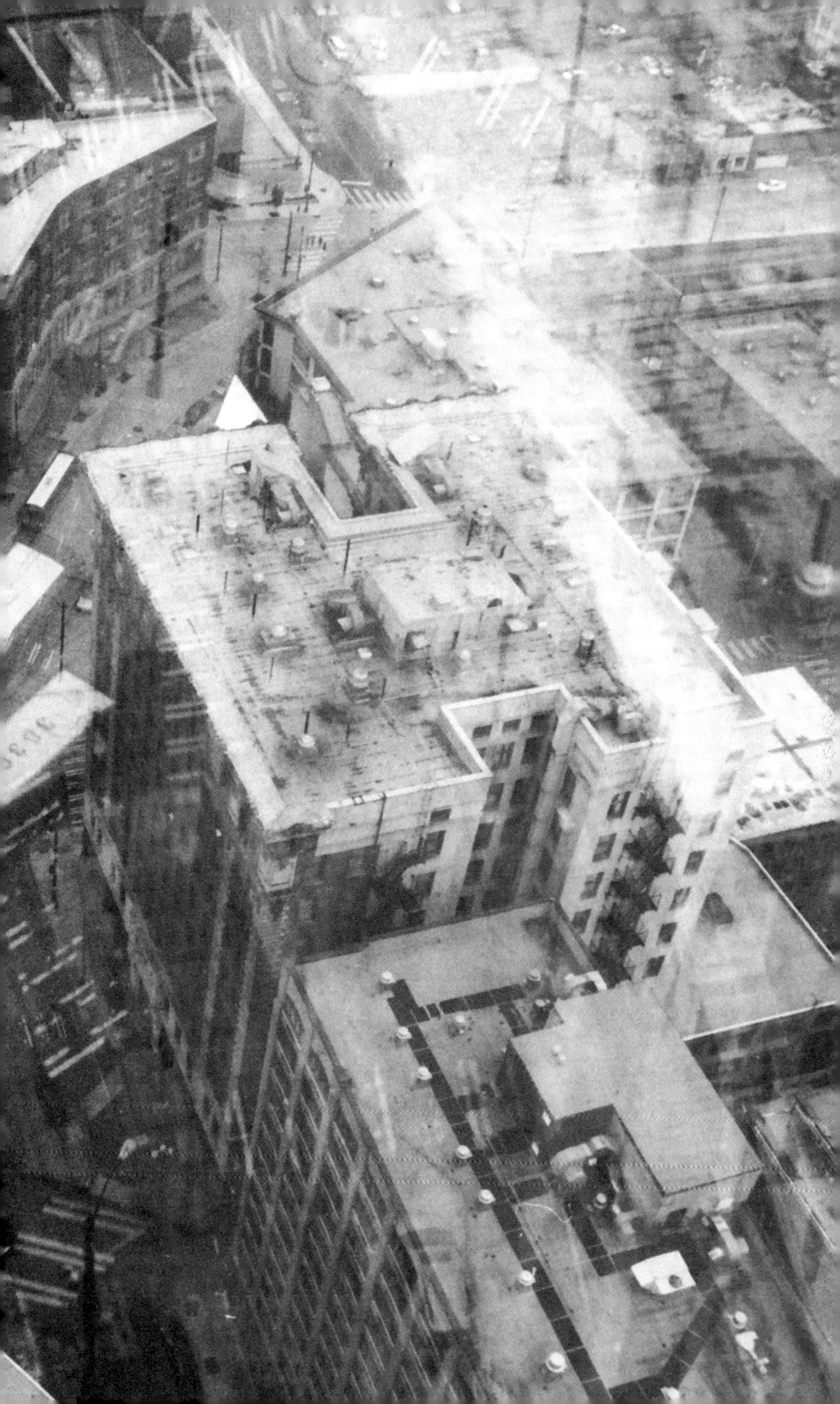

THIS HAPPENS TOO

4/6/15

Martin Luther King Jr. Way, just south of South Seattle's Rainier Avenue. We have one taker, a middle-aged man, close-cropped shave growing out again, with a paper bag under one arm; he's wearing faded blue running pants and a tattered blue sweatshirt, one of Manet's beggar-philosophers come to life.

"Hey," I said.

"What's goin' on."

"Not a lot, how's it goin'."

We're so far speaking in a pleasant monotone. He seems the stoic type. The genial timbre of the questions asked is its own answer. Aren't pleasantries always in fact reflecting something deeper, the acknowledgment of an equal plane? He pauses after my last question, and I'm thinking he won't speak further, when he does:

"*Good*, for a change."

"Oh, excellent!"

"Real good, actually."

"Happy to hear it."

I'm about to ask him for details, and he jumps the gun— "I was just sitting on t' street corner mindin' my own, right back there, when *six cars* stopped to ask me if everything was okay."

His stoic vibe is quickly disappearing as he relates the experience, becoming more animated. More lifelike.

"Six!" I say.

"Yeah, six different cars! And I didn't have my head in my hands, nothin' like that, I wasn't cryin' or nothin'! Didn't matter what they was drivin' neither, new cars, old ones . . ."

"Oh that's so beautiful—"

"Aw yeah! And I'm talkin' in a *row*!"

"Thaaat's amazing! That makes me so happy about humanity!"

"They're still out there!"

"They're still out there!"

On simple reflex I clap with joy, both of us rising up in uncomplicated rapture, living that burgeoning high you hear in the voices of gospel singers. Why am I reminded then of the line, once told to me by a visiting German student and which I have never forgotten: "Realists are forever doomed to mediocrity because they lack the necessary naïveté for believing in the possibility of great things." Only in real life could something as improbably beautiful as this happen. Our friend, continuing:

"Every single one, makin' sure I was okay. And one of 'em came back, and we had a looooong conversation, prayin' and talkin'."

"So beautiful!"

When he leaves, we wave at each other through the glass, and he's winking a wink I can almost hear, a signal call to joy and belief, putting rich color into this cloudy evening.

NOT BECAUSE IT IS EASY

4/27/22

I like the ten P.M. crowd.

If you drive buses through Downtown at the top of this hour, you'll notice it contains what I call a "rush hour echo"—a spike in activity entirely benign in nature. These folks have just finished their swing shifts and they're ready to go home, grateful to see you. They have completed their toil at a panoply of interesting worksites, those places where you use your hands, developing calluses and camaraderie; the humble and hidden jobs which are not confusing but easy to explain to others, elemental, and which keep the city running. I have a soft spot for these guys.

I am one of them, after all.

Here is a tall, able-bodied regular with flowing light brown hair down to his hips, running from the opposite corner at 21:59, almost too late as I pull up across the street. The man always waves a silent hello as he boards through the back of my E Line, and it is in appreciation of his friendly waves that I tarry for him tonight—I arrived one light cycle early and *could've* taken this green and left him in the dust. But no.

These are my people.

I gesture at him across the roadway, letting him know he's good. The timing allows another fellow to squeak in, a thirty-something with a well-groomed Afro, the round halo surrounding his excited face in an unapologetic '70s style. He will thank me verbally from the middle doors as he leaves later tonight—notable, in these terse and antisocial times.

In between zones in Belltown, I pull over for two figures waving their arms in the dark. I sense something of myself in their companionable yearning gestures; I know what it's like to plead to get on a bus at night. As passengers, they're the sort I'm grateful to pick up. Probably coworkers, two Black American gentlemen, effusive in their gratitude toward me and happy to be chatting with each other, their soft-spoken banter lighting up the bus's middle section.

Rounding out the crowd are a scattering of your expected E Line neighborhood flavors, but of a mellower stripe tonight. An elderly army vet, built like an ex-footballer. A woman who hears my *Have a good night*! at the last second, her hand waving *thank you* from the back after the rest of her body has already deboarded. A bedraggled grandmother twice my age with her belongings in hand, including a fishing rod and 101 Dalmatians pants, catching a nap in the back. A stentorian but amiable fellow up front I'm chatting with, who tells me what you learn as a footballer if you're small and have a tough father: "You can't meet force with force. You have to go around it."

So true.

There were his thoughtful words and more, other faces you forget, the youthful outcasts you're surprised to discover do have destinations. Here is another man at the end, Aurora's answer to Gary Payton, only less lucky. We're at Aurora Village and he's very lost, asking where Salvation Army is. I perk up when I realize he's actually trying to get someplace, and he perks up when he perceives I'm giving him genuine real directions because I *care*, explaining the slightly confusing path for how to get there—all the way at the other terminal.

We have a good group tonight.

I look at them in my rear-view and smile involuntarily, deeply contented by the opportunity to serve these folks, to get to be in their presence. I feel a motherly caring for my fellow humans, and I embrace them with my bus.

This is what we can do, while the institutions slumber around us. It is what we can do as individuals, and what we have to do. As a passenger once told me, "We have to allow ourselves to love so other people can receive it. People need to feel loved in their lives.

It's not just for us, it's for them." She phrased it as a responsibility done on behalf of others.

I know that's harder to do now. I know you've heard the horror stories of bus routes like mine. You may even have lived them, as I have. But can we take a moment to remember all the rest is happening too? Can we remember that during your day, the terrible thing that happened probably lasted less than five minutes? That we can be our best not only then, when it may accomplish little, but for the other hours too, when it's just as worthwhile to keep community alive?

We try for the right things not because they are easy, but because they are hard. Because they tell us something about ourselves, about the person we'd like to be. We try not because we will succeed. We do not expect an outcome. No, we try because doing so inches us incontrovertibly closer toward a better definition of things, gently shifting our listeners and futures and notions of truth.

That is enough.

THE DAY THE EARTH STOOD STILL

5/3/17

Blue sweatshirt, flat forehead. It was the last time I ever saw him, a street character I encountered not infrequently on my 7; not homeless, you understand, just scruffy. I liked saying his name. He was the definition of boisterous, but I didn't mind. He was a sweetheart when you got right down to it, and always reacted well when I called out: "Inside voice, Little Leon, inside voice!"

That morning both of us were strangers in a strange land. I can't remember why I was driving the 70 at seven A.M., and I'd never seen him in glossy Amazon tech-head land before—definitely not at the crack of dawn. He was more an evenings-in-South-Seattle type of guy. Like me. But Fairview Avenue was beautiful in its own quiet way, one of those cloudy Northwest mornings, the brightening grey that blurs the moments before dawn and afterward.

"Little Leon, good morning!"

Even as I said it, I could tell something was different. Leon's eyes were more than sober; they were shell-shocked.

"Hey, man, what's goin' on," he mumbled, his eyes trained on an invisible distance far beyond the material. He stumbled into the front seat, right next to me. The intimacy felt appropriate for our conversation, though given Little Leon's volume habits, everyone in the sparsely populated interior was surely within earshot. Somberly: "Hey, guess what."

"Tell me," I said.

"My mother died last night."

"I'm sorry!"

I looked at the moistness of his eyes, two deep brown pooling wells. There was something wrong with this day, something particular that had never been wrong before. His hush following the sentence contained volumes. We're all of us going through this life for the very first time, beginners in this racket, and we have no preparation for something so new, so large and silent and terrible.

I'm sorry. How forgettable. People who've lost know how meaningless the phrase can sound. But what can you say? Sure, it's overused, but the sympathy is real. You want to say it. You want to reach them, let them know you're trying to bridge the chasm, and this is the phrase we have.

Little Leon, a thin-framed broken man, Black American, too early to middle age, today clad in a blue sweatshirt, blue jeans, and battered white sneakers. Survival already trumps style for many of my street friends, but for Mr. Leon today, as would be the case for any of us, fashion was especially meaningless. He sat as a man consumed entirely by the past, the present an afterthought too bitter to bear.

"Thanks, man," Little Leon said, pausing. "It's so many ways we can go."

"Gotta go with dignity."

"What?"

There's a film that's special to me—I won't spill the title because I'm giving away the ending—about a man who slowly loses everything, including his life . . . but not his dignity. I've always remembered that and voiced it now.

"We gotta go with dignity."

"Dignity, that's right. And she did, she was beautiful right up until the end. It just hurts—"

"Aaat's heavy—"

"It hurts 'cause I was uh only child."

"You and me both!"

Little Leon leaned forward. He meant every word he said.

"Hey, lemme ask you a favor, king bus driver. By the way this guy's the best king bus driver in all the whole a Metro. He's he's he's—"

"Nawwww—"

"There ain't nobody else, 'cause every single time he sees me, he treats me the way he would wanna be treated."

"Thanks, man. I try!"

"You do. But lissen, I gotta ask you one favor."

"What's up?"

"Just, next time you see your mom, just give her a big hug, man, hug her tight. Don't matter what she's doin', she's comin' out the bathroom, hug her anyway."

"I will. I will."

"It *hurts.*"

"I'm glad you got to spend time wit' her."

"Oh yeah, my mama raised me. My dad, I never met him." The raspy inflection, halfway between tears and a hard place, the plaintive voice rising, helpless: "I tell you, when I make it to those pearly gates I'ma ask him just one thing." Trying not to shake. "I'ma ask him why he was never around, why he was never there, so I coulda maybe learned somethin' from him." His voice cracked, and cracked again.

"Oh man, Leon. I'm sorry."

"It hurts."

"Death is so huge."

"Just hits the bottom of your soul."

"We're gonna lose everything we love in this life," I said, half to myself, gazing out at Mercer Street, reflecting as we waited out the long light.

"Well, we won't lose it, it'll just . . . . you know, king bus driver, I saw somethin' a long time ago that I couldn't believe. I saw this guy just bawling. Just heaving, cryin' and cryin'. I said why and he said he'd just lost his wife."

"I don't blame him."

"Oh no me neither. But I didn't know grown men *cried.* But he was. Tha's why I'm cryin' now, I understand."

"It's like you lose one person and the whole world seems empty," I replied, paraphrasing Joan Didion. Didion, Little Leon . . . doesn't matter what world you come from. These things are all the same.

"Yeah," he agreed. "Exactly. Yeah."

He paused. He spoke. He told me he was writing a song in anticipation of the funeral, at which he planned to sing. "I ain't done with it, but the first part goes like this."

And then he launched into it. Reader, would that you were there. A century and a half of the gospel blues tradition had existed for the purpose of building to this moment, a broken man on a city bus singing to his friend. To hear his deep, sorrow-stricken, gospel-inflected voice . . . this was a blues with no affectation whatsoever. It was shattering in its heartrending truthfulness. Was I really going to tell him to quiet down now? Did I care what the other commuters thought about their morning trip to work?

Not for a second. They one day will be where he is, and we'll give them room then, too.

I couldn't help but consider myself in his shoes. "I don't know if I'll be able to handle it," I said.

"What?"

"Oh, when my own mom passes, I's thinkin' I don't know if I'll make it."

"Well, don't rush it, man. That's pain."

"You know though," I said after another pause, "It's better than the opposite. This is better than us dying before our parents do. Ain't nothin' worse than a parent losing their only child."

"Yeah. Yeah, that's true. Yeah."

"This is part of the cycle."

I could see he was noticeably buoyed by this idea. Mourning happens in waves: a step forward, and three back. Though they may seem as nothing more than drops of water in an ocean, every one of those incremental steps forward is a milestone. This was a step forward, and it was just what he needed then. As we came to his stop, he exclaimed, "Iss a *reason* I ran into you this morning, king bus driver!"

"I'm so happy you got on my bus, Little Leon!"

"You're tellin' me! Love you, be safe!"

"You too!"

I watched him walk away, a man in blue, shivering in the wind. He wasn't Little Leon anymore. He was just Leon now, and his grief will be our grief, has been our grief. Do we lose everything we love in this life? We do, but we don't lose their spirit. We don't lose the good they built in us, the most important part. In your good actions, in the grace or humor you learned from them . . . that's *them*, reaching out at life through you, with you.

Keep that goodness alive.

FIGURING IT ALL OUT IN THE BULLPEN

8/4/16

At the base, there's an operator hang-out area called 'the bullpen.' I avoid it, but on this particular afternoon I was comfortably ensconced in one of the chairs listening to an operator friend air his complaints. Albert was hung up on littering and wanted to hear my perspective. People littered on his bus all the time, and he was tired of it. He drove the E, and I the 7; two routes whose coach interiors you can instantly identify by the sheer amount of wanton filth (I prefer the term 'neighborhood seasoning') left by the passengers. He wanted to know how I maintain a positive outlook on people.

"I don't get it," he said.

My initial reply was a line you've likely heard: if you can't control it, let it go.

He said, "Yeah, but . . ."

I tried all kinds of things. I told him how littering is a form of asserting control. It may be the only opportunity available to effect change on your environment. I told him how if you feel society has wronged you, you may not feel inclined to follow its rules. I talked about a lack of role models. I talked about how these guys who act entitled by littering and not paying aren't exactly living luxurious or untroubled lives. Their entitlement comes from a place of frustration different than other forms of the same: they act entitled because they're not.

The lines above are what I tell myself when frustrated, and I thought I was laying down some pretty good stuff. But Albert remained perplexed. He expected other people to have similar values and perspectives (that is, experiences) to him, and was surprised and disappointed when their behavior revealed otherwise.

He said, "I just wanna know, what's going through their head when they throw a bunch of chicken bones on the floor. What frame of mind could make you think, *this is the right thing to do*?"

The indelicate thing to say here is, that line of thinking will get you punched.

Albert believed there was a wrong way to do things and a right way, which sounds okay in a principled sort of fashion, but when people say that they usually mean *their* wrong and right way, which everyone else should follow. Don't we all do this by habit?

"You know what my problem is?" Albert asked. "I have no empathy. I believe everyone is in the situation they're in because of their own choices, their own actions."

The conundrum he was outlining is one I wrestle with myself. There are attitudes of my own that creep up in the night, easy ugly answers for what I'm seeing rather than the more nuanced view, questions I berate myself for asking. There's a line of thinking in East Asian thought that says we are responsible for our own actions. We are creatures of free will; instead of apologizing for making mistakes, the idea goes, just don't make them in the first place. Hold yourself accountable for your behavior. Albert and I are both Korean American, and I know this perspective is as familiar to him as it is to me.

The problem with that outlook, of course, is that humans are fallible.

America is the land of second chances. It's where people come to start again. The imperfection of us mortals is not a concept exclusive to western thought, but in our contemporary culture it figures as a universally accepted truth. Intelligent people do make mistakes. We're disappointed when it happens but not surprised. We believe bad things happen to good people; we believe in forgiveness; in wiggle room.

Albert in the bullpen was not of this outlook. I lean toward it not because I think it's more truthful, but because I have to. I appreciate the high expectations of the first mindset, but I have thrived only because certain people have been kind to me, offered me a second chance.

I said something like, as a bus driver, if you need the passengers to act as if they're well-adjusted and highly functional, you'll go insane. You can't expect folks to be reasonable or do things that make sense. Sometimes I have to give up on understanding the things I see, resign them to the mysteries of the universe, because I simply have no idea where people are coming from.

Albert really was trying to listen, but I could see I was getting nowhere. By now a few other drivers had gathered round. One was a tall fellow I hadn't seen before. We'd nodded with our eyes while I'd been struggling with what to say.

Now that man spoke up.

"In my country, there used to be these wild birds."

There was his height. There was his accent, dignified, somewhere Mediterranean, Greece maybe. There was the fact that he'd been listening for a while without speaking. The person who speaks the least always appears the most intelligent. He had a certain stately gravitas, a polish, such that when he butted in with something about wild birds, we didn't interrupt him. We had no idea the relevance of this bird business. But he surprised us into attention.

"In my country there used to be these wild birds, that if you shot them, if you shot one of them, you would get five dollars selling it on the street. And that five dollars would feed your whole family for a week."

He coughed before continuing. The storytelling pause.

"So, for you, the farmer with a family and mouths to feed, it's very important to shoot the bird. But the government was saying, these birds are endangered. You can't shoot them because they are rare, endangered species. It's bad for the environment. But if killing one of those birds feeds your family of four, five people for a whole week, you don't care about that at all. It doesn't matter if it's endangered or not! You have to feed your family." Now he looked directly at our conflicted friend Albert. "So. You want the people on your bus to clean up after themselves so you can feel more *comfortable*? No. These people have nothing. They don't even know where their next meal is coming from. They have different priorities."

We were all silent when he finished. I'm pretty sure that got through.

KING TREVOR

7/6/19

You would know if you've seen him. No one else here in Seattle, whether mentally stable, housed, employed, or otherwise, has the happy-go-lucky gall to dress up like a king outside of Burger King. I don't even know if the restaurant has anything to do with it. Trevor stands out there most every day, like any number of folks you see at freeway exit ramps or major intersections. If you spend enough time in such places, you'll notice a pattern: there's often a second figure standing in the wings, waiting for the first to vacate his position so he can "start his shift," as it were.

But no one else panhandles in Trevor's spot. Who could follow a king? You'd be forever doomed to be second-rate. Look at that stubby smiling fellow, complete with flowing black cape and gold crown, sword and shield, a grin ever visible beneath the appropriately regal beard. His sword remains sheathed, and instead of holding a sign he moves between the cars offering a gesture of prayerful supplication and a well-wishing smile. Like my older friends who don't need to wear logos or slogans on their shirts, who simply are themselves and you have to *talk* to them to know them, his being, his life force, is his sign. I'll open my driver's side window for a brief chat at the light, or else tap the horn twice as I roll by. He always knows it's me.

Today, though, Trevor was a mile or two further down the road, collapsed on the concrete expanse of Mount Baker Transit Center. I opened the doors while other passengers boarded. He cried out from his prone position on the ground.

"I need somebody to help me up."

"Hey, Trevor," I called out.

"I need somebody to help me up."

I stepped outside, toward him. "Okay, let's see here." I had to do *something*. You don't just leave a monarch sprawled on his belly on the side of Rainier. Especially a benevolent monarch. "How're we gonna do this. How 'bout I reach under your arms like this, and then we'll both stand up, okay? Let's do this." He's a smaller guy. This was doable. "Okay there we go. Great. You got it. Now do you wanna go sit on that bench, or do you want the bus?"

"I want the bus."

"Okay, let's go get on this bus. But listen Trevor, if you sit down on the bus, are you gonna be able to stand up again?"

"I'll stay standing."

"Great," I said. "Cool." I wondered how long he had been lying there. I didn't ask.

"Hang on, lemme put my sword down," he said as we settled inside.

"Yeah, they say no sword fights on the bus . . ."

After a chuckle he said with complete seriousness, "Nathan, thank you. I'm so glad you came by."

Me, trying to brush it off: "I'm so glad I did too!"

"I'm so glad it was *you*."

Actors try for sincerity that unvarnished. It was a simple sentence, but it answered my unasked question: he had lain there for no small part of the afternoon.

"I'm glad I get to see ya! It's an honor to have a king onboard . . ."

I kept it in between a joke and earnest gravity, the better to let him lead. I like that he chose the latter. "Man, Nathan," he mused, "I remember the first time I met you."

"Me too. You were just in from what, Texas, right, Austin?"

"Yeah. You make me feel better every time I see you. Thanks for every single moment."

"You too, it brings me up every time I see you! And I love what you've come up with, bein' king and all. Nobody else out here has even thought of puttin' together a cool outfit like that, havin' some fun with it. You know?"

"Hey, I'm trying to make Seattle happier one smile at a time!"

"I think it's down to just you and a couple others doin' that, but I think we're doin' a bang-up job!"

"I think so too. I just don't like fallin', man."

"Yeah, fallin' down's no fun. Falling can be a bigger deal than people think."

"Yeah it is."

"But even a king needs a lil' help every now and then. Gotta help each other out, right?"

"You make me feel *appreciated*, Nathan."

"Right back atcha."

"I'm so glad it was you. I love you, brother."

"Love you too, man. I'll see ya soon."

He stepped off on his own, slowly. You could say regally. Trevor pulls off the king act so well because he's humble. He's an educated man, well-spoken and with a sizable knowledge of the law. He has reason to be proud but isn't. The gaze of pride is inward, and as such it risks blindness. Trevor walks with his eyes open.

"That's the king right there," I said to whoever was in earshot, half to myself, as I drove away. I felt lucky to know the guy.

A figure seated behind me called out in response: "Yessir!!"

Two weeks later Trevor's longtime girlfriend would step aboard my 7. I don't know her name. She's almost pathologically quiet, but on this day, and for the first time in the four years I've known them, she would lift her eyes up to me and speak. She said, "Hey. Trevor told me you helped him up onto the bus when he had fallen down."

The years of silence beforehand, knowing of her introverted character, vested the moment with enormous size. It was the sort of sentence you worked on, rehearsed, you who for whatever reason don't like talking to strangers. But you did it on this occasion because it was important.

"Yeah, I did," I replied, my jaw slightly agape with wonder, still processing the fact that she had spoken to me. "He's a good guy."

"Yeah, he is. Thanks for doing that."

"Oh, of course."

Years would pass before I heard her speak again.

COMPTON, GENTLY

7/6/03

This was lifetimes ago. Summer of 2003, one year of high school remaining. I strolled the flatlands of Compton with camera in hand, up early by choice and searching the shadows and light for an angle that would show how I felt. Rush hour had burned off with the marine layer, and I loitered about the rail station in the midmorning sun, Willowbrook and Compton Boulevard. I used to love riding up and down the Blue Line, Los Angeles's equivalent of the 7, with photography on the brain. Mornings were the best time for doing so; better light as always, and safer.

I'd just snapped a double exposure and was winding the film when I noticed the man in my viewfinder coming closer, walking toward me. I nonchalantly concealed my camera. As he got to speaking distance he cleared his throat.

"Hey how's it goin', little man."

I wasn't good at talking to people then. Shyly: "Good."

"You enjoyin' your summer?"

"Yeah, it's good."

"Hey, you live alone or with roommates?"

I was staying with my aunt. I said, "with roommates."

"Some of them are boys?"

"Sure."

"That must be nice. Do they ever walk around with their dick and balls hangin' out?"

"What?"

"Like walkin' from the living room to the bedroom, casual shit like that. They ever walk through the room with their dick and balls hanging out?"

"No . . ." Nervous teenage tittering on my part.

"Well but okay hypothetically. If they was people walking around with they dick and balls hangin' out, how would that make you feel?"

"I guess I'd feel kinda uncomfortable!"

"Oh. Ah see. Well, it would make me feel comfortable, 'cause I'm gay, and there ain't nothin' that's ever made me feel so lonely in all my life. You got no idea, lil' bro." He spaced out the words as he repeated the phrase. "You. Got. *No idea*. You count yourself lucky."

And with that he walked away. He became smaller now, much smaller than the perspective he was walking into, a lonely fellow with a weight on his shoulders, ambling at the pace you take when you've got precious little to look forward to.

I should have said I'm sorry it feels lonely. Or something about how I cared, I appreciated and welcomed the skin-thin openness of his fragile heart. Something to let him know he wasn't alone. But I was seventeen and I didn't know anything. I wasn't brave enough or self-aware enough or empathetic enough to say a thing like that. I just watched him walk away. I remember reflecting with surprise at his candor, how uncharacteristic it felt in that hypermasculine milieu. How refreshing his sincerity was, both because I wasn't expecting it in that environment and because young people aren't very good at being sincere, and forthrightness wasn't something I found a lot of in high school.

These are the things we think and feel, the tender reflections we don't know how to share.

I wonder if he knows I still think about him from time to time, wondering if he's alive, if someone's shown him kindness or even love across these spanning years.

I hope so.

CHOSEN

10/24/18

Third and Prefontaine Place, northbound. Nobody's first idea of a safe place to wait for a bus at night. You know the terrain, the way the little things all add up: uneven sidewalks; an out-of-commission reader board; the magnificently poor lighting, almost as if on some city planner's evilly gleeful purpose; the tents and cries from over there, tensions boiling across the street; and you, clutching whatever you clutch in your pocket, trying to be gracious in your thoughts as figures lurk about, shifting on the dark urban floor, letting you know they're alive.

I roll up slowly in my 7/49. I open the doors to a zone with two people, neither of whom wants my bus: a young White woman, early twenties, in a demure white puffy jacket and nondescript ponytail and jeans. She looks at me through the open bus doors.

The other person is called Chosen. Chosen is a Black American man two generations too old to be sagging his pants, but he does it anyway; every tatter of clothing on his body sags, and the phrase "dressed in rags" is here, finally, not an exaggeration. If you depicted him in a painting as he is, exposed skin and frayed dead fabric, viewers would accuse you of caricature, saying no man over forty really stumbles about in this bad of shape . . . with a face like that.

Because his face is magical.

The unkempt beard cannot conceal the beauty of his features. Look now at those high cheekbones, the perfect cheeks below them, hollow, like I wished mine were when I was little; his symmetrical eyebrows and sockets and the big emotive eyes within them.

Expressive eyes. Thin, skin and gaunt bones, with a perfectly proportioned and evocative face: He should be in the movies. You want this guy to play a Black Jesus. I think he'd be perfect. He may have a drinking problem, sure, but so did Richard Burton . . .

I will always have a soft spot for Chosen because I once saw a group of girls pepper-spray him on my bus for no other reason than that they thought it was funny.

"You know you want to, nigga," they laughed at each other, with the same voice you'd use for ordering fast food or trying on jeans. They violated him because he was helpless and homeless, and it amused them to destroy something beautiful, like a child stepping on a butterfly. It was the second ugliest thing I've ever seen. The stinging tears streamed down those beautiful cheeks of his, the Jesus cheeks, and I sat with him as he sat blinded, after everyone else had run off, and tried to guide him toward the doors.

Tonight, Chosen is in far better circumstances; same tattered garb as usual, but no apathetic gangster gaggle of girls to worry about. Between the two of us, hopefully I'm the only one who even remembers the incident. He is slinking about on the sidewalk, mildly disoriented as per character, closer to me than the young woman in the white jacket. I recognize him and call out a nonchalant hello. Just another acquaintance at the office:

"Oh hey, Chosen!"

"Hey."

"How ya feelin'?"

"Aw pretty good."

"Right on, man. Have a good one!"

"Aight," he said genially, slinking onward, receding into the night shadows.

The high point of my entire night was the woman's smile.

She had watched the interaction, and the two of us locked eyes now. I grinned in return, cheekily. Her smile was the smile of relief, where you don't realize you're letting down your tensed shoulders.

Everything's fine. Sometimes everything's just fine. She almost laughed: the inherent silliness of our banal pleasantries and good-natured tones juxtaposed with Chosen's terrible appearance, and the pleasure of her discovering what this bus stop can be. That guy wasn't a threat. He was just Some Guy, with a name, and a friendly bus driver who knew him and who was clearly enjoying being out here, at this hour, on this block.

We both smiled wide, teeth gleaming, and I think we both kept smiling our separate ways for a while after.

OUR LADY OF CONTEXT

2/6/20

Only her eyes were visible beneath her niqab, but isn't that all you need to feel someone's friendliness?

I forget the first words of our exchange. Something banal. But within seconds, we were off to the races, the story tumbling out of her with the desperation of thoughts that must be shared.

"You know, my daughter has been missing. I paid private investigator one thousand nine hundred dollars to find her, and she is living with her dad."

I asked, "Is that good or bad?"

"Bad. Her dad is terrible man, stole her away from me, him and her stepmom and her sister they tell her bad things about me, not true. So I think if I go there and talk to her maybe she will listen. Because if I don't then it's three voices against one, the three will win, you know?"

Makes sense. "Where is she?"

"Minnesota."

"That's so far away!"

"I know but I have to. I am her mother. I will go and wait for her in the street if I have to, homeless if I have to. I love her. I'm gonna go over to her and try to get her back. Because that's what mothers do."

There is no substitute for life, real life experience. Art is closest, but even it falls short: What I heard in her present voice was the tangible power of belief. Of love. It was beautiful.

I said, "What does her dad say?"

She spoke quickly, a headlong passionate rush. I suspected she was similarly zealous in many areas of her life; a woman who coursed her journey forward with tumultuous confidence.

"He thinks I am too American," she replied. "That I am a bad influence. But you know what, he is wrong because she, my daughter, was born here! *She* is American!"

Her excitement was making me excited. "And also, we can learn from every culture! He doesn't need to shut her out of here. It should be her choice."

"That's what I'm saying! I am her mother and I will love her no matter what, as long as she is kind and compassionate to others, good human being to herself and those around her, I don't care her choices her religion sexuality. It doesn't matter," she exclaimed, alight with enthusiasm, and though I couldn't see her mouth or gesticulating hands beneath her garments I could feel her verve.

I said, "It doesn't matter. As long as she's a good person."

"Yes. And her dad doesn't think like that."

At the next red light, I turned around in my seat. "You know what, you are a great mom. She is so lucky to have you. I don't know how many other kids wish they had a mom like you."

"Thank you."

Her mind was already whirring on to other topics, and she continued anew: "It can be hard in this country if you don't read or write good English."

"Yeah."

"When I first come here, I got tricked into signing paper. My husband gave me papers to sign and I didn't know what they were. It was divorce and custody papers and now the police tell me I can't do anything about, because I signed it, it's a legal document."

"Oh my goodness. Oh my goodness! That's awful!"

"I had her young, my daughter. I met a man in Somalia, him and some others said they would take me to America and everything would be fine, but they beat me and forced me to come with them here. So I had her when I was thirteen."

"Oh my gosh that's terrible."

"And I feel like she should know the whole story. About me, about who her dad is."

"Definitely. Oh she needs to know, because it's what happened!"

At this point a man walked past. She asked him, "Are you sober?"

"What? Yeah."

"I am too. The reason I ask is because I remember you from before. I was the girl on 12th and Jackson, really skinny, always on drugs, crazy."

"No way!" I blurted. She was the picture of responsibility.

"Oh my god," the man said. "That was you? Yeah, I remember now. You *were* crazy."

"I been sober twenty-four months now."

"That's amazing. Nine months for me."

"Congratulations to you both," I said. "Seriously." To see these two connecting—opposite races, religions, attires . . . but survivors of the same strife. Her monologue could sit alongside Tennessee Williams:

"Yeah, when you are depressed sometimes you just want something, anything. I was hurting from losing my daughter and being betrayed by my husband, and this Somali guy at 12th and Jackson gave me three hundred [unintelligible] pills and told me I would be happy. And I took all of it and said oh my god this is everything I ever wanted. But it destroyed my body, my mind, my life. That guy, he does that to so many girls. They say they wanna help you, but they don't care. They ruin your life just to make some money."

"Yeah, he sold to me too. Andrew is his American name."

"I hate that guy. But I realize I have to take responsibility for my life. No one is going to help me. People help me now. If I miss my medication, there is someone who will drive me, but the only reason they help me is because they saw my dedication to helping myself in the beginning. You have to show them you are for real. That you care. Because no one can change you but you. Right now I'm sober, I have a job, an apartment, a car. Twenty-four months. And I'm going to find my daughter, no matter what it takes."

You felt elevated just listening to her. Inspired. You need this as a civil service employee, day after day with so many folks of less perspective, less self-awareness on the motivations behind their actions, less galvanizing views on responsibility. I was uplifted.

We talked about her impending Minnesota adventure. I worried the journey might be disastrous, and wanted to ensure she had the best chances possible; I don't often hear stories like that turning out well. She had three friends in Minnesota who could help. I told her about attorneys, public defenders, how you can request a different one if you choose. She talked with the other passenger, commiserating on the challenges of sobriety. "It's all about an hour at a time," she said.

"More like a second at a time," he said.

I found myself grateful for the degree to which she gave context. Her willingness to vociferously share with an American stranger, especially on these sensitive subjects, was somewhat unique in relation to her cultural background. In sharing she dimensionalized the many covered faces I see from around the world, offering a concrete example of the complexities even a single life contains. No matter how many such stories you learn, you can always use a few more. Each is different. She deepened my understanding of the desperation I see at 12th and Jackson. She gave those anguished lives a narratival heft and profundity.

I was grateful for the reminder.

OF ANGELS AND ALCOHOL

11/29/15

"Young driver!" he slurred, three syllables a bit much to handle in his intoxicated state. He's a young thirty, this Somalian man, saliva pooling around his lips, in a sports coat and beanie.

"Hey!"

"Young driver, how old are you?" *Di-ryvah.*

"Sixteen."

"You *are* young driver!"

The subsequent clarification and understanding weren't terribly exciting. He was too drunk even for a fist pound, gazing confusedly at my proffered fist and then grasping it like a tennis ball.

"Okay, come on in," I said.

My notes now read, "young driver 50x," and I think this is an underestimation. For a solid forty minutes or so he bellowed from the back inarticulately and repeatedly, "Young driver! Young driver! Young driver, are you twenty-nine?" I'd told him my age. It was hard to discern anything of substance beyond the repeated "young driver." It's a strange feeling knowing someone is talking about you, but not knowing if the talk is negative or positive. Periodically I'd holler things like, "I can't hear you, my friend, come on up! I can't hear nothin' you're sayin'!"

Eventually he did stagger up. "Give me your bag," he said.

"But I don't have a bag."

"Give me your bag!"

"Oh, I see, you want a bag." This was no attempted robbery, but rather a request for some basket-like object to carry his eight-pack of orange Fanta and six-pack (now five) of Heineken. The drinks were on the brink of collapsing out of his cradling arms.

Some archeologists assert that the basket stands alongside the wheel, paper, and printing press as the great human invention. The concept of carrying an extra item in order to carry other items *is* revolutionary. Baskets and bags. I actually remember thinking this while the guy was accosting me. I'm sure he would have agreed.

"Give me your bag," he begins yelling to each individual passenger.

"You gotta say '*please* give me your bag,' yeah, that's the only way people gonna give you their bags!"

Delicacy is not his strong suit right now. Free bags are not forthcoming, and he stumbles back to his spot in the rear. "Young driver," I hear amidst the traffic noise. "Young driver . . ." A woman sitting near him comes up to the front to exit, and I ask her, "What's he goin' on about back there?"

"He's drunk."

"I hope he's a friendly drunk. That's more than we can ask for."

"Yeah."

"Good. Thanks for being patient!"

That was at Boren Avenue, outbound. Ten minutes later, at Broadway and John Street, he staggers up to the front again, struggling like Sisyphus up the mountain.

"Young driver!"

"That is me! You wanna step out here?"

"Wha . . . ? No, I wanna go back," and he dodders down the aisle, teetering by the middle door, finally collapsing in a heap at the bottom of the stairwell.

"Y'all right?"

I open the doors and walk back there. I step around him and out of the bus, speaking to him from my position on the sidewalk. "Wanna step outside, cool off for a bit?"

"No—"

"I think it's time to step out, man."

"No, I wanna go back in . . ."

"No my friend, it's time for you to step outside." Say it with confidence. "It's time to jump out the bus, I'm gonna help you. I'm gonna take your hand—" didn't think I'd be saying that to a drunk man today, but the world is full of surprises— "I'm gonna take your hand like this and we're gonna get you back up."

"No—"

"I'm gonna help you out." His body is diagonally laid out on the stairs, with his head at the lowest point, near the bottom step. "I'm gonna reach under your shoulder and lift you up like this, okay?"

"Unh—"

"Yuuup, it's time to step outside, get some fresh air. Here we go."

"But I wanna go back and get my drink!"

A visiting German student at this moment stepped in to assist. Thank goodness we'd once had a conversation about realists and optimists and had gradually bonded over time. Thank goodness he was here tonight. I love it when angels help out.

Lukas ably grabbed the drunk figure's other shoulder and we lifted—*dragged* is more like it—him into a standing position on the sidewalk. In response to the cries for his drinks, Lukas retrieved them while I kept reassuring the guy everything was all right. He was becoming darkly anxious. "My friend is getting your drinks; he's helping you out. Look, there he is! Fanta! You have your Fanta back, everything is good!"

I think he was more excited about the beer.

"Okay, you have a good night now!" I said.

"Young driver!"

"Yup!"

Having another person helping out in a situation like that is huge. I thanked Lukas the Angel of Broadway and John profusely. We got to talking afterwards.

"Hey. Were you the driver who was missing in Paris?"

"Oh my goodness, how did you *know* that?"

"You had a bunch of people worried. I talked to five or six drivers who were worried about you."

"Oh my goodness, no way! Yeah, I was declared missing and presumed dead by the US Embassy for three days. Them, and the French Police, and CNN eventually found me." The memories were coming back, but I kept up a smile. Focus on him.

"Wow," Lukas said. "Yeah, I was on a 49 when the radio message came out that you were okay. The driver told us about it, and the whole bus gave a round of applause! They broadcast that on all the buses!"

"WHAT?!" This was the first I'd heard of such a thing. "Are you serious? No way! Wow! That's humbling beyond belief. A round of *what*? Oh my goodness, I had no idea. I didn't know that! Thanks for telling me!"

For some people, their ego inflates from such acclaim. I think I'm closer to the opposite: it's my opinion of people at large, not myself, which skyrockets. That there were that many people who *cared* about the welfare of me, the friendly stranger? That this guy Lukas *wanted* to help carry a drunk man down some stairs, for nothing in return? Moments like this are as real as any other, and they make me ask, with wonder:

What glorious space are we living in?

PART II

THE THINGS WE CARRY

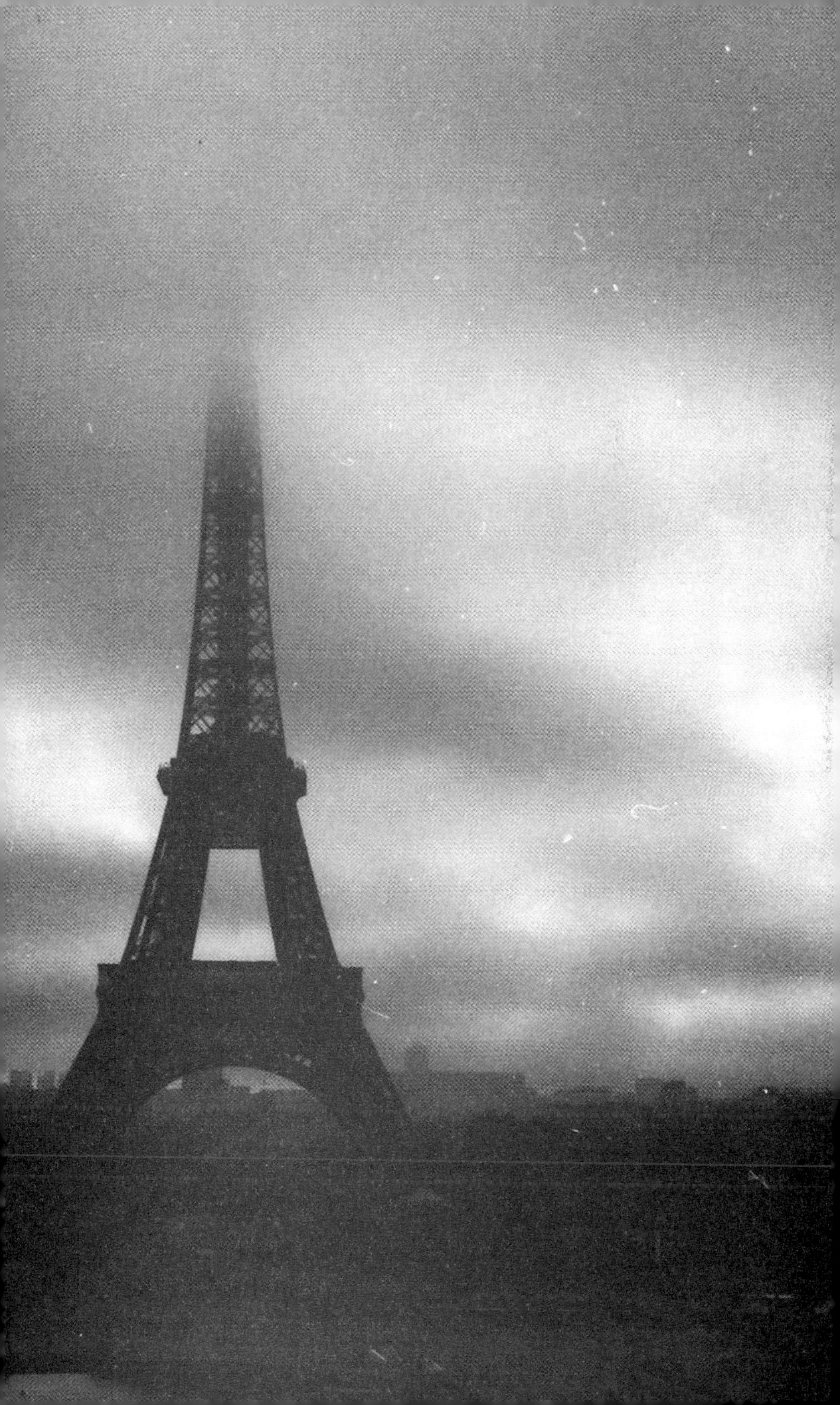

PARIS

11/13/15

On Friday, November 13th, 2015, I was sleeping fitfully in a small room on the upper floor of a hostel in the 19th Arrondissement. I may have been dreaming of my parents. Earlier, I'd been lying in my lower bunk studying the city map, memorizing where I'd explore tomorrow. Examining the metro system, the phrasebook. I didn't travel with electronics then; why let your phone do all the heavy lifting, when you know you can?

I couldn't have known then that none of those plans would materialize. I didn't know that mere hundreds of feet away, ordinary folk like me had just been murdered, and that by morning there would be 547 newly dead or injured bodies, the lives of all who knew them forever altered, shaken by the size of history replacing daily life. The city would shut down for three days of mourning, by its own will and that of its leaders. Empty streets in every direction, hollow, missing human life and heavy with something else; a fraught and massive bulk invading our thoughts, the nameless weight that makes grown men stand still.

For me there is before Paris, and after Paris. The event began when I was three blocks away at a laundromat. The city was loud enough that you couldn't hear gunfire. Laundry is important to me when traveling: I pack only one pair of black jeans regardless of duration of travel, plus one pair of sweatpants to wear while washing those jeans. I was enjoying the mix of domestic bliss and urban exposure laundromats offer. That's what I was thinking about, zening out to the rotating whir, trying to understand the French dryer instructions.

I changed and met a hostel mate for dinner, as planned. It was Yi-Syuan's last night in Paris, and we treated ourselves to "a real French dinner." Our restaurant was hardly any different from the ones down the street getting shot up—festive, busy, delicious. She was a student about my age from Taichung, also traveling alone. We sat by an open window, oblivious to history. We knew we'd never see each other again, which meant we could discuss anything, anything at all, our deepest secrets, confusions, fears, hopes. It was a dinner for the ages. I've never had another like it.

Mere blocks away.

During exactly the same moments, nineteen people were murdered in two adjacent restaurants while probably having similar conversations. An unknown further number were injured or hospitalized. What staggers me into bafflement is that the universe has space for these two utterly opposed worlds to happen simultaneously, *in almost exactly the same place*. I hardly know what to think. I'm reminded of Joyce's description of the sky as a "vast, indifferent dome," always there, forever silent.

The following morning the night-shift receptionist wouldn't allow me outside, as per the instructions of the television. There was no functioning bus or metro, and makeshift encampments were established around the city for the millions who couldn't make it home. After an hour of pleading ("I'm a photographer!") I convinced the night guard to let me outside, and I immediately returned to the intersection of Rue Bichat and Rue Alibert.

I arrived before police or news did. There was punctured concrete from bullet strafing throughout the entire intersection, and splintered bicycles and motorcycles from the same. Blood pooled on the entry steps to Le Carillon, some of it gristly with the remains of flesh, elsewhere leaking into crevices and gutters before anyone could bring flowers. It was still wet when I got there. Cleaning crews were laying down sawdust on the blood, in a feeble attempt to absorb it.

I was part of a very small group of strangers, and as light came to the morning so did more and more people, with roses, candles, cameras, and consternation. We staggered around each other, stupid and raw. No matter what we did, or where we looked, at the evidence of violent death, at the spaces between each other, up to the unblinking sky . . . what was the name of this thing that had happened here, just a few hours ago? The terrible question lives now as it did then.

Why did I live?

Locals congregated in groups familiar and new, filling up the still-open cafés—nothing could ever close the cafés in Paris—but they were talking differently now. The tones were hushed, somber, torn. Laughter had been replaced with silence. Women with faces paler than ghosts, haunted; men with red eyes, ugly from crying but who cares, tears running down their stubble as they pointed at blood on the ground. Language, a thing we used to turn to, no longer a solace now. It was losing relevance. We were slipping into realms unimagined, unimaginable.

The date will be remembered as its own noun. The names of the concert hall, the restaurants, and stadium will forever shift in meaning, something sinister about them now, sounds which carry the weight of lost years.

Why did I live?

Why did Yi-Syuan live? Imagine the nightmare for the 138 who were dying, the last moments, the final view from dying eyes, the final view and also the worst. They met their end on a Friday, out on the town as I was, taking in food and good company in that huge, beautiful, complicated metropolis. Until that night, many of us had something sacred, which we held dear in our different ways; some notion of a just universe.

How do we keep that notion? Where do we go now, and how do we think?

AAOGHUU

10/23/13

I'm riding the 124 late one evening, chatting with the driver after my shift. Nishant (whose name, appropriately, means 'end of the night' in Marathi) is one smart guy. It's dark in here; just one row of the bus's pale-blue fluorescent bulbs is on. We're talking photography, sharing in the roving expanses of the late hour. A few of the old sodium streetlamps pass us by as we make our way through town. I'll miss their orange glow.

As we approach Union Street, a young man comes up from the very back. He's dressed in armor—thick, bulbous headphones, a baseball hat pulled low, with enormous reflective sunglasses useless at this time of night for any purpose beyond covering one's own eyes. From his invincible cocoon of a shield, he leans in close to Nishant, speaking quietly. I'm in the front seat, and I can't even hear the guy.

Evidently there's a sleeper in the back. To me this hardly qualifies as newsworthy; why, as a young, armored man, with your headphones and hip jacket, would you trouble the driver about it? Maybe he's just awfully considerate.

Or perhaps this sleeper is a little different from the rest.

Nishant walks back there, and after a moment I follow. I'm curious. Our movements draw the attention of the crowd—ten, maybe fifteen people in here; a motley but subdued crew. Evenings on Pac Highway have a singular atmosphere, similar to the no-holds-barred environment of Seattle's infamous Aurora Avenue but more ethnic tonight, and slightly younger. The dim lights amplify the sensation; we're in another world here. Armored Youngster, still too cool for school, points out the sleeper in question, and the motley crew keeps watching from all directions.

The figure is draped against the seat, head pushed up in the corner by the window, formless, melding with the surfaces like a chameleon who's trying to hide by changing color but can't. Nishant goes through the routine of trying to wake a sleeper; he and I make noise, first speaking, then clapping, then gently pushing on the back of his chair, and then not so gently. Nothing works. It's an East African man of no more than forty, looking emaciated to the point of starvation; his angular cheekbones protrude so far they seem to pierce the skin. I notice how his head is unnaturally cocked back, not unlike that of a CPR dummy. Nobody sleeps like that. I take in all these observations, but they aren't the first thing I notice.

The first thing I notice is, his eyes are open.

Wide open, body frozen, staring straight up. Completely unresponsive to light or sound. The faint fluorescents offer a feeble glimmer in his pupils, but no spark; this isn't a sleeper. This is a body. He's dead.

The men around us—no women sitting in the back of a 124 at this hour—begin to come closer. What's going on? Can't we wake him up? The ramshackle assemblage, hulking and disheveled, begins to form a village, as we all try to rouse him. He looks dead; he sounds dead; but it doesn't matter. Who cares? You find yourself still making the effort.

We all come from the same place.

I keep clapping, right in the body's face; another man pounds the back of the headrest; Armored Man takes off his headphones. There's a united feeling among all of us, multifarious group though we are: the shared sensation that we, no matter what roads in life led us to this night, would really prefer this person to be alive.

Finally, Nishant decides to touch the body. It's against the rules for safety reasons, but with this many people helping out, safety's no longer a concern. No need to worry about him reacting violently. Anyway, he's dead. Someone reaches to his neck and presses against the jugular vein, firmly.

"Aaoghuu," says the man's throat, his face still expressionless.

We're elated. A collective sigh of relief, audible and true, followed by exclamations—

"Whew!"

"Awesome!"

"Okay!"

"Great," I say, beaming. The young man with sunglasses smiles wide. In any other circumstance the raspy guttural exhale would've been cause for concern, but tonight this, the only sound or movement we are able to elicit from the 'sleeper,' is enough. He is alive.

A phlegm-filled grunt never sounded so good.

IN CHINA

1/3/12

There's something formidable about the place. It surpasses the American understandings of boundaries and size, sidesteps our notions of fealty and social constructs. Remember the childhood feeling, overwhelmed with the realization that the world is more than you know? Travel does that for adults, and China does that for those who travel a lot.

Shenzhen is a port city connecting the mainland to Hong Kong. In 2012, when I was there, it had the indefinable adventurous grit port cities have, the fractal conflations that slip and slide against each other in a concentrated space without borders. The city was burping upwards in fits and starts, a somber sort of puberty evinced by skyscrapers and leveled villages; no corner of communist China reeks more heavily of late-stage capitalist strife than Shenzhen.

My partner and I looked out our window at gleaming laundry and sky-high glass.

We lived obliquely, at the limits of our comprehension. We wandered, coloring in the names of our feelings without language, sussing out the real in a place that moved at a pace beyond. Shenzhen is as different at the end of a month as an American city is after five years. The shanties and open fields I photographed there exist no more, but they *were* once. In cities like Seoul and Milan, I ruminate on the complicated intersectionality between past and present; Shenzhen is another beast entirely. It dreams faster than we can *think*. It speaks not in objects, or echoes, or sanctity, but Motion. It propulsively bulldozes forward at a rate quicker than life. But that isn't what grabbed me.

There are whispers. Sometimes you pause, drawn beneath a tree on a street corner, or stilled by the momentary plainness of an open field. As a government China—at least in Shenzhen—seeks not only to obliterate its past but also its present, chasing the image of progress at the expense of itself, historical identity be damned. But you cannot erase the fact of existence. What is it you can feel in those moments, when you let yourself hear the world speaking softly? What is the essence that so much blind speed tries to cover up, but can't? You take a deep breath and pause, opening your eyes afterwards.

The skyscrapers have nothing on you.

You've absorbed them into your goodness. "If you slow down, you kind of know everything," the painter Laura Hamje once told me. I walked through the melee that is modern China, most fully in the exploding-imploding industrial border-town riot that is Shenzhen, seeking stillness. I would pause, listening. There is something underneath the surface of all things. It is near; it is quiet; and it doesn't insist on itself.

I found it in the beaming eyes of a Uyghur boy I ran into every morning. He didn't speak Mandarin and neither did I, and he also knew no English; no doubt he felt something of the enormity that so bewildered me. He stood there every morning, early, selling his family's flatbread from a tiny rolling cart. I saw him as I saw myself once, a quiet boy from another culture with nothing stylish or exciting to offer, hoping to be taken on my own terms.

Even if we could speak a shared language, it would've been hard to hear each other on the massive sidewalk of this ten-lane road, already buzzing with traffic at sunrise. The bread was simple; there were no tourists; and the locals ignored him, looking sullen and harried. I wondered how many of them worked at the nearby Apple plants, whose infamous mass suicides several years after my visit would draw worldwide attention to a city that was moving too fast.

We made our own glow those mornings, speaking in the language of smiles. I conveyed how much I liked the humble flavors of his family's handmade goods. Do you know what it feels like to see someone react to your kindness in a way that reveals, clearly, that being so treated is for them a rare and cherished occasion? I could almost see him growing taller, so deep was his happiness at my enthusiasm. We made something together, he and I, a mutual appreciation as tangible and real as any flickering candle.

The skyscrapers had nothing on us.

IN PRAISE OF SILVER HAIR

4/30/15

The last thing George Orwell wrote in his diary was, "at [the age of] fifty, everyone has the face he deserves." Meaning, by then your life has overtaken genetics in bearing itself out on your face. Harsh words, yes, but not entirely untrue.

There's a storytelling event I attend each month. The storytellers recounting their experiences come in all shapes and sizes, but lately I've found myself drawn most by a number of the senior women there. Do you ever surf the channels and think, enough with the attractive twenty-somethings already?

The verve these oldsters possess, the vivacious glowing light, a rich twinkling humor you know is earned and strong, still here after all these years . . . *this* is what I find inspiring. Everyone's bitter over something, but I hope I can confront loneliness and loss as they have, and have space leftover to laugh during the fading of the long day.

A woman of similar demeanor recently boarded my bus. On the older buses, which have stairs, the passengers rise into your view as they ascend the steps. From the driver's perspective they become closer and taller all at once. For her it seemed appropriate, in keeping with her confident stride; I saw frizzy silver hair, still cut long, with blazing grey eyes and an unusual knit sweater—a sprightly sense of the individualistic. She paused as she took stock of me, staring as equals and children do.

"Oh wow," she breathed. "Aren't you a little *young*!"

“I am! I should be at home doing my homework! Gettin’ the chores done!”

She grinned, and with a hint of joyful sarcasm replied, “And I should be in the garden, doin’ the yardwork, cleaning the house!” Hers was a tone which said, *there’s a role I’m expected to resign myself to, and I’m so glad I’m not*. She continued with, “but we’re not doing those things.”

“Somehow the world will survive.”

“The world will survive.”

“It’s good to be here.”

“I’m all the happier for it.”

“You and me both.”

The glow on her face was writ large. Orwell would’ve been impressed. Let us continue to be ourselves, conforming to no man’s template, thoughtful and sharp, defiant when we need to be, that we might follow in her admirable lead.

LULIT

5/18/14

Picture yourself on a southbound 36 on Third Avenue, the heart of Seattle's Downtown, back in the days of the older buses with stairs, wherein the first passenger seat was very close to the driver and the layout practically cried out for small talk.

She's coming aboard, a face I've picked up before, but now there's time to converse. When she's with her friends she emits a buoyant youthfulness. I don't understand Amharic, but it's easy to tell when someone's joking, bringing out light in those around her, a soul unafraid to dance. Trim with sparkling brown eyes and a bouncing, playful demeanor; she has on a habesha kemis laced with floral patterns of purple and red, and a glowing starch-white netela. The latter is loosely wrapped round her head, that gauze-like fabric and its aquamarine trim which somehow seems so appropriate today, a literal halo surrounding the radiant elation on her face.

"Hey! Nice to see you!" I say, as she enthusiastically proffers her arm for a handshake. She waits up front, wanting to talk more, and I gesture toward the chat seat. Thank goodness for the old bus. The masses bustle in. She watches as I energetically greet everyone boarding.

Her, leaning forward once we're moving again, with an expectant smile: "Haven't seen you in a long time!"

"Where are you going today?"

"Church! I go to church now, I pray, then I go to work, then I go home see my family, my daughter!" She nodded conclusively with a self-aware affirmation, cognizant of the humor of lists. I laughed. We were at the stage where every sentence has an exclamation point.

"It's a good plan! Where do you work?"

"Sea-Tac."

"Oh, long way."

"Yeah, I take train. I live in Lake City—"

"Oh, I live there too!"

Her eyes brightened. Such enthusiasm for life. But who talked to her? How often do you *really* think someone outside her culture group approached her pleasantly, with no motive, for just a chat and hello? Light rail and Lake City became that much more rewarding to talk about. Something ineffable in the air.

"Yeah, I take the 41!" I said. "I go to the Fred Meyer up there; you know the Fred Meyer?"

"Yeah!" she exclaimed.

"I was just at the Fred Meyer."

"When?" Laughing: "I did not see you!"

I replied, "It's true, just last night! What kind of work d'you do at Sea-Tac?"

"Clean cabin?"

"Say again?"

"Clean cabin." She showed me her shirt. Beneath her elegant dress was, in a hilariously anachronistic surprise, a neon green uniform T-shirt. I asked if she liked her job.

"Yeah," she replied. "I learn a lot. About the engine, about the fuselage, about the cabin . . ." She wasn't being sarcastic.

"That's great! I was just down there yesterday, coming back from California."

"Oh what time!" She was asking a question, but an exclamation point better conveys her spirit . . .

"We landed at 9:05, but it was late, maybe 9:30."

"Oh, I was there! I do four to ten."

"That's amazing!" I declared, without irony. Much has been written about the extremization of language, in the sense that words formerly used to describe things like hurricanes and fear of God are now used to define items like toothpaste and cupcakes. The downside to this is that when something truly astonishing actually occurs, we're left speechless, having no vocabulary remaining to describe it.

For me that's not the case. I really do think certain toothpaste is awe-inspiring. I'm so grateful for whoever ingrained this perspective, whatever chemical imbalance, who knows, that exists in me which allows me to be so thankful—and therefore so easily excited—about life's many offerings. My dear friends are kind; they patiently listen as I continually express astonishment at things like cars letting me merge or sunlight filtering through trees.

"I'm easily thrilled," I'll say, by way of explanation.

"We know," they'll say.

I'm guessing the eavesdroppers on this cluttered peanut gallery of a bus were chuckling at us. But can we help it if we get excited easily? Are we going to stop just because others might disapprove?

Nope.

"I should have said hi!" I exclaimed to her, despite the obvious unlikelihood of such a thing happening. How much of any conversation is really a search for togetherness? Belonging? We are at our best when we reach out with no agenda.

"So do you have other children besides your daughter?"

"No. Just one is enough!"

That got a laugh from more than one person listening. I said, "Good! Me too, I'm an only child."

"Ha! Perfect!"

"She is five. She does not want any other brothers sisters. When I hug other children, she cries!"

By now everyone was laughing. She pointed at her church, standing up.

"It was nice talking to you," I said. "What's your name?"

"Lulit!" *Looleet.* Her smile was infectious.

"Nathan!"

A second handshake, firm and strong. "So nice to see you!"

Strangers bring us up. They deepen our experience. I feel impossibly spoiled sometimes, working a job which affords me the luxury of exchanging bubbly banalities with so many outside my class and culture. I can develop opinions based on primary contact with these people, my own experiences, rather than secondary and tertiary sources of questionable motive, like news channels and targeted articles. Many of us aren't as fortunate. I pity my friends who don't get to be in my position, the ludicrously fortunate position of working with such an uncurated mass of humanity. I can see things I wish they could, too. My words often don't reach them, and I don't try to change their minds. But I get to see it firsthand:

Most humans in most circumstances, everywhere, have good in them.

CONVERSING WITH MY COLLEAGUES: I

4/21/17

I was sprawled out up front on the 41 headed home, exhausted but content, chatting it up with Robert, the driver. He recognized me from my regular presence on this, the last 41 of the night.

"How was your day?"

I sighed happily. I love when people ask me this question with genuine interest. "You know," I replied, "I don't usually do this, but tonight I just let the sleepers sleep the night away on my last trips. I can't do it normally or else everyone finds me and we have you know, hygiene and sanitation problems, but . . . tonight was different because there was no other bus at my terminals to put them on, the way there usually is. So we just hung out. Have you ever done that?"

He thought about it for a moment. "Well, it's good to establish some ground rules."

"Yeah."

"I had an arrangement with this guy once when I was doing the 124," Robert continued. "He asked if he could sleep on the bus and I said yes, and he would get on and go find somewhere to crash, not where everyone wanted to sit, and he would sleep the whole night through. And we did that for about nine months."

"Oh okay. Long time."

"And after ten months, he came back and said, 'Thank you.' And I said, 'for what?' And he said, 'Well, because you let me sleep, I was able to hold down a job that whole time, and now I finally have an apartment.'"

"Wow. That's amazing."

"'Cause sleep is so important. You have to be able to sleep, get good sleep, if you're gonna keep a job. And these guys out here, they can't really—"

"You can't sleep out here—"

"They can't sleep out here. It's too dangerous."

"It's a friggin' zoo—"

"They have to keep one eye open, or move around," he said. "Some of these guys . . . now if they're drinking or whatever, no, no, no. I can't help. It's not that I won't help. I can't. If *they* can't help themselves, *I* can't help them. But if you can develop a relationship . . . when he came back to say thank you, it hit me that it's because he got sleep that any of that was possible. Yeah, and he told me he played music, he'd go down to Pike Place on his days off and try to make a little extra money playing. AJ, or PJ, or something. It was a two-syllable, or rather a two-letter name."

Something stirred in my memory, but it remained buried. A two-letter name. I said, "Wow, he stayed busy! All things considered."

"Well, you can't be too busy when you're homeless."

"Yeah, true."

I take comfort in stories like this. I need to be reminded of the successes. It takes willpower to avoid getting bogged down by certain behaviors I see on the street. Who am I to judge Albert in the bullpen? It's too easy to assume the worst in people we don't know.

That car cutting in front of you—have you noticed how natural it is to assassinate his character . . . until you pull up and recognize him as a friend of yours? Watch how quickly your brain then backtracks, coming up with explanations for why he's in a hurry. They're all just humans, sometimes motivated, sometimes not, imperfectly working with the cards they've been dealt toward approximately the same goals we all have.

Be unreasonably kind and trust the universe to sort it out later.

I couldn't help but think on how I struggle if I miss a single meal or sleep badly for a night. Boo-hoo. What about entire *days* without eating, weeks or months of interrupted, inadequate rest? Add to that the complication of searching for jobs and housing—try getting one without already having the other—and the hurdles of things like birth certificates and social security cards. That stuff is complicated and annoying for *us,* who have easy access to resources. Should I really expect these guys to be civil, pillars of unswayable conscience when faced with easy access to the distractions of drugs and alcohol? I seek here not to excuse, but to explain.

"So many drivers, it's just, get the bums off, get the bums off. But if you see someone who's trying to do something—"

"Man, thanks for sharing that story," I said. "That helps me."

Robert smirked. "So, when you're homeless, just let me know, and I'll be happy to let you sleep on my bus!"

"Ha, it's a deal! You're very kind!"

IT'S NEUTRAL BEIGE'S NIGHT

10/25/14

I still wonder if it would have gone differently had I been a little more present when they got on. These two men were the last two to rush aboard at Fourth and Pike, just in time now, right as the light turned green.

The first was a squat and burly older figure with an ex-football frame, that familiar silhouette of muscular shapes gone plump. Shorts and a torn T-shirt, forties, White. He asked if I go to Broadway. "Yes," I answered distractedly, checking around to see if it was still possible to clear the intersection.

Just behind him the second man boarded, a tall thin fellow in his sixties, dressed in a neutral beige jacket, khakis, and walking shoes that curiously didn't identify any status affiliation. He may have been working-class or a millionaire, European or American. He nodded as I said, "Glad you made it." I closed the doors and announced into the mic, "Okay, we're gonna take this light here, hang on," smoothly accelerating away with six seconds left. Plenty of time.

We continued up Pike without incident. Ex-football man sat up front watching the proceedings, grunting with satisfaction as I dove into the bus lane to skirt traffic. I thought about engaging him but didn't, enjoying a moment of quiet time. Maybe I should have. Neutral beige fellow was seated next to him, but they didn't speak with each other and were clearly strangers.

At Bellevue and Pine, we rolled to a gentle stop for the red light.

Mr. Football stood and came up to me, saying, "Hey, can I get out right here? I kinda wanta go to that store, what is it, Benson's, back there on the corner."

"You know, I've actually gotten in trouble for doin' that, so I gotta say no, but there's a stop around the corner."

"But I wanna go to the store."

"Yeah, there's a stop just up the block here. Didn't you say you wanted to go all the way to Broadway?"

"I know. I wanna go right back there."

The light is staying red, and staying red, and staying red. "I can let you out around the corner here, we got a stop just up the block."

"You can't let me off right here?"

I say, "We're almost there."

"How about if I go out the emergency window?" He points at the first door-side window that has a red emergency lever, which happens to be directly behind those first side-facing seats, where the neutral beige man is sitting.

"Well, I can't stop ya," I say, not expecting him to.

Mr. Football stalks his squat frame over to the window and pulls down the red lever, pushing out the window, preparing to stick his leg through, but—there's one small problem. The beige guy is in the way, sitting right in front of him. He's been sitting there, oblivious to the above conversation, and is now confused: There's a burly guy with a handlebar mustache standing right in front of his face, doing—what? Sticking his leg over my shoulder—

"*What? What the fuck are you DOING*?!" Neutral screams.

"Outta my way," mutters Football.

"Stay the fuck offa me!"

Neutral Beige lifts his legs to his chest and shoves them with all his might into Football's stomach. Football is propulsively thrown backwards, crash-landing into the wheel well directly behind me. A young woman sitting in the midst of all this stands up, disentangling herself, and walks to the back. I imagine she's thinking, since when did fights happen at the *front* of the bus?

The burly man lunges forward—"STAY THE FUCK AWAY

FROM ME" from Neutral, hollering at top volume—lunges forward and grabs the old man's legs and yanks backwards, as though trying to pull Neutral's legs apart from his body. Now the old man's waist and legs are on the floor with his top half following quickly behind. He is on the floor but not completely, his neck still pinned on the seat bottom, and Mr. Football is collapsing on top of him, going at it with his fist. A right into the man's face or left shoulder, hard to tell, somebody's knee hitting the floor. Neutral Beige flounders with his arms, blocking, rotating rather impressively out from underneath, shouting in stammers. "Get the, fuck off . . . fucking asshole . . ." We're moving into the language of grunts.

All this in less than ten seconds. That red light is still red. I open the front door, saying loudly, "Guys guys guys, okay," and Football stands, extricating himself from this mysteriously capable older fellow and running into things on his way out the door, howling in tongues, throwing scraps of paper at me, trying to get back inside but I'm closing the doors, yes just in time thank you, and the light is mercifully now turning green. I roll slowly away. He's out there, a fairy-tale monster who won't go away, still chasing after us, smashing his fist into the front side window, shattering it into a thousand spiderwebs. So much energy. Where does it come from? Why do fights always happen over the most picayune matters?

Eventually he's gone. Neutral Beige is gathering himself, talking to others around him. I ask, "How ya feelin'? Can I call the police for ya, do you want to maybe make a statement . . . ?"

"Nah, it's up to you."

"You sure?"

"Oh yeah, I'm fine."

I looked at him. He was sitting there, much like before the incident, but there was something new in this scene. His sixty-something self was completely energized. He exhaled with a relief that couldn't fully hide his excitement.

"You feel alright?" I asked.

"Oh, yeah, it's nothing."

Actually, he felt great.

You could smell it. Exhilaration was coursing through his veins, and he was no longer old or young or tall or whatever; he was the original version of himself, the invincible youth we all remember being, and he had just proved his quality in no uncertain terms. Wouldn't you feel great? The worst thing you could imagine, the worst possible scenario had taken place on his bus ride home. He was attacked by a younger, bigger, stronger man without provocation, and he had held his own with no assistance. *I've still got it*, and everything is in its right place. It's not something you discuss with others. He just sat there, trying not to smile.

"I hope you have a great rest of the evening," I told him when he got off.

"Oh, I will," he said, allowing himself a small grin. The vitality beaming through.

I think he was the happiest person on the bus.

LOVE IS IN THE AIR

9/21/15

Begrimed is such a perfect word for this man, sitting in the front seat, staring at me. I love the English language. With over 615,000 words, you can nearly always nail down the subtlety you're after. The unlaundered trench coat, kinked and torn and growing stiff with organic filth, fits right in on this ancient, dilapidated vehicle. The non-slip flooring is streaked with peeling paint, and the metallic panels and glass are carved about with various slogans and namesakes, their angular letters vying for attention with the natural blemishes of age.

Several of the interior lights are out, and the resulting gloom emphasizes the shadows of our friends, the bulky figures. As a youngster on the 174, I remember thinking that freeloaders and sleepers seemed larger, occupying of more space, due to their need to carry all possessions on their person. Jackets over hoodies over sweaters, and bags within bags. There's been a lot of napping tonight; beds can be hard to find for those who need them most.

The begrimed man at the front is no sleeper, however. He's wide awake, stubby fingers working as he regards me between thickset, narrowed slits. You know when a face in the shadows is watching you, even if the unkempt mustache conceals the mouth, even if nothing but pinpoints of light mark out the pupils.

He's growling softly. Slowly his growls become discernible. He growls, "After you get off work, I'm gonna take you home and make you mine."

To think of such come-ons as genuine flirtation would be amusing if they didn't end so awfully for some. You almost want to ask, *has that approach ever actually worked*? But of course, it's not about sex, but rather asserting power, fear, dominance. Control.

Somehow my first impulse is to laugh. I do so, saying with friendly confidence, "Oh, I don't know about all that!"

"As soon as you're off, you're comin' with me." A husky rumbling gnarl. "I'll warm you right up."

I did what a female night operator once told me works for her—accept the implicit compliment and then steer the conversation somewhere else. Lead this dance, don't follow.

"Yeah, tonight's my last night before vacation, nine days," I say.

"Lucky you."

"Yeah man, I'm thankful. Doesn't happen often, lemme tell ya."

"Where you goin'?"

"Mostly I'll stay here, but I'm takin' a couple short trips out to the East Coast, then down to LA, that's my hometown."

"What parta LA?"

"South Central. You know South Gate?"

"Yeah, I'm from Orange County."

"Oh, cool! What part?"

"Anaheim." Which, though it's a big city, has zero street cred compared to South Central. In the ongoing (and ridiculous) SoCal geographical status sweepstakes, there's a hierarchy here which works in my favor. The thing to do is let him feel respected despite that, bring him in.

"Oh, cool. Friend of mine went to Chapman, the school there."

"Yeah, it's a good school," he grunts.

"So I've heard. You know what's interesting? They have a piece of the Berlin Wall there, and it's one of only two Berlin Wall slabs that size in the whole US. In Orange County! Go figure." He's not overly engrossed by Berlin Wall remnants, but I don't care. I need to keep leading! "I don't know why. It's like you know the Lenin statue up in Fremont? That's the only Lenin statue in the whole country. I don't know what it means!"

"Huh."

The man's interest in discussing Communist revolutionaries and Cold War artifacts is approximately zilch. He lapses into silence.

As he gets out, he starts saying something about penises, but I heartily steamroll right over the guy with an enthusiastic and concerned "*Have a good one*! Be safe now!"

On my last trip he reappeared.

A distinct difference between taxi drivers and bus drivers is that taxi drivers can choose their fares. Bus drivers can't. I opened the doors at Mount Baker Transit Center and a few people boarded, our begrimed friend included. But there was no cause for fear. We only talked about bus matters. There was no mention of trench coat removal, no dark muttering about fornication and temperature adjustment. I asked how his last hour had been, and where he was off to next. There'd been a mix-up with his keys. He needed to go to his landlord's to drop off a pair, and there was no bus going that way for a while. We discussed landlords and bus routing in SoDo. As we approached Chinatown, we considered the remaining distance and figured it might be quicker for him to walk.

This time as he left, he said something about beds, but once again I was entirely too busy thanking him to hear: "*Be safe walkin' out there*! Take it easy!"

"You too!"

Like nothing awkward had ever happened. I let out a deep breath. Thank you, female colleagues who work alongside me, you champions of the night, who navigate moments like this more than I have to, and who so kindly teach me how to follow in your footsteps.

I bow to you.

THE BULLET TRAIN

2/9/18

Ibrahim laughed. His perfect teeth shown in the reflective dark; it was one of those dry nights, clear, where the silhouettes of trees and buildings are not foreboding but comforting. We stood outside our respective coaches, both one trip away from going home.

"Why do you like the 7? What's your trick, Nathan? Every time, even before I became bus driver, I saw you only on this one."

Ibrahim's wise. I think he knew the answer. As an operator he's new, one of many recent hires, and from his youthful appearance and movie-star-smooth good looks you might not expect wisdom . . . ah, but the world is full of surprises.

"I like the people," I replied. "Really!"

"Yeah, they all know you. Once they know you, they don't mess with you."

"Yeah, usually it's good. I like to go with the flow, you know?"

He nodded. "If you act tough, *they* will act tough. We got stuff to lose. But they have nothing to lose. They don't care about going to jail, they have already been there many times. What could possibly go wrong for them? They don't have anything."

"Yeah, it will never work, acting tough. They can always outdo you." I was repeating his words mainly that I might better remember them; he'd just coalesced a hodgepodge of good instruction into a single succinct sentence, and I wanted to fold it up in my pocket for later. "I like to just make friends, be nice, and forget about it!"

"And once they know you're nice . . . Hey, you know that one lady?"

I chuckled ruefully. I knew exactly who Ibrahim was talking about. He didn't even have to describe her. Twice my age, half my height, and as hateful as I am happy, she's the yin to my yang. I search for the positive in life because it works for me; in some fashion, her bitter, profane "Irish temper," as she calls it (it's a lot more than that), must do the same for her. Orwell's last journal entry about faces came to mind; I wonder if he was thinking of Iris, who looks like you'd look if you'd frowned and cursed without stopping for a half-century. Ibrahim managed to get on her good side once, and I listened, flabbergasted.

"I'm impressed," I said. "She's so . . . I wanna be like *you*! You know, I know someone who used to know her, decades ago."

"Oh wow."

"And she used to be better! Had a different name then. She drank too much, but she was much more normal."

Ibrahim sighed, shifting his weight. He looked out at the stars, exhaling into the cold air. He spoke.

"You know, this country is different. It's like a train that's moving too fast. One wrong move, and you might fall off."

"So easily!"

"So easily," he said. "Just one thing."

"A couple of paychecks—"

"A couple of paychecks, or your house, or child support. Man. I know a guy, homeless guy, and he goes to UW!"

"I know him too! Older, wears a hat?"

"Yeah yeah!"

"Yeah, he was telling me, he used to live on Queen Anne, everything . . ."

Ibrahim nodded. "Or this Somali guy, one of those guys who hangs out at Fifth and Jackson. His name is Amal. He used to be truck driver, had a wife and a son, but his wife started acting up, and they split, and he had to pay the child support, started drinking—"

"And then you just go down—"

"Yeah. Lost his job, everything. Now he's out there in the rain. He used to have a family and a job! I talk to him like man, you still have your license. You could figure your stuff out. And he says no, now I have pneumonia, my kidneys, this, but I told him you got to just get up and start working on it."

"*Do* something," I said.

"Yeah. Or else he's gonna die on the street alone."

"And that would be too tragic, too sad. Somebody's father."

"Yeah."

We're all fighting our own big, complicated battles. Take it one step at a time. Nobody ever achieved the summit otherwise.

PLACE DE RÉPUBLIQUE

11/14/15

Certain moments resurface whether you want them to or not. The image of those girls attacking poor Chosen continued sticking in my craw, a pain in my heart jarring thoughts loose. You see iniquities out here that you can't fix, too many, people you can't help . . . and you know dwelling on certain things will lead only downward, into the helplessness of no-control, a self-induced suffering that will help exactly no one. You remind yourself that simply bearing witness can be enough. It is a significant act, and sometimes all we can do.

And yet. Chosen was on my mind, because he brought into focus what was really brewing inside me: Paris. The thoughts cycled, tossing like my clothing in that French dryer:

There is something I don't understand. I cannot, for the life of me, grasp why such horrible badness befalls good people. I realize this has been debated since the dawn of time, implying no one else knows the answer either, but that does not comfort me. There are nights when I am haunted by the unblinking silence of the world.

I try to remember all are good and bad, and none are good and bad. Our nuances transcend such categories. In my own life, it seems the finest people I know consistently receive the worst agonies; but maybe everyone feels this way. We know best the misfortunes of those whom we love most, but everyone else has their hardships too.

For a long time, there was a part of me that was always waking up on November 14th, 2015. Always wandering Paris's empty streets. They would never be so desolate again, not even during COVID. As the days passed I walked further, revisiting the improvised plaques and flag-draped statues. There were things I did not photograph; sometimes it feels wrong to take a picture. I read the graffiti, all of which was for once the same new topic and tone, a reflection of our stunned, city-spanning grief. *Même pas peur*, a banner read. Tucked away in a corner, English scrawled on stone: *Be a helper*. Writ large across a construction zone wall barrier: *Si peur & ignorance = haine & guerre . . . confiance envers autrui & connaissance = amour & paix?*"*

Despite announcements urging against congregating in public, we found ourselves drawn, we strangers, toward Place de République, the historic square. Did we only number in the tens of thousands? Or was it hundreds of thousands, or more? To this day no figure has been settled upon for how many mourners appeared, there and elsewhere. At the time it felt like all of Paris. This was a crowd unique among crowds, where no small talk was necessary, no silence awkward. Although I crave connection and community, I hope you never have to know what it feels like to share a plaza with innumerable other people as mute, stricken, and trauma-shocked as myself.

We gravitated toward the central statue of Marianne, the national personification of France whom you've seen in the old masterworks, and who represents liberty and reason— two qualities which did not exist on the previous night. It felt right to mourn here. All around the statue's enormous base, thousands of letters, flowers, and candles formed an impromptu memorial. A printed photograph amongst the candles stood out; there were not many photos. I knelt down to look closer.

Landscape letter, cheap Xerox-printed black-and-white. Four figures nicely but modestly dressed for a night out, all standing, with balloons and flowers behind. Perhaps a birthday party. A printed caption in block capitals runs along the bottom of the image: *REPOSE EN PAIX, MAUD*. Which of the three women is

Maud? A couple have the expectant smiles you don't know you're making when the flash goes off. Another is beaming, the brunette in the center. Is it her? The man on the right wears a Santa hat and the kind of enigmatic half-forming smile capturable only by da Vinci or Vermeer or photography, a record of emergent thought. Of life.

One of those faces, or maybe more of them, was living no longer. The mourning figures around me, the candles and slogans and statues and blood all receded into my periphery. There was only this picture. I thought of Maud. I looked at their faces, young people with goals and dreams. I thought of the men who killed them, young people too, children once. I had never before cried in the company of thousands of strangers, but I did then.

These people are my friends, I thought, internally addressing the terrorists. *Why did you do that? Why did you destroy them, and break the lives of all who knew them? You are my friend too, in that you are human. Did you not know it would break you too? Have you ever known anyone to get away with anything, ever?*

When we discuss the meaning of life, we are usually talking about the meaning of tragedy in life. Aside from the question of why we exist in the first place, the rest generally makes some kind of sense. But what to make of the suffering foisted on good people? This cruel riddle is both smaller than the fundamental query of why we're here and at the same time more relevant. Because if we knew the answer, we would achieve the miracle of being at peace with all acts of man and nature. The philosophies and religions we offer each other are suppositions, the best of them based on experience, each carrying their different rings of truth.

I recall now the definition of optimism my parents once taught me: being comfortable looking at truth, even when it's negative. I recall the Taoist principle of accepting everything in front of you without wanting it to be any other way. These maxims make life easier, but one day you will encounter a situation where abiding by them feels like a crime. A dying loved one; a permanent injury;

bodies in the streets. It is so hard sometimes, so impossible.

But we have to try, or we will never find peace.

---

* *If fear and ignorance equal hate and war . . . trust in others and knowledge equal love and peace?*

IN SUPPLICATION

9/2/15

"HEY, DO YOU KNOW WHAT TIME IT IS?"

Southbound Third and Marion, as the world is going home. I love when I know people's names.

"Hey, Mr. Hau Ling! It's 7:17." He's a spirit I know from the late-night runs, thirties maybe, angular, with a childlike sensibility unnoticed by those distracted by his penchant for stentorian volume.

"SEVEN SEVENTEEN?"

"Yeah."

After staring a moment, my face starts to make sense to him. "OH HEY, IT'S YOU!" he thunders. "DO YOU LIKE ME?"

"Yeah, you're a nice guy."

"SOME DRIVERS DON'T LIKE ME," he roars. "They won't even open the GODDAMN door."

"That's no good," I reply in an agreeable tone.

"Do you know why? DISCRIMINATION!" Pause. Reflecting. Then: "WHY DO I TALK SO LOUD?"

I find him endearing in a way, with his sweatpants and no-frills jacket, clothes your mother would choose for their practicality, though she'd have found a cleaner pair; and his baseball cap, not the trendy flat-billed kind, no, just the old-school regular, a person outside the peaks and valleys of fashion. His comment about "goddamn doors" and subsequent answer were articulated with an uncomplicated passion I consider oddly adorable. The last question was asked innocently, as though he really was curious. Why *do* I talk so loud, after all?

I was reminded of a long-ago memory: A girlfriend and I were waiting to cross Third Avenue in Belltown, and she circled to the other side of me, further away from a homeless gentleman on the sidewalk. The man saw this and said to me, "Why's she afraid of me?" I looked at him with kind eyes, caught dry for words. Then he sighed, saying, "Why's everyone afraid of me?"

"I don't know," I said. He swung his arms in the afternoon sun, one part bored and two parts frustrated, pondering how the world saw a type, not a person, when they looked at him. I wish I had bid him a good day.

Mr. Hau Ling likewise seemed to be asking a question not to me but to the universe. "I don't know," I said once again, in a friendly tone I haven't always known how to use so comfortably.

"DO I NEED TO SEE A DOCTOR?" he bellowed. Which sounded like, *is there something wrong with me*?

"No, I bet you could talk quiet if you wanted to."

"I CAN HEAR PEOPLE AND CARS PERFECTLY!"

Mr. Hau Ling grinned with pride, and without trying I couldn't help but reflect his smile. "That means you got no problem, it's all good!"

He gave me a thumbs up, his grin toothy and crooked, unfeigned, one of the evening's many sparkling whispers of the bona fide.

Let me hang on to every little moment like that. Let me have the eyes to note the positive, no matter how minute, and recognize its substantiveness, that I might not rot into jadedness, or miss out on some of the very real events surrounding me, twinkling like so many fireflies in the night.

Maybe this can be the way forward.

RICHARD

1/2/18

Richard rides a lot. He's homeless, but not a sleeper. He's always going somewhere. He has a limited wardrobe and an ungainly wheelbarrow-like stroller to which are strapped all his possessions, but the questionable odor one might expect is nowhere to be found. This guy's got it figured out.

The longer I'm alive, the more I realize the degree to which a person's character and appearance today is but a surface ripple over the iceberg of their past. There's always more to a person, and they were never quite how they appear now.

Some of my homeless friends suffer from limited educational opportunities. Others clearly finished school, but their intelligence is clouded by untreated mental health issues (like Nefarious Peripheral, whom I once listened to for forty-five minutes as he told me how aliens and communists relate to volcanic explosion cycles, just to stay on his good side!). Richard's of neither stripe. He's just another smart, thoughtful guy with reasonable opinions. He listens. I'm always happy to see that familiar figure, an urban Santa positioned at the ready in the zone, blue eyes peeking out from under a weathered baseball cap, his bag of treasures in tow.

He once got on my bus because the previous operator had passed him up, on the grounds that Richard's lil' cart was a "fire hazard." I expected Richard to be frustrated by that and was ready to give him room to vent it out.

"Well that's super lame," I said.

"Well, not really," he replied amicably, referencing his experience as a former union shop steward. "It's his prerogative to assess if it's a fire hazard, and if he says it is, well then, on his bus it is."

Prerogative. I love Seattle. In the country's most educated city, even those on the class ladder's lowest rungs know their way around a dictionary. Another night he was expounding on the "new lady in my life"—a stray kitten—and pointed out that he's "never been able to divine a cat's age strictly from their appearance." *Divine*. When was the last time you heard it used as a verb? Oh, how I love life!

For months he rode my 7/49 without saying much. Only lately do we sometimes have scattered conversations, punctuated with the silence and rhythm of the world walking on and off. Some nights it's trivia he'll share, relating to conversation I'd been having with someone else: Archibald Leach being Cary Grant's real name. Or, it'll be the twinkle in his eye as he asks me, in a dead-dog serious voice, "Can you do me a small favor?"

"Sure thing. What's up?"

The comedian's pause, and then: "Enjoy your day off."

I sometimes think I was born twenty or thirty years too late. I assume most people do, because we're comfortable in the world we spent our childhoods adapting to. Richard's beyond that. He thinks he was born 600 years too late.

"Well now," I said.

It turns out he had a previous career in welding, and his thesis at LW VoTech was a period-accurate re-creation of a medieval knight's armor. It weighs seventy-two pounds. We talked—or rather he talked, and I listened—about the difference between steel and aluminum as building materials, the way shield and chest armor are carefully surfaced to deflect spear throws, and how the gauntlet is the hardest part to build, because it has the most moving parts.

I wasn't on a bus. I was at a graduate seminar. He was excited because he recently got to wear the armor with some fellow medieval enthusiasts. I was so happy for him, hearing his tempered but entirely unaffected enthusiasm.

Maybe it is profound, the way he surprises us with his gentle wit and history. I was surprised when I learned he got ten solid hours of sleep the previous night, automatically making him the envy of the entire homeless community. How does he manage that? Prerogative. Divine. Gauntlets. He and I discussing Michael Wadleigh's use of three-strip 16mm in the landmark documentary *Woodstock*. I couldn't believe it. Somebody in my life besides me knows about that . . . and it turns out to be this guy on my bus?? Richard almost made it to Woodstock in 1969. He had tickets. Too many crowds though, miles out. But he was there on the sidelines of history, as we all are from time to time, and here he is forty years later, chatting with a youngster half his age and weight about the same details, finding excitement and brotherhood in the unlikeliest of places.

If it was in a movie, we wouldn't believe it. We'd call it too cheesy, too cornball to withstand real life. Let us however remember that in real life, in our world, corny does not track. There's room out here for the best in people, for surprises, deviations from the narratives we've been told to believe.

We just have to look for it.

I BET YOU APPROVE UH GAY MARRIAGE!

9/23/13

"We're just goin' to the nex' stop."

Somehow that's often the way it begins. He slurred it out as best he could, stumbling around up front. In tow was a woman about his age, forties, with her grandson, a boy of about eight. The boy was chubby and had a chocolate milkshake in hand.

The speaker was a dedicated drunk; worn-down, nondescript blue and black clothing. His friend and her grandson were a little more put together. They were sober. Our bus being somewhat full, the boy stood in the aisle while they sat near me.

"Ey, sit the fuck down, boy. Got to play by th' rules," he said to the youngster, who didn't respond.

Quietly, the young Grandmother: "Don't talk to him like that."

The boy in question impressed me. Not only did he seem utterly unfazed by the father figure's barbs, but he didn't feel the need to put up a front, either. He wasn't stoic, or too cool for school, or any other defense mechanism. He was simply there. Doing his best to ignore the negative energy and enjoy another sip of that milkshake.

"Stop holdin' on them bars like a li' girl and sit the fuck down."

"But I like standing," the boy replied in a kind voice. It's the kind of voice you could never yell at, not if you were sober.

"Keep runnin' your goddamn mouth, you little motherfucker. I'ma show you how this world work."

"It's okay."

"Watch what happens, boy."

We're at a red light. I turn round to face him. "Hey," I say in a normal voice. No response. Again, loudly: "HEY! MAH FRIEND!"

He snaps to attention. Everyone is instantly silent.

Back to normal volume: "I don't think you need to yell at that boy."

"Fuck is you talkin' to. I got nothin' to say to you."

"Don't yell at him, man. Yell at me."

"Wha . . ."

"Yell at me."

"Man, shut the fuck up. I say the fuck I wanna say—"

"Go on, man, get it outta your system—"

"Little kid tryna stir some shit—"

"Aw, don't stop now!"

Every minute he's yelling at me is another moment of respite for that boy. My heart goes out to the youngster. I wonder if he has to listen to this all the time.

"Grabbin' them bars like a pansy," he says to the youngster, turning to me again. He contemplates life for a moment and then says to me, in a tone of revelation, "I bet you's a *faggot*!"

"I said *get it outta* your system—"

"I BET YOU APPROVE UH GAY MARRIAGE," he lurches out.

"Yup yup yup, lettin' it all out, good—"

Into the microphone I say, "Have a good night, everyone—"

"—Faggot—"

"Thanks for hangin' out—"

"Wearin' nice pants and shit—"

"You folks stay safe this evening—"

"Crease down the middle—"

"Maybe see you tomorrow . . ." Now our friend is getting up, balancing, as we pull into the next zone— "Broadway and Jefferson, everyone, hope you all have a *great evening*—"

"Muth-a-fuck-in asshole, tellin' me the fuck to do, you all dressed nice, lookin' good for the ladies and shit—"

We're almost at the zone. People are getting up, milling about, thinking let me outta here. He stands.

"Fuckin' buttons and shit, gay-ass—"

I get off the mic and look him in the eye: "Hey, listen. You have a *good* night now."

There's a way to say that line that cuts to the bone and twists like a knife. I'm a little ashamed to say that that's exactly how I said it. Perhaps I shouldn't have. Why?

Because he used to be a toddler once, who was probably yelled at exactly as he's yelling now. Deep down there, buried someplace, dwells a kernel of goodness. He must have heard my tone, because he paused and said, in a measured voice of furious confusion—

"What the fuck?"

You could almost hear his voice crack, like a teenager whose surprise has overtaken his anger. He's towering over me now, teeter-tottering, a spinning top starting to slow. In his mind though, he's still Genghis Khan. He's Patton at Messina. Hostile, belligerent, snarling pugnacious: "*What's your name*?"

Say it with confidence.

"*My name is Nathan*!! You have a goooood night!!"

There isn't anything else the poor guy can say. He stumbles down the steps, onto the sidewalk, one foot crossing out, balance going and there he goes, tipping on the slanting pavement, slipping, falling, everybody watching, the boy sipping his milkshake, this dark, lanky figure crumpling out against the white cement squares, collapsing into a young tree. His body slides into the landscaping, arms almost laconically reaching up for air, rolling through nothing, small bushes and beauty bark, a victim of gravity and vice.

Not a soul offers help. They just look on.

Young Grandma watches her friend try to stand up. "Sorry 'bout this," she says to me. She means it.

"Are you gonna be okay?"

"Oh, yeah. Yeah, Ah be alright."

Two hours later she got on again, alone. Was that her?

"Hey," I said. "Are you the woman from earlier . . . ?"

Yes, she was.

"Your man back there looked like he wasn't having a very good day."

"Yeah, he just my friend. I ain't seen him in a while, we went and had a couple beers."

"A couple?!"

"Yeah! He kinda gets like that."

"Guess we all have that friend drinks a little too much."

"You got tha' right!"

"You know, I'm glad you got on again, 'cause afterwards I felt bad about yelling at him. I shoulda been nicer to the guy." I was worried about him seeing me again.

"*What*? Oh dude, don't worry about it. Yeah, he's legally blind and pretty deaf. Always thinks people are out to get him."

"Okay, okay. I felt bad for your boy!"

She explained he was her grandson, and I told her to congratulate him on his attitude. I should have taken that chubby kid by both shoulders and said, *You are awesome. You deserve all the insight this life has to offer, and you should run this town someday.* I should've done everything that can be done in five seconds to balance out however many hours, weeks, and years he's had to receive such hate. But I couldn't think fast enough. Seeing Grandma replenished me, brought the noise down to something comprehensible.

A few weeks later, the same man got on again. Which attitude to take? Should I harbor the past, even out the score, make judgments? No. There are so many reasons why those are bad ideas, but frankly, they simply take too much energy. I remembered only that I needed to speak up.

"Hey," I said in a friendly voice. "How's it goin'?"

"Good, good," he said. "Thanks."

"Right on."

KIND HEART

8/15/13

We're crowded today. Somewhere amidst the throng back there is a young family. Two toddler girls, with their father, mother, and stroller in tow; Mom's wearing purple, her hair in braids, tied back in a high ponytail. Dad has a puffy white jacket and close-shaven hair, no sunglasses, with heavy blue jeans and basketball shoes. For lack of a better description, he looks exactly like Big Boi on the cover of Outkast's double album *Speakerboxxx/The Love Below*. He'd been watching me do my thing, as I greeted and chatted up all the passengers.

They, the family in back, seemed weary from what looked to have been a long day. The daughters gazed out the window, or leaned against Mom, drifting in and out of slumber. The crowd was a mixture of everyone—happy, tired, impatient. From the back lounge, Big Boi looked on in silence, taking in my behavior.

At 15th and Pine, the family came up to leave. The girls ("Bye!" "Bye!") were first out. "Thank you," said Mom to me in a subdued but truthful voice.

"No, thank you! Take care now!"

Big Boi brought up the rear, carrying the stroller, holding his big jacket in close to keep it from hitting people. When he got to me he said quietly, "Hey. You're doin' a great thing."

"Thank you!"

"Carin' about the people."

"Thank you," I said, wishing I could convey how much it meant.

As they began walking away, he turned back and added: "Kind heart!"

He said it with the muted enthusiasm of a quiet hope. There was a gentle sadness in his face, the way God's might look were she to survey her wayward children. The late Roger Ebert once wrote that it wasn't the tragic events in films which brought him to tears, but rather the moments of people being enormously good to each other. To see empathy, to see compassion; these are the actions that stop us in our tracks.

PART III

THE CHILDREN INSIDE

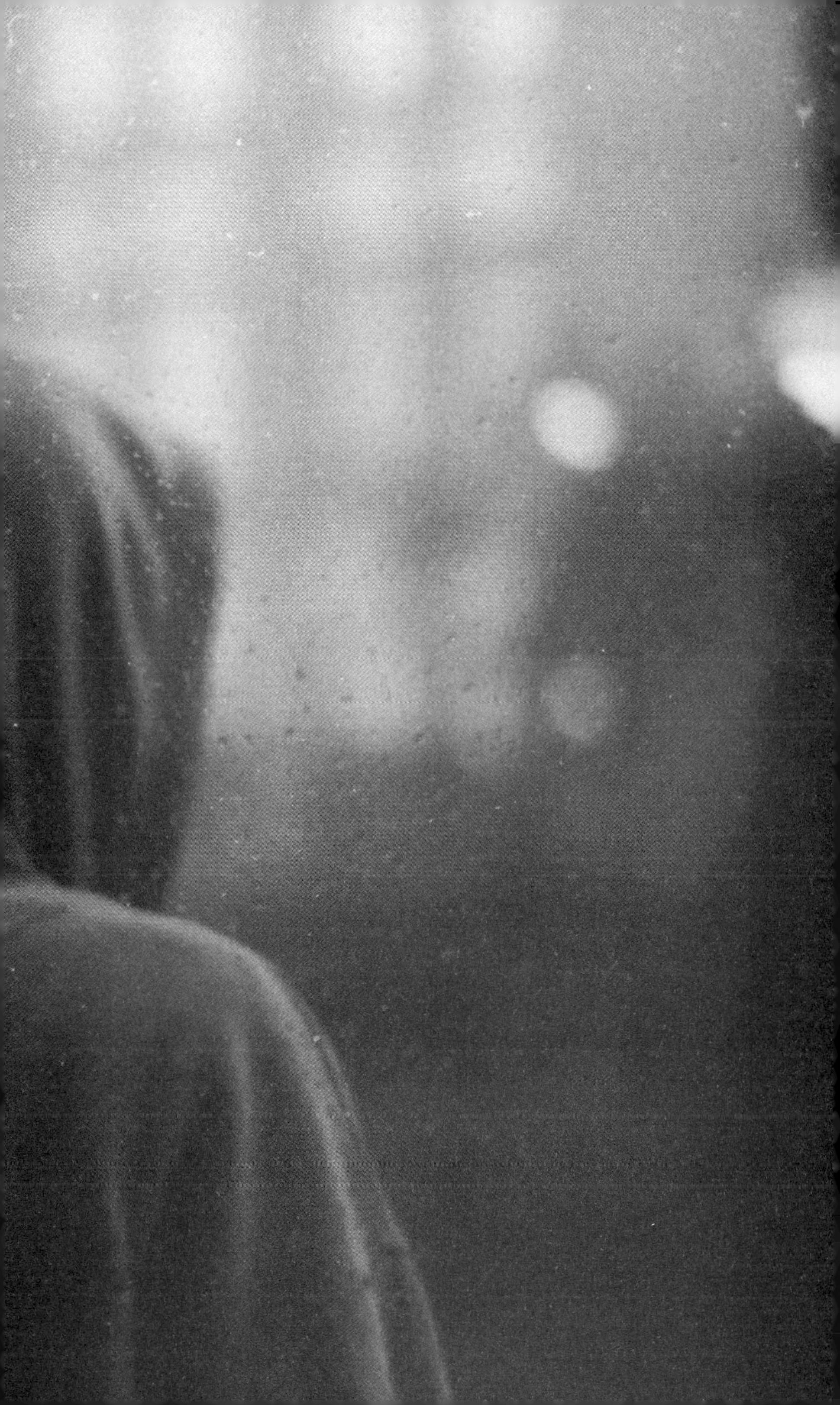

EULOGY FOR THE DAMNED

5/23/19

Oh, Darlene.

No other phrase encompasses the spectrum of thoughts and feelings I have for this god-forsaken creature. She dared you to hate her, pity her, dismiss her, and love her, sometimes in a single breath. If you walked more than once through Third and Pine, Third and Union, or Third and James, you would have seen her, that unruly daughter of an outcast god, a litmus test of a person who caused in you reactions which revealed more about yourself than her.

I once spent the better part of an hour chatting with three homeless teens. Among other things, I learned that as a homeless person it often behooves you to pretend your circumstances are more dire than they are. To lie.

Housing and other services get prioritized for those with more extreme hardships, and if you tell them you're schizophrenic and bipolar, for example, rather than (or better yet: in addition to being) merely thrown out by abusive foster parents, you're going to get a leg up. If you tell those unwitting tourists the bruises on your leg are from something truly tragic, rather than the stupid fall you just had, it might further convince them you're in need. It's a curious position to be in, and one brought on by too many people fighting for the same resources:

You're lying in order to emphasize the truth.

The thing is you really do need help. You're on the street. But that's not enough anymore. Everyone's on the street, and your problems are too complicated to explain quickly.

How the pain medication from your on-the-job injury has developed over the years into a full-blown hard drug addiction.

How the continuous sensation of being treated like dirt because of your race and appearance makes you want to fight the world.

The thorny family situation you could return to, but which would actually be worse than being out here, if you can believe it.

Or maybe you do have housing, but it's in a roach-infested subsidized building with enough crime and drug issues as to be so far away from anyone's definition of a home that it feels more accurate to just say: you're homeless.

It's real and it's dire, the three kids explained to me, but it's too convoluted. People only listen to extremes nowadays. Sure, being homeless and hungry is a big deal for you, but you have to compete with people who actually *are* suffering the extremes you end up having to pretend, or who really do have the sanctimonious moral fiber you wish you possessed. They're getting sympathy and solutions from social workers, strangers, and others, and you need sustenance.

Time to come up with a strategy . . . and maybe not an ethical one. Because ethics are a privilege of those who are doing well. You'll be your good self later. Right now, you've got to survive.

And thus, it begins . . .

Darlene's strategy is to pretend to cry. Few, if any, street people look as utterly and spectacularly miserable as hers truly. Yes, American homeless people are much better off than the maimed, deformed, and starved souls I've met abroad, but as far as US streets are concerned, you haven't met Doing Poorly until you've met Darlene.

How long have those inadequate rotting slippers been on her feet, melded and twisted in her flesh as they are? Which actual color is the fabric of her pants? What precious few teeth does she have left, and at what point did her slurred, nigh incomprehensible torrents of speech become her norm?

She reeks less of the expected smells than of a particular brand of dirt I used to encounter when I drove past a certain landscaping plant in Bellevue. She'd step on board and my nose went right back to afternoons at Pacific Topsoils, Incorporated, maybe with a little human putrefaction thrown in. Ah, memory lane . . .

Don't get me wrong, dear reader. I like Darlene. Street people, especially at the volume and level of mental illness at which we in Seattle now possess, are not an embarrassment of themselves but the chagrin of those with the power and position to do something constructive . . . and don't. The homeless person carries a cross of shame belonging less to her than to the society that would pretend her problems don't matter.

Any individual before you is a result of the cause-and-effect timeline that is their lives, and if you think people end up where they are because of their choices alone, brother, you've lived a charmed existence. Someday life will just happen to you, and you'll shake your fist at your god or your devil, wondering why. It isn't because you're an awful person, my friend. It's just life.

Darlene's body vibrates from withdrawal with a persistence you sense she must not notice, twitching shudders made invisible by their constancy, known only to her as a pain she must fix. It's obvious she's an addict, that she's unappealing, even repugnant, and you know she knows it too; what then is a girl to do for sympathy?

This is where the crying comes in. Like the best of actors, she can manufacture tears at the drop of a dime. It's impressive. An unsuspecting commuter will round the corner toward her, and her eyes and lips crinkle and split sideways, instantly at the stage it should take hours of grieving to get to.

Watching her perform, I'd sometimes find myself genuinely touched. Who am I, after all, to say how fake those tears are? What great sorrows, hardships of the soul and body, roil beneath her drug-fueled haze? I happen to know this: She was once a nurse practitioner, an educated woman on her way. Her husband would beat her in their younger married days, regularly, such that she fell into heavy drinking. Then came the drugs.

I first met her during grade school, offering her a handful of change which she accepted, and from which she immediately picked out the pennies and nickels, throwing them on the ground. At twelve years old, I was disgusted. I'd worked for that money. But she had other problems.

Single-minded is a euphemism you think applies to many people, until you know Darlene; it's a veritable science, how she's streamlined her actions down. If it doesn't have to do with cocaine, opioids, Red Vines, or Twizzlers, it's not even remotely on her radar (though she did mention Skittles and once, incongruously, spaghetti with chicken and marinara sauce . . .). But crack, mainly. Crack and little else.

Darlene died recently, in the dried-up turtle fountain at the northwest corner of Third and Yesler. It's a terrible place to die. Not many will miss her.

But with whom will I have conversations about Red Vines versus black licorice, or the merits of peanut M&Ms? Whom will I marvel at as I did her, this strange asexual beast who didn't walk but shuffled, who could shuffle into the busiest street without looking for cars (Darlene never looked for cars; far too prosaic for her focuses) and never get hit? Did she know how she would later be killed, and that it wouldn't be by a car or bus? Is that how it works?

I want to believe she had some secret bulletproof gene that separated her from all other hard drug users: she was invincible. There's her, Hunter Thompson, and Keith Richards. I swear these people are bionic. Darlene destroyed her body every day in ways that daily kill many younger souls, but she kept right on into late age.

Usually, she wasn't able to say much besides the street name containing the subsidized housing in which she lived. "JAMES," she would scream repeatedly, a scream which will echo in many an operator's head, including my own, until the end of time. I loved responding with the same word yelled at equal volume, the two of us creating our own echo chamber, the glee in my voice deeply confusing the other passengers.

No, I can't solve her problems. But I can yell a duet with her down Third Avenue that befuddles people and makes me laugh—with her, you understand, not at her. Wouldn't it be funny if every passenger roared their destination stop with guttural force, saying little else?

Darlene's strategy for absorbing life's blows was to turn away. Addiction provided a solace she was unable to find elsewhere, and before it claimed her life she lived in a hidden place of her own mind's making. It was distant, this place, some other planet, but it was just near enough for me to hear her yelling *James*, and for me to yell back.

She always threw in a few coins for bus fare—perhaps vestiges of a childhood in which she was taught to pay her way. I now realize the coins she tossed in were pennies and nickels; she found a use for those things after all. Sometimes I'd get a sentence or two of conversation besides out of her—I always tried—and blushed when she'd croak, "YOU TH' NICE BUS DRIVUH. YOU KIND." Yes, her spittle would come flying at me in ways I didn't particularly appreciate. And yes, I don't exactly love being involuntarily inundated with the smell of Pacific Topsoils, Incorporated.

But I will think of the young woman who lived inside her, deep down and far away, the newlywed who didn't want to get beaten, didn't want to go home, couldn't stand the pain.

Who hurt.

Emotional pain hurts worse than physical pain, and domestic abuse cuts deep because it is both. She was the woman who had no one to turn to, and looked for answers in all the wrong places. It doesn't matter if those tears were real or fake.

There was a reason they were there.

THE QUESTION

2/2/17

They can still be one of your favorite passengers, even if you hardly see them more than once or twice a year. The last time I saw Jacqueline was two New Year's Eves ago. She'd just acquired keys to her new apartment, further north on Rainier, and she was excited. We spoke of reduced commute times, new roommates, and the adventure of transporting possessions by bus.

She was a unique compliment to the riders around her, especially after dark in the Southlands. Her demure ponytail and sensible attire, chosen with warmth in mind, couldn't disguise a certain electric vitality, unafraid and insistent on being herself, regardless of circumstances. Her, the rare White passenger on this line, the rare female passenger at night, sitting cross-legged on the bench seat. Something powerful in her slight, unassuming frame, radiating from those sharp blue eyes—or maybe sharp green eyes, I can never remember.

We bonded over literature. How refreshing, this lettered, erudite young mind steeped in books not just from school, more than able to hold her own against her busmates, unsuspecting older men trying to tell her the state of things. Some among the younger set try to hide their intellectual acumen, not realizing there's a way to be smart and stylish at the same time.

Jacqueline's likely in her post-collegiate years but has the relaxed confidence of someone either older, or much younger. Her voice doesn't need to broadcast her affinities, feels no pressure to proclaim her quality. I'm impressed by people like that.

Tonight, two years later, our conversation isn't about books or moving furniture. She's telling me about her new squeeze, and it's next-level stuff. They've eloped. *Serious* is the wrong word, although that would be true; potent is better. Spirited. She's been in long relationships before—very long ones—and knows what heartache is. So when she, with her battle-scarred heart, shares how excited she is about this new fellow, I pay attention. It's an unusual mixture; she's Juliet on the balcony, walking on air, but she's been through so much more. I expect this ebullience from teenagers. How does she do it? Listen to that voice, those sparkling eyes.

The fact that she possesses the very same is a *cause de joie,* proof that we can rebuild without putting up walls, that we can still find it in ourselves to be vulnerable, that hardest and most worthwhile thing, and the place where beauty is born.

Jacqueline asked me, "Have you ever been in love?"

She put the question forward with genuine excitement. She asked because she knew it was the most beautiful mode of existence, and that it was exceedingly rare. She asked because she knew it lived in fiction more frequently than in life. That being in a relationship was no kind of guarantee, and sometimes the loneliest place of all. She asked because she knew it sometimes never happens, but if it did, you cherished it, no matter how awkward or strange or new. She asked because she trusted I was smart enough to know these things. Her voice carried the wisdom that was nimble enough to be foolish, brave enough to be open.

I thought for a long time before answering.

IN NAPOLI

1/8/15

For whatever reason, all the boys in sight had basically the same haircut: a semi-close shave on the left side, and on the other side, longer hair with fashionable curls, echoes of the flapper aesthetic. The look was absurdly specific to be so ubiquitous, but there you go. It was all the rage in 2015 southern Italy.

I was traveling alone, late-twenties restless, eager to feel for myself the bewilderment, the joy, the soul-filling melancholy of seeing a thousand things for the first and last time. No other experience more closely approximates early childhood. The bombardment of stimuli, languages you don't understand, every word and color something new—settings where memory is insufficient to comprehend existence. This is where I needed to be. We are taught how to think, but not how to feel; any first-time life event involving emotions is one we stumble through. We will always be amateurs.

I drifted through the cluttered square, an open oblong plaza from which extended five or six ancient cobblestone streets heading off at odd angles. You felt a weekend sensibility here, adolescent gaggles of arms and legs and dreams. Must have been school break. Do you remember what it meant to be that age? Timid and loud together? I rode the subway into town, and they were everywhere. I imagined similar scenes on the other subways coming in. These were the nights of possibility, humid air rife with hormones and longing.

Even in Napoli, people look put together; it's still Italy. I was by far the worst-dressed person in sight, with my stocky black raincoat, unwashed hair, ill-fitting black jeans, and dirty boots. I hid my film camera in my coat and tried to keep a low profile. Rione Sanità, Centro Direzionale, the infamous Vele di Scampia (now demolished) . . . places with the stench of death, stifling in their danger and callous malfeasance. Tourists don't come here. You, the photographer, survive by being invisible. I wouldn't go back now, but I had then something of the youthful chutzpah these teens surrounding me possessed, the vitality that feels like a safeguard against the city's looming threat. The irony is that I slipped through these truly deadly locations unscathed, only to nearly die later in tourist-paradise Paris. I suppose there is no escaping such things.

I did what I often did as a lonely child, and what I'd come here to do: observe. Observe, reflect, and create. I wandered aimlessly, my thoughts drifting along the above lines, when *it* caught my eye.

The only English language wording in the entire space, in this burgeoning chaotic plaza with its teens and cars and signs and stores and vendors and alleys . . . was a phrase written in sharpie on the side of a girl's right shoe—on the welt, to be exact, the bottom outside wall just before it touches the ground. The welt of her shoe was white, and the black sharpie thusly drew my eye. She'd scrawled in neat, bubbly handwriting a lyric from Lana del Rey's beguiling "Art Deco," new at the time.

Lana's sultry voice, with its strangely energizing despondency, wasn't literally playing, but in that scrawl it flitted through the air like a whispered secret, at once giving the plaza rhythm and making the whole place wink. We are like you, the wink said. Our hearts are the same shape as yours.

A woman was performing on a sidewalk portion of the open space. She stood beside a seated musician who accompanied her singing with classical guitar. He didn't make much of an impression, perhaps the better to let her shine, for shine she did: she resembled the older Sophia Loren of Ettore Scola's 1977 *Una giornata particolare*, with the same grace of self, the poise that comes with age and deepens your beauty. This woman's dark hair was long, and her voice rang out elegantly, if wearily. The kids paid her no mind, but occasionally a soul would pause.

I took up a position across the street and listened from a distance.

She sang what sounded like Italian traditionals, and the melancholy chords they required she suffused with histories of pain comprehendible in any language. What was her story, this striking figure who'd surely lived more than the street-performer life in which she was now engaged? As she wrapped up her final song, the few listeners who'd gathered scattered off, some leaving a few coins.

I approached, and she looked up while boxing up her microphone and related paraphernalia. Deep emerald eyes matched her flowing dress, a contrast to olive skin that had seen better days. I fumbled with my Italian, but she knew some English too, and caught my meaning. I needed to tell her how good she was. I needed to contrast the ignorance she received from the others. Most crucially, I needed to somehow express that she wasn't alone, not even in this precarious place.

We communicated most in the spaces between our words, in the universal language of look and gesture. I gave her a big handful of coins, mostly one and two-dollar Euros—a hefty figure for pocket change. I complimented her singing and spoke my appreciation of her being here tonight. She warmed, realizing we were two people who know something about the debilitating solitude of crowds. We looked at each other, divided by generations, culture, geography, and language. We held the moment, knowing we'd never meet again.

You can dream an entire life in an instant.

I dreamt of a world where she was appreciated by those around her regularly. Where love played a greater defining role than struggle, and her loneliness was assuaged often and with ease. I could observe by her surprised gratitude that such things were not customary in her life. Nothing makes us belong more broadly than a meaningful encounter with a stranger; the moment made me feel part of something shared, something vast and knowable.

I hope she felt similarly.

THE NAMELESS HEROES

12/10/09

I can remember it quite clearly. In the late wintry days of 2009, I was riding in the passenger seat of my partner Alicia's small two-door car. She was driving. We were eastbound on 45th, approaching University Way and looking for dinner, hoping to turn right. In the left lane, at the head of the intersection, was a semi-truck with its emergency flashers on. The right lane, which we were in, was clear, but we stopped behind the truck while remaining in our lane because Alicia wasn't sure what he was planning. The way through looked narrow, what with the huge truck on the left, and the looming overhang of trees and uneven sidewalk on the right. The light was a stale green, and we let it cycle out. Maybe the truck was going to attempt a wide right, or back up, or something.

After a full light cycle, nothing had changed. The semi was still sitting there in the left lane, at the very front, with its four-ways on, motionless. The light was newly green.

We began to drive forward.

Her car was passing by the truck, which was still stopped. We were getting through, about to make our right turn. Soon, we would be clear.

But we would never be clear. That moment would never arrive, because now the truck was a moving shape, simultaneously fast and slow, an unstoppable living glacier, a beast awakened and angling into us, with force. I do not remember sound. There was only the inexorable quality of this massive object, a figure in your dreams coming closer, governed by laws outside your understanding, the kind you know you can't escape.

The truck's trailer now, filling our vision from the left, a mass of aluminum white cast in sodium streetlamp orange. He was also turning right onto University Way, whether or not we mattered. Alicia's little car didn't stand a chance. I wanted to tell her to honk, to really lay on it, but the moment was too large. In times of extremity we are reduced to children, awestruck by the strange and terrible newness of it all.

Here is her car on the sidewalk, tires forced sideways, the trailer forcing us up and over the curb, me briefly wondering is that even possible. We are on the corner, with the moving semi-trailer on the left and a steel utility pole on the right. The car is getting smaller now, crunching together but without sound, as the truck continues pushing in from our left with the utility pole standing firm on the right. I remember Alicia's hair, lit by the light of the drugstore opposite, her hands on a now-useless steering wheel, a frantic question in the darkness. The side door on my right is crumpling, and I notice my passenger seat is becoming smaller . . .

People are starting to stare.

The ever-moving crowd is slowing. I register still figures in my periphery. But against that stasis, one of them is running out there, a middle-aged woman. Hers is the only voice I can hear, screaming, clapping her hands at the truck driver, her arms making big waves as she races in front of his gigantic vehicle. It's a homeless woman, steadfastly standing in the truck's path and yelling at him, pointing at us. She's thinking about our lives, not hers.

Only then did the truck stop. Alicia checked if I was okay, then immediately got out to ask if the truck driver was alright. Wow, I remember thinking. What a tremendous soul she is. I learn from such giants, the lovers and friends who've been kind enough to share their passing lives with me.

I stepped out of the vehicle slowly. We three involved were uninjured. Alicia and the truck driver and the homeless woman were talking. People were pointing. The time for rapt staring was over, and the period of gesticulated arguments was underway. I wandered around, stopping often.

Sometimes someone would ask what happened, or if I was okay, but I didn't feel like answering. I found myself looking up beyond all this noise, noticing the age of the upper stories of the buildings. How long had they been here? I looked at the contrast of the indigo sky with the neon brilliance of the storefront signage. I noticed with irony that we were blocking a bus. Hands in my pockets, walking with legs that worked. I was alive.

Where was the homeless woman? I needed to thank her. Her life had offered a half-century's worth of experiences which collectively led her to be the type of person who would run out there, without a second thought. Who believed this was the right and necessary thing to do. My able-bodiedness was due to her decision and nothing else.

But she was already disappearing into the crowd. I returned to that intersection often in the months afterwards, looking at the faces lining the sidewalk, hoping to see her again and thank her. What did she even look like? The face was receding from memory. I can still see the figure though, to this day fresh behind my closed eyes, a spirit who cares for others without thinking.

If someone saves your life, they will probably be a stranger. Whether following cruel chance or my own stupid mistakes, there are people who've stepped in to help me when they didn't have to. If by a twist of fate you come upon this book, know that I am forever grateful. With reference to the above story, I've heard the homeless crew on University Way described as lowlifes, losers, hobos, garbage, gutter trash, parasites, bums, bloodsuckers, scumbags, grifters, and indigents.

I have to add another name: angels.

ISLAMOFRIENDIA

12/13/15

I'm wandering around outside my bus at the Rainier Beach terminal. There's another 7 parked in front of me. The idea at terminals is that the bus parked in front pulls forward, creating more room for other coaches coming in behind. The 7 at the head of the line ought to have left already, but the driver's nowhere to be seen. As a third 7 pulls in behind me, it's now become an issue, as we're running out of space on the block to park. While I was wondering if perhaps the guy in front is new, the operator behind me hopped out of his bus, yelling, "What's goin' on?"

He's a buddy of mine, salt of the earth American, a little older, with a booming baritone.

"Hey!" I yelled back, as we walked toward each other. The block was deserted.

"These things are pieces a shit," he grumbled, in full salty dog mode, growling in the tone you use when you love complaining. He's referring to the new buses, which have quickly developed a reputation for being insufferable. Essentially giant but woefully finicky computers, they came preprogrammed with multiple auto-shutoff "safety" features that must've sounded good on paper, but which are a headache making no room for the complexities of real life. I was already missing the fleet they were replacing: grey-and-white behemoths, so massive and ungainly they looked like they should be illegal everywhere except Russia and Eastern Europe, with gloriously unstreamlined '80s body styles that took me right back to childhood . . . not to mention the torn, stained, cut, molding, half-lit interiors, which I thought were perfect for atmosphere. That might have just been me though.

The new coaches are another matter. Everyone's got a different theory for why they don't work properly, but I chalk it up to growing pains. New buses always have kinks that need working out. I'd like to discuss this with Mr. Salty Dog, but I'm more concerned about getting the 7 in front of us out of our way. Any minute now a fourth bus will pull in and be forced to block the intersection behind us, because this operator hasn't pulled forward.

"I don't know where this guy is!" I howled into the empty block. "Supposed to've left a few minutes ago!"

"Oh my God," Salty Dog said as he walked closer. "He's s'pposed to left already and fucker's not even at his bus? I'm 'onna pull it forward myself. Fuck this . . ." He reached for the toggle switch to open the doors and get in—and then he paused.

From my angle, I couldn't see what he was seeing. He peered inside, looking down the main aisle, and relented. Salty Dog didn't open the doors.

"Oh, he's prayin'," he said.

Just then the operator within stood up and began rolling up his Muslim prayer rug. He didn't know we were there. I could just make out the rug's intricate decorative weave in the evening light and remember thinking this would be a perfect place for him to pray, since the bus is already facing east, toward Mecca; no need to awkwardly squeeze yourself perpendicularly between seats.

"I'm not gonna mess with that," Salty Dog said. "He's gotta do his thing."

"Yeah, you gotta do whatcha gotta do."

"I'm 'onna let him do his thing. Don't wanna interrupt that."

"Yeah, it's important."

It didn't occur to him for a second to otherize what he'd seen, poke fun, or express any sort of ethnocentrism or prejudice whatsoever. He innately knew the meaning of equivalence, and though that operator in the bus wasn't praying in the manner Mr. Salty is likely accustomed, that didn't matter. All he saw was a man praying. We walked back to our coaches together.

"Yeah, so these fuckin' buses," he continued, reverting to the original subject without another thought.

"Okay, here's my strategy," I said, diving into jargon-land. We shared our solutions with forceful and deep-throated gusto, trading in the high-flying fraternal bonding of insider tech talk. We exchanged tips of our own ramshackle making, the shortcuts which work so well—*too* well—that you could never tell your superiors, laughing together in the camaraderie found uniquely at work: these were the gearhead intricacies you could only discuss with a coworker.

My heart swelled with pride for my fellow people. Salty's immediate return to complaining about equipment was something I actually found optimistic. It was a further sign of his respect toward our Muslim friend within—as in, he is who he is, doin' what he's gotta do, and there's no need for us to go on about it. We'll just take it right in stride—

and this was the month after the Paris terror attacks.

No Islamophobia here. Salty Dog, a middle-aged White man and self-described conservative, nevertheless looking right past the outer trappings of different religions, simply respecting the core within, giving the man room to be himself. Such notions came so naturally to Salty he hardly needed articulate them. He said it all in his tone.

We all have more in common than we don't.

ANGRYNICE

5/1/16

She was standing there at Dearborn Street, and I sighed. She was Iris, and the question was whether or not to let her on. Elderly, infirm, and heavyset, with a stuffed stroller, as quick to snarl as I am to smile, with stringy silver hair and corresponding eyes, tiny ones, which nevertheless had enough bile in them to rage and rage against all about her, all the time. I don't think this is what Dylan Thomas was talking about. How had Ibrahim gotten on this person's good side again?

A line of people boarded before she did, and I sat there wondering what to do. She'd been on recently and wreaked havoc. Memories were coming back, against my will: among other abrasives, she'd yelled at an elegant Somali woman in the aisle in a manner completely confounding to the lady, who seemed as bewildered as she was hurt, as if wondering, *when did people of* this *age group behave without manners*?

The thing is, I just don't like refusing service. I believe these folks, insufferable though they can be, deserve to ride as much as I do.

"Iris, hello," I said, with no great enthusiasm. "How you feelin'?"

"Good," she replied, shifting her weight.

"Okay. In that case, come on in!"

I began the process of deploying the ramp. Iris ambled forward at her pace and no one else's. Should I begrudge her the right to be unhurried? It's difficult when fifty people in the vicinity feel differently. I like to be the one person who *is* patient, who *does* give them a small oasis of acceptance, here in the desert of the harried and overtaxed.

Iris's attitude doesn't exactly make this easy.

"Goddamnit," she mused, pushing her stroller forward with numbing deliberation. It was a puny affair and long past its due, flimsy and dirtied by time, buckling under the weight of several huge bags no stroller designer *ever* thought of. The wheels had rusted and no longer swiveled in the direction of travel, and some didn't even roll. She grunted with effort, cursing, each small impediment a vigorous cause for fury: the lip of the ramp where it meets the cement; the geography of the bus's floor layout, requiring her to turn the stroller; the bags slipping; and more than all of this, the weight of the years, the accumulation of strife, seeds of misery now grown, long percolating as only she knew.

I'd already gestured to the neighborhood youngsters outside behind her, saying, "You can get on the back door if you want to!" They were thrilled. Forget fare; this got them nearly *five* whole minutes—an eternity on the road—of comfort.

"My wheel is stuck, the wheel on the stroller," she bemoaned.

"I know," I said. "That's okay, come on in. I'll make some room for ya." I walked back to the front seating area and flipped up every seat that was empty, saying to those uncertain whether they should move, "we'll let her decide where to sit."

As she arrived in the seating area—which I know is only a few feet from the door, but you really have to imagine slow motion here, like a cargo freighter docking at port—she snarled, "*Put that seat down! I want that down*!"

"What do you want, Iris? Tell me what you want."

"I want that down."

"This one?"

"That one."

I flipped the seat down. "Alright," I said, mostly to myself.

Back in my own seat, I gave her a moment to get settled before saying, "Alright, I'm just gonna roll out slowly—"

"STOP THE BUS YOU FUCKING BITCH NOW!"

"You're all right, Iris, we're stopping."

"Bus driver won't stop the goddamn bus, goddamnit—"

"You don't need to yell, Iris—"

"Motherfucker—"

"If you yell at me, I won't pick you up again."

She continued muttering. I was thinking how much her raspy tone resembled Honey Bunny's (Amanda Plummer) voice in the opening scene of *Pulp Fiction*, where right after Tim Roth suavely tells everyone to stay calm, Plummer's ungainly form clambers atop the table and in the very opposite of cool-headedness shrieks, with hair flailing and to excellent comedic effect, that everyone needs to do exactly as she says or else!

Wouldn't Iris and Honey Bunny make a terrific dynamic duo?

I'd watch that movie. Iris mellowed into a hesitant silence as we got underway, and I let my musings wander. My first thought was, well, I'm definitely not boarding her in the future. No need for all this drama. I'm not kind so that people will be kind to me, but when kindness is returned with such vitriol, one's enthusiasm wanes. I thought about a route 41 driver I used to see regularly, older guy, generally rude to the folks, sometimes cringe-inducing. It went that way for years, until one day he was friendly. What gives, I wondered, and I asked him how he was doing. He shared that finally, after decades of excruciating back pain, he'd at last had a surgery that took the agony away. I felt embarrassed for ever having judged him and thankful for the context.

What travails had Iris endured? What collusion of life events had led to this unglamorous present you knew was not her high point? To ponder the disappointments those small grey eyes had been privy to. I would never know the details, but being kind certainly wouldn't make things worse. It also occurred to me that she, a longtime Rainier Valley resident, wasn't going anywhere. What was I going to do, pass her up every other week and force some other operator to put up with her? No. Too selfish, too cowardly. I needed a different solution.

She always gets off at Mount Baker. When we arrived, I didn't deploy the lift just yet. "One second," I gestured to the people waiting outside. I walked back to where she was and took my right hand out of my pocket. I was ready.

"Okay." I stood directly in front of her and spoke clearly, firmly. Everyone was watching. Everyone always watches when you get out of the driver's seat.

"Okay, *Iris*. You need to get a new stroller. This is twenty dollars so you can go get one. If you do not have a new stroller the next time I see you, *I am not gonna pick you up*. You have to get a new stroller. Okay?"

I think her day started over right then. Sunset and sunrise, in the moment between my "okay" and her reply. She looked at me, dazed into confused silence.

"Okay," she said.

She said it quietly, accepting the bills I almost never carry but happened to have that day. Once again, I asked the folks outside to use the back door, and Iris gathered herself and began the procedure for liftoff. When she passed me, sitting in my driver's seat, she stopped and patted the hair on my head. Her way of saying thanks. "I know you're not supposed to touch the driver—"

"Well. I guess that's okay for today."

When she was outside, just off the ramp, she turned back slowly and asked, "What was your given name?"

"Nathan, like Nathan's Hotdogs. Yeah."

"Okay."

"I'll see you again, Iris!"

"Okay!"

I drove in silence for a minute. We sat at the light at Martin Luther King Way. Maya, a regular rider, was sitting up front. She'd seen everything. We were silent for a moment longer, and then we laughed. We cackled together, at the joy of it, the comic absurdity of it all, laughing out my frustration, Iris's anger, her pace, at the ridiculousness of my tone giving her money, practically demanding—angrynice, feeling good that we'd done something. "You know?" we told each other, grinning wide.

I said, "Hopefully, we just made life easier for her . . . and *fifty* other bus drivers!"

"And who knows how many passengers!"

We chuckled some more. In my mind though, I kept returning to the sight of her on the sidewalk at the very end, clutching two tens and one very dilapidated stroller and looking around, calm now, bewildered. Rested. The things she thought were rules had changed a bit.

It was a new world.

I'LL STILL DO IT AGAIN, THE SAME WAY

3/1/18

I've been out here long enough to watch people grow up. André stood beside me now, once a high school student, now a thoughtful young man with the sort of maturity you don't often find till later age. He had the sober insight that can only be won from heavy disappointment—in his case, a debilitating sports injury. To fail and become anything other than bitter: that is real accomplishment.

Tonight, he's wearing a beanie and '70s-style gold frames, big, with fitted jeans and a dark jacket, not a Letterman but similar in shape. He's tired, and it lends him an unintentional gravitas—the soft spoken, world-weary Black American intellectual, but young and athletic too, dignified and hip all in one breath. It's hard not to like a guy who covers all the bases.

We were talking about the track and field program at Arizona State when he pointed out another young man running for the bus—a White guy, unusual in this neighborhood, at this hour—running fast tonight, really sprinting.

"Wow," I said. "He must *need* this one. He's puttin' in the effort!"

The runner, probably eighteen or twenty, dropped his sweatshirt in his exertions and didn't even pause, racing ahead to the zone at 39th Avenue. The sweatshirt was in my path on the roadway, on my way to the stop.

"Okay, we're gonna be super nice and make his day, because why not," I explained. I stopped the bus by his sweatshirt, jumped out and grabbed it, jumped back in to drive up and land at the zone.

Perfect timing. Our new friend bounded in. I had a big happy grin pasted on my face as I held out his sweatshirt and said, "It's your lucky day . . ."

My smile withered away. The young teen received his shirt without looking at me and stared wordlessly—at André.

I haven't seen that much hate in years.

The boy looked at André like you look at a spider that's too big to stomp out, but you can't wait to do it anyway. Like it was crazy they weren't fighting already.

I have a lot of friends, and they have many differences in ideology, religion, politics—but they all share one commonality: kindness. They represent all class, status, race, and gender groups in Seattle, and at gatherings of mine they have a swell time. Only one ingredient is needed to make it so, and they all have it.

But I still live in a cocoon. I forget the attitudes my friends have to tolerate, and what it feels like to take the brunt of hate.

My friend Dewayne, walking home in Greenwood—not Greensboro—the 'progressive' side of town, you understand—when a pickup truck of White frat boys pulls over to dump buckets of water on him and tells him to go back to Africa.

My friend Glenn, hustling two jobs to pay off his loans from graduating the Art Institute and driving home from his real estate work, almost home in the innocuous suburb of Shoreline—not Birmingham—when a young White woman cuts in from of him, parks, and exits her vehicle in traffic to scream much more than this: "Fuck you, nigger! You almost killed me! My life is more important than yours!"

What do my friends have to tolerate, daily, that I only hear echoes of? I know so little. Should I be surprised when some of them act distant, or have a more caustic perspective?

André didn't mirror the hate. He kept a neutral gaze, soft, non-committal. That takes talent. The racist youngster walked past; I got the sense he felt scared and out of place, perhaps thinking that demonstrating readiness to fight was a solution.

Afterwards I looked at André, and André looked at me. I

shrugged my hands in the air, and he shook his head, almost a smile. I didn't have to say what I knew we both innately grasped:

Whatever, man.

I wasn't going to let this be a teachable moment for me. If another person is sprinting for my bus and drops their sweatshirt, I'm going to do exactly the same thing. I will pick it up, wait for them, and default to a smile when they step in. I'm not going to let this boy's hate proliferate. I'm just going to keep on keepin' on, stayin' strong. Like André.

He said, "What were we talking about?"

BRAVADO

5/1/20

We talked of all manner of things.

Grover went by Samuel too, interchangeably, though I never learned the reason why; a middle and a first name, perhaps. A squat fellow who looked good for late middle age, with defined features and a ready smile, a boylike grin that took me back to the days of playgrounds and soccer and the great unknown.

Most people talk about themselves, which I'm fine with at work. I'd rather listen than speak, and always learn more from the former. Grover and I talked about each other. I'd tell him my thoughts on the job, and he told me about his life. When I temporarily switched from the 7/49 to the 5/21, he was the one face I still regularly saw, as he used both routes, and we accordingly formed a closer connection.

He cleaned three buildings in different parts of town and could show up whenever he chose as long as the facilities were closed. Pretty swell deal, I thought. He'd been at it for years. Like me, Grover favored routine; he never missed an episode of *Happy Days*. He loved the show. "You get to feelin' like you almost know them, like they friends in your own lives, seein' 'em for that long, knowin' they troubles."

He'd been with his ladyfriend for twenty-two years. He saw his son intermittently, a young man now out of jail and married to a lawyer ("She's a real catch," in Grover's words. "He don't know what he got."). Grover hoped his boy could rise to the responsibility and aptitude of his wife. I hoped he'd go easy on his son. Nothing's more sour than a parent who takes their child for granted. Grover was one of those tough-love types, proud in a matter-of-fact sort of way. I think you know the kind: a front that's convinced it's right.

Sometimes chatting with him was a struggle, other times a joy; it'd be an exaggeration to say he was a man at war with himself, but I noticed moments of sensitivity shining through from time to time, a conflict to the confident front and a reminder of the child inside.

One night he said, "I adjust my whole schedule so I can make your bus."

I jokingly replied, "No way, I don't believe that."

I immediately regretted my tone.

The briefest hush revealed he'd been telling the complete truth, and that it wasn't the easiest thing to say. I thought of Trevor's girlfriend. You work up to sensitivity like that, especially if it isn't your style. I spent the rest of the ride trying to make up, letting him know what I now realized: he wasn't being Tough Grover but Real Grover. It was one of the nicest sentiments I could think of, what he'd said, and I wanted him to know it meant something to me. But I couldn't get through.

"I think that's beautiful, man," I said.

"Naw, you don't think that! I heard you laughin'."

"Seriously though! Now I'm just worried about could I ever make a bus ride worthwhile enough to reschedule your whole day for!"

"What choo talkin' 'bout, you know everybody loves you."

Who knew what was inside? He'd tried to open up, clearly something he was careful about. It's a risk. I get it. I was grateful to have known even a glimmer. No matter how gruff, there's always a human being somewhere in there. That was why his grin reminded me of childhood. Those days are fraught with insecurities, and you hide them as best you can, especially as men who are taught to not show emotions—or better yet, to not have any in the first place, unless it's anger.

Can you imagine what a better place the world would be if men had the equipment to express themselves with something besides bravado? If Descartes's famous line* had been rather translated as I *feel*, therefore I am? Would our society be a different place if feelings weren't believed secondary to thoughts?

"I been wondering where you were at," I say to Grover, whenever I haven't seen him in a while.

"No you weren't," he says, staying strong.

It's a game we play. I really was wondering.

I hope deep down he knows it.

*_Cogito_ could as easily be translated as such, for it just as much means to ponder, reflect, consider. Descartes's line comes into greater meaning with context: _dubito, ergo cogito, ergo sum._ "I doubt, therefore I think, therefore I am." As he explained, we cannot doubt of our existence while we doubt. And doubting, as any human knows, is as much a feeling as anything else.

THE KNIFE'S EDGE DANCE

3/24/17

What is the Knife's Edge Dance, you ask? I will tell you. It's the duet you play as a bus driver when you know one wrong word, or tone, will cause the whole thing to collapse. All operators have had to play this game. It's no one's favorite way to pass the time, even for someone like me, who likes talking. The risks are way too high, and you can't screw it up.

"Fucking 7," this man grumbles, after I said I don't go to Bell Street. He'd lobbed his body into the bus at northbound Seneca, saying he 'just needed to go to Bell.' A twenty-something White man with nothing to lose, hair stringy and matted, dressed in every shade between brown and orange.

"What's that," I bark, too sternly. I hadn't eaten. Wrong tone, I instantly realized. Where's my A-game? Can't sleepwalk through this one. I attempted a more genial pitch. "Come on up," I said, trying to get his angry self away from the other passengers. "Where you trying to go? I go to Pike."

"Fuck Pike."

"I also got a terminal at Virginia, you wanna go to Virginia?" I don't usually mention that, but now seemed a pretty good time to throw that bone out there. There's a time for everything.

"What," he replied, looking up vacantly. "Yeah."

"Best I can offer, you know."

"That's my destination."

We're sitting in bumper-to-bumper bus traffic in the dead heat of afternoon rush. Of all the twenty-four hours, the stretch from 16:30 to 17:30 is the most heavily traveled, and we're right in the middle of it. If there was a blockage ahead, I'd never know; all I can see is the back of the two enormous buses right in front of me, one in each lane. I try to assuage him. We could be here twenty minutes. I need to stay friends with him for however long this takes.

"We might not get there fast, but we'll get there."

"I gotta be there in . . . five minutes." He speaks erratically, standing and sitting again, a live wire ready to flame.

"Uh oh, that might not happen with this bus, dude, we got some traffic tonight. I mean if it was up to me, I'd just run 'em all over."

"I know you'll get me there on time," he rumbles. "We got, we got three minutes."

Three minutes from Seneca to Virginia, arguably Downtown's busiest six-block stretch? I almost laughed and tried to set him up for noble failure: "I gotta say, we might not make it. But who knows! Just don't get mad at me if we roll in a lil' after, you know?"

"Oh, I know you're good."

"Thanks man."

"You got a horn. I know it works."

"That's true."

His voice, pushing toward irritation: "You got a nice big horn right there."

"Yeah, he probably wouldn't hear it though, he probably got the air conditioning on."

"Oh yeah! Ha! Hum." As I throw a hand up toward a fellow operator, he chortles, "Waving at bus drivers, I LIKE how you guys do that."

"Yeah you know, keeping it positive! Never know what they might be going through, bringin' up someone's day even just a couple minutes." Pause. "What takes you up to Virginia? If I may ask. Just hangin', or . . ."

"I'm looking for my friend."

"That's nice a you, hope your friend appreciates that. We gotta look out for each other sometimes, help each other out."

His voice, husky and dark: "Don't ever question me again."

Let them win. If you can let people get away with having the last word, life becomes so much easier.

"Okay," I said.

His mind was now free to go elsewhere. "When is this traffic gonna MOVE?"

"We'll get there. It all depends on when *he* gets there! I don't think I can run him over though."

"You can do it!!!"

I smiled, and a few minutes passed in silence. He studied the clock on the bus pass reader, counting down the minutes. Then he looked at me. He stared unapologetically, stepping closer. A drawn-out glare, piercing and slow. Finally, he spoke in a low voice.

"Are you intelligent?"

From his tone, his bearing, and those penetrating eyes, which I avoided for longer than a glance, you knew there was definitely a wrong answer to this question. I forced a chuckle. "Ha, I'm not that good!"

He kept glaring. Remember your training: *pretend to be confident, and it will turn into real confidence.* I said it again.

"Yeah no, I'm not that good. I got a little something, but I'm not up there." Pause. Keep going. I still had his full attention. He looked ready to pounce.

You can't meet force with force. You have to go around it.

I glanced at him again, with a smile. "I don't have all the answers. Anybody tries to tell you they have all the answers, ahhh . . ." I made the wishy-washy hand motion. He nodded with a grin, dirty yellowed teeth, making the same gesture with his hand. He understood. We've all got something in common.

"But you *look* intelligent," he growled.

"No, that's just the glasses!"

"Haha!"

"That's all it is!" Like Samson's hair! We're pulling reasonably close to Virginia Street now, on the same block, still sitting behind mounds of traffic. It's a veritable bus doggie-pile out here. What a perfect opportunity to coax him off the bus early. Aren't some rules made to be broken?

"Well here, it's a red light, and that's Virginia right there, do you wanna jump out here while it's red?"

"No, I wanna go to Virginia. That's my destination."

"Right on." Stay friendly, I told myself, and calm. Engage him. I ramble, searching around for a topic. "You ever go there," I asked, pointing at the storefront. "Bed Bath and Beyond?"

"Bed Bath and Beyond?"

"Yeah, right there? It's all right. I used to have the biggest crush on this girl that worked there."

"Where?"

"Yeah, at the register. She's gone now though. One day she was there, one day she wasn't. I never told her."

"Where she go?"

"I think she went to Chicago."

"Chicago?!"

"I know!"

"Lemme off right here."

By now we were in the middle of turning the corner, so close, mere seconds away from an acceptable stop on Virginia Street. I replied with, "For sure, lemme finish this turn real quick, I can't let you off in the middle."

"Yeah you can. Yeah you can!"

"Yeah?"

"Lemme off right now!"

If you can, let them win. People like winning. This would be easy to explain to a supervisor anyways. Safety is paramount, more so than finishing a turn and potentially waking the dormant beast inside this man.

"Okay," I said. I opened the doors.

And that's the story of why there were no police called to Third and Virginia, or Third and Seneca, no additional traffic blockages, no security incident, no further delayed service, no injuries to me or others. Just a weird blip of a moment where a bus downtown, for some reason, stopped in the middle of a turn, and let someone out.

PRIVATE

9/24/15

I'm in a mellower state this afternoon, contentedly focused on giving the smoothest possible ride on this 70. A youthful man in a sweater, one of those young professionals returning home from the Amazon corridor, comes forward to stand for a while, watching the proceedings up front. After pulling the bell, he says in a congenial Indian accent, "There is something so satisfying about being the one to pull the cord!"

"Say again?"

"There is something strangely satisfying about pulling the bell cord!"

"Yes, there is!"

How lovely, that he felt comfortable sharing such offbeat innocence with a friendly stranger. We all have thoughts like this, but how often do we refrain from sharing our love for the simple pleasures, just for the sake of sustaining petty sophistication, irony, coolness? Being ourselves, in the purer sense, is both easier and much harder. It requires a belief that we'll draw toward us those souls who are similarly minded, and a genuine disregard for the judgments of everyone else.

In an enthusiastic sense of *esprit de corps* I exclaim, "I think so too! It brings out the inner child in us."

He sighs happily and says almost by way of explanation, "I think my inner child is always out!"

"I think that's good. I try for the same."

"Well, thank you. Like seriously, your cheerful attitude brightened my whole entire day!"

I didn't realize I'd done much of anything, in my mellow state. "Thank you so much!"

When I see photographs of myself as a child, I sometimes think that little person knows so much more about being happy than I do. He flutters on ahead, beckoning and unreachable, dancing a little further onward on the path of life.

One day perhaps I'll catch up.

SLOW HEALER

5/14/18

"Hey," she said slowly, pausing as she stepped onboard. "How long has it been?"

Far more people recognize me than I them, and this was another instance. Where had I seen her before? I smiled, waiting for my brain to catch up.

I said, "twelve years." I assumed she was referring, as passengers often do, to when they first saw me. For some reason folks tend to assume this moment was also my first time driving. Maybe it's because I'm happy. People will eventually stop thinking I'm young . . . but hopefully they'll always think I'm new. My stock answer here is to state how long I've been driving in total, because who knows? Maybe they were there in my first days on the road.

"Twelve years," she repeated. "That sounds about right. Maaaan, iss been a while. I remember when you first started this job. And you still here?"

"Yeah, I like comin' out here. Lil' different each day, people to talk to . . ."

She chuckled, looking on in wonder. She was a mother's age, mildly heavyset with a sweatshirt, ponytail, and baseball cap, and the sparkling eyes of someone around children often enough to absorb their youthful flair, but not enough to be exhausted by them.

"Man, you still doin' it, huh. You still got that *hair*! That's how I recognized you!"

"Ha! Thank you. But yeah, I try to put out that positive energy, you know?"

"I know that's right."

"'Cause that karma comes back around in unexpected ways!"

"It sure do!" she exclaimed. "You brave though, goin' out there every day."

"I just try to keep puttin' those good vibes out."

Which is all I can do. I get varied replies in response to the line; pessimists won't hear a word of it. Neither will anyone who thinks our actions are meaningless, without consequence. For myself, I haven't lived long enough to know if being good has the slightest effect on our lives. But I know what I want to believe.

She was no pessimist, and I found her attitude infectious. She whispered: "Oh, you know they ain't gonna mess with you!"

I laughed. "I got my fingers crossed!"

"You don't need to keep 'em cross', you got somethin' special. Somethin' nobody could take away. 'Cause they woulda done that by now if they could. Twelve years, sheeeeeit. It was the *hair*! Wha's your name again?"

"Nathan."

"Nathan. I saw from a distance and I said naawww, that can't be him, from all those years ago!"

"And we're still here! You're still here! That's a modern miracle now, we're still doin' our thing day in and day out!"

"One day at a time!"

The words summoned thoughts I wasn't expecting. My mind swam back to Paris, as it so often does. As a youngster I used to think if we were good, we'd be fine. Didn't you?

What a shock, then, to step over blood and glass. To watch a woman my age unable to keep from suddenly screaming, howling till her breath ran out, giving way to gravity and heartache as she collapsed onto sodden concrete. To feel the common language of crowds, not lonesome anymore but tragically united in having no idea, no concept anymore, empty of notions for how to live. All touch was platonic, concerned; all silences were sober. We were children again, in all the ways we never wished to be.

I was back at Place de République now, drifting toward the enormous impromptu memorial, trying not to step on flowers, moving through the silent figures and closer to the ancient and towering Marianne at the plaza's center, as if somehow hopeful that it might speak softly, guide us out of our listless oblivion. I remember squatting down, having my own sort of Carlton Pearson moment as I looked at that lone photograph, reliving the now-haunted eyes of Maud and her three smiling friends. They had no idea. I distinctly recall having the thought: *there is no way these young people deserved to be killed as they were.*

That was the beginning. Then things would happen to loved ones of mine, people whose actions I know well, and then to me. There was cancer, apathy, selfish cruelty.

We were struck with violence and implacable death.

And I knew incontrovertibly that neither they nor I had done anything to suffer these iniquities. The realization terrified me and altered for the worse my perspective on going out into the street every night. I began to assume evil rather than goodness, defaulting to suspicion and fear over the peace that comes with giving the benefit of the doubt.

There's a colleague of mine who goes out there, on the worst routes, like I do—did—enthusiastically, without a care in the world. Carla's a trim young woman in her later thirties or forties and nobody's first idea of an invincible tough who can fight off anything. But that's exactly what she is, and she gets her poise from her strength of belief. She's Christian to what I would call an impassioned degree, devout in her every word and act. She is so confident that she will thrive.

I would look at her and think, *I used to feel like that.*

My confidence didn't come from a religious source, but it achieved the same end: I trusted the world. I desperately wished to find that again.

Her carefree joy seemed inaccessible to me, and the prime impediment in my mind wasn't that evil might happen to me again, but that I lived in a universe that didn't seem to care whether evil happened to me, or anyone else. It was tempting to snipe at Carla. Others did. *She's never gone through anything*. But you know that's not true. You don't make it to forty without suffering, not in this world. What did Carla have to resist, to sustain her course? How many operators once told me with great conviction that this or that route, this or that experience, would "wipe that smile right off my face"? Just the way they patronizingly tell her? I've held strong this long, to their great surprise, but maybe my faith in existence has a limit. Terrorist attacks.

I felt bitterness creeping in. You find yourself trying it out, testing out its flavors. Cynicism instead of optimism. Everything random, or worse, with goodness an accident slipping through. Maybe Cause and Effect don't even exist. What could be more profoundly terrifying? I roiled under gray skies, feeling the hypnotic pull of despair. It seems to explain everything. And yet. And yet, it gradually occurred to me:

This way of thinking isn't working very well.

It lacks motion. I struggled, as if in paralysis, to get through what were formerly the best parts of my day: pulling up to Fifth and Jackson with a welcoming spirit, saying hey to the guys; pulling up to Rainier and Henderson inbound with joy, not trepidation.

How did I used to do that?

Carla reminded me of my pre-Paris self. Was it possible to return to my own version of her fearless assurance? How do you put your hand to a stovetop again after you've been burned?

THE SOULFUL STENCH

7/13/17

I'd never smelled anything more horrible in my life—and I've driven the E Line! I've walked through LA's Skid Row and strolled down alleys on the wrong side of Napoli. But this took the cake. My bus had a huge driver's side window, and I put every inch of it to use, barely able to keep from vomiting. I'm ashamed to say I described the smell as "poop death" in my notes, as I could conjure no adjective more appropriate.

How do you politely tell someone they smell rancid?

He was a big man, twice my weight and a head taller. In one hand was a full-size plastic chair which he carried as though it were a paperback book. He may have been forty, Black American, clad in a large black top with a scarf of sorts wrapped around his neck. He had kind eyes.

When you're doing a short route, issues like this are less urgent. They'll be gone in twenty minutes, or ten.

My route is ninety minutes.

Did he intend to stick around? I wasn't prepared to undergo this level of suffering regularly. All the other passengers had scurried to the back of the bus en masse. I felt compelled to speak but didn't want to embarrass him, waiting till he got off at 12th and Jackson and then following him outside, saying, "Hold up, I wanna tell you somethin' real quick."

He tarried a moment on the sidewalk, chair swinging in hand. He was tall enough that he formed a silhouette in the sky, dwarfing nearby buildings from my shorter vantage.

"Listen," I said. "I respect you. You're a good dude. But I *got* to ask you to take a shower, bro, we can't have you ridin' the bus smellin' like this. If I see you next time and you haven't taken a shower, I'm gonna have to pass you up. I don't wanna do that." I rambled. I was nervous. "I di'nt wanna embarrass you in front of all those people . . ."

He heard me out. "Alright," he replied. I wished him a good night.

A few weeks later I saw him again at southbound Marion Street. He was sizable, but bulky mostly in the upper part of his frame, less so his legs; perhaps a former athlete. He moved with relative agility toward my front doors, nodding and looking me in the eye.

"I cleaned up," he said.

And he had. The smell had lessened. I figured he'd taken a shower, and I appreciated the effort. "Thanks, man," I answered. This time his scarf was slightly ajar. I noticed something beneath: in the area of the lymph nodes and thyroid were masses of overlapping subcutaneous spherical globules, quite large, swelling to the point that there was no separation between neck and chest.

That was 2013.

It's 2017 now, a summer night on an empty route 12. I've traded my usual number 7 for the evening, pinch-hitting to fill an open shift. I haven't driven this thing in years. Here comes Boren Avenue and Madison, in the midst of hospital row, and there's somebody at the zone: an enormous figure, appearing even more massive with the lightweight black coat worn over his head as a hood. I see the scarf but can't place it. In shape and state of repair, he reminds me of an ancient Germanic warrior; something untethered about this beast of a man on first impression. Feeling apprehensive but willing to take the dive, I take a deep breath and open the doors: "Hey, how ya doin'?"

I recognized the kind eyes first. They had a mellow quality to them, somewhere between frustration and sadness, teetering on the brink of hopelessness. He was a barbarian warrior in silhouette only. The agility was gone. I wondered if he remembered me.

I certainly did him, and instinctively tried to stop breathing.

"Been a while," I said amiably.

"Yeah," he replied. "Comin' from the hospital."

"I hope they're taking care of you in there."

"What?"

"Oh, just sayin' I hope they're lookin' out for ya."

"Not really."

"I'm sorry to hear it."

"There's only so much they can do. I have cancer."

"Gosh, I'm sorry," I said.

"That's why I smell bad, it's not 'cause I'm just some . . . I want you to know, 'cause I remember you told me I gotta clean up, but it's 'cause of this condition I got."

"I'm sorry, man. I appreciate you tellin' me what's goin' on."

"Yeah, I wanted to tell you 'cause . . . some drivers aren't cool with it, and I was worried 'cause I remember you said you wouldn't pick me up if I didn't clean up, but there ain't nothin' I can do 'bout this condition."

Why did I live?

He remembered everything. I felt ashamed. I felt the deep, lacerating melancholy in his voice. "No, I totally hear you," I said this time. "Man, cancer . . . I've lost good close people to stuff like that, and also, I just . . ." Paris was too complicated to explain. I shook my head, stuck for words at a red light. The thought suddenly burst forth, intact; he of all people would get it, the fundament of the dilemma which haunted me so.

"What's crazy to me is, there seems to be no correlation, *at all*, between whether or not you're a good person, and how long you're alive. Cancer just tears up the best and worst of people."

These are the things you can't discuss with just anyone. I was thankful for his contemplative pause before responding. We were entering the zone of shared silences, of burdens and aches nursed in solitude, now finding a meeting place.

"I'm a good person," he said.

"I can tell, you're a good dude."

"It's just this thing eatin' me up . . ."

"I respect you, man, and I'm so sorry you got this thing goin' on."

We moved to other topics. He laughed incredulously at how I liked the 7 ("What about all those crazy people??") and emphatically suggested I pick the 12 instead. We bantered back and forth over which route was better. He got off Downtown. We wished each other a good night.

Later, I walked through the bus checking for lost items, and the odor lingered, strong, present. But I wouldn't call it rancid now. It had a different shape in my mind, not putrid or foul.

It was the smell of immeasurable sorrow.

What plans did he once have? How wide was his smile, how rich his joy, before it all began? Did he know, in the year which would mark the halfway point of his life, that *that* was midway, and would he have spent it differently? Regret, despair, guilt, woe; these are the names of a present overwhelmed by the past, a past whose possibilities once felt tangible, now forever encased in glass. Like Maud, he was a child with a dream once. He likely thought about family, accomplishment, romance.

He wasn't thinking this.

A deformed, outcast body with exterior growths, destroying itself against his will and revolting everyone within shouting distance. When was he last looked upon with anything besides pity or disgust?

I opened the doors at the terminal, but otherwise made no attempt to eliminate the smell. It was nothing compared to what he was going through. I thought back to Little Leon, the gospel voice still echoing in memory. To Paris, hollow and haunted. Grief is the act of being profoundly confused. We enter this world not knowing how it works, and we gradually figure things out . . . until we further discover we leave this life knowing about as much as we did coming in. We never stop asking Why.

Can doing so be a distraction?

How easy it is to forget the impact of making others a little happier, the heft and worth of leaving a mark in a heart or two. I wonder if the most substantive part of our conversation was the jokey small talk. I hope that just for a second there, when we were laughing about bus routes, he felt appreciated as a regular human being.

PART IV

QUOTIDIAN HIGHS

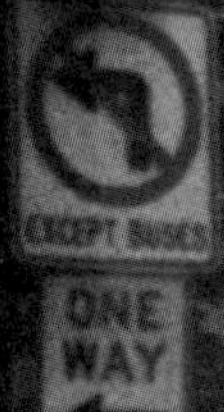

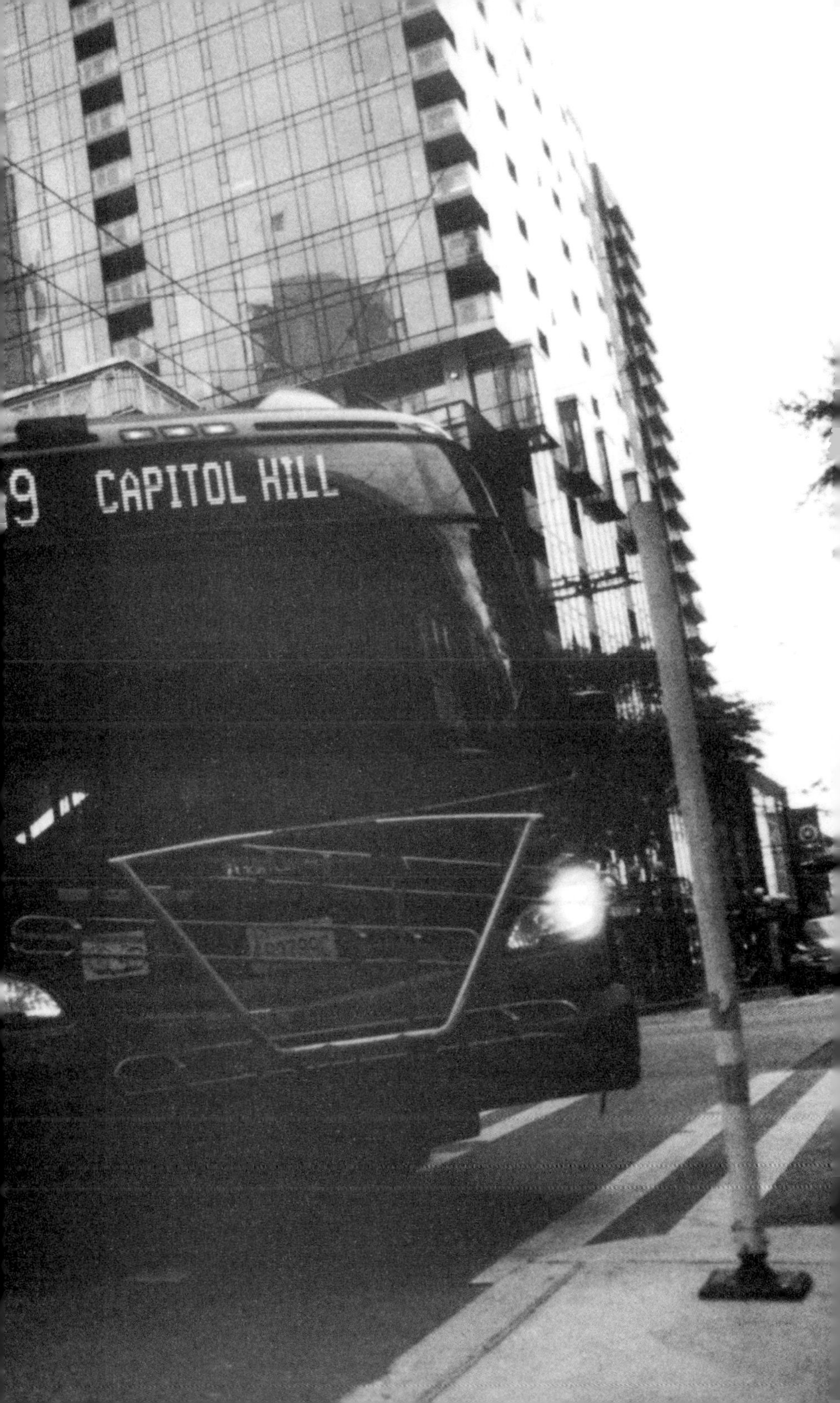
9 CAPITOL HILL

THE BENEVOLENT ROAR

7/24/16

The night was silent. We ambled forward, a mobile living room of people sitting alone together, each nursing their own thoughts. Nothing but the gentle hum of the bus's electric current.

Then out of the silence, like cymbals crashing after a mellow adagio, I hear that ear-splitting stentorian roar:

"DRIVER DO YOU LIKE DONALD TRUMP?"

So inquired the great Hau Ling. In retrospect, it was strange he'd been quiet until that point. Maybe he belatedly realized he was out of character and felt the need to set things right. Time for some classic Hau Ling. This funereal silence won't do.

I responded in a normal, easygoing voice: "Um, we're not gonna talk about politics on the bus tonight."

"OKAY," he boomed.

"Yeah, we're gonna keep that to ourselves." Talking to him, and to myself.

"OKAY. I'LL KEEP IT A SECRET WHO I'M VOTING FOR."

"Thanks, man."

Hau Ling's howling is like no one else's. He might be my favorite shouting person to listen to. Yes, the list is short, but he's at the top. His diction is precise, like Christoph Waltz's, and unhurried, like Jason Robards's.

The difference, as I've mentioned, is volume.

Kakapo parrots and Blue Whales have nothing on this guy. Reader, I'm not making fun at his expense. He possesses an innocent sincerity not everyone has, and that I admire.

Plus, doesn't all this make the evening more exciting? His line above was reeled off slowly, and the effect was unique; we're accustomed to yelled declarations that carry significant meaning or emotion. We expect them to be said quickly, heatedly. Less ordinary is hearing thunderous levels applied to innocuous statements of minimal emotional import. I couldn't not smile.

I recalled a moment strolling down Third Avenue some weeks previous. Hau Ling was a bit ahead of me, his short, compact figure bobbing up-down amongst the dense crowd—we as a city were impersonating a packed New York sidewalk. His hunched shoulders, furrowed brow, and italicized forward momentum were the very picture of determination. He stood out from the others in that he was giving himself some positive self-talk—something I hope we all do, but he was unique in not exactly keeping it to himself. Repeatedly, he roared, "TRY TO TELL ME I CAN'T? I THINK I CAAANNNNN! TRY TO TELL ME I CAN'T? I THINK I CAAAANNNN!" He howled to the skyscrapers with malicious glee, practically shaking glass, flattening imaginary antagonists with each step. Nothing wrong with a little self-confidence, I thought.

"I LIKE YOU AS A DRIVER," he slowly screamed, if a raspy bass voice can scream. "YOU'RE A NICE GUY."

"I try."

"I'LL TELL YOU WHO I WANNA BE LIKE." He paused dramatically. Let's take a moment and consider his use of *wanna*. Contractions are used to accelerate delivery. Nobody says *wanna* slowly . . . but Mr. Hau Ling isn't just anyone. He's Hau Ling. He wrapped up his dramatic pause by concluding with the exclamation, "MY FATHER."

I was about to say something admiring, something about it's nice to have good parents one can respect, but he bulldozed in with, "HE'S OVER SIXTY-FIVE YEARS OLD, AND HE'S STILL WORKING."

"Really!"

At this point he stood. Which made sense. There was no remaining way to emphasize his upcoming point: He was already bellowing. What else can you do?

He's Dr. King at the Lincoln Memorial. He's Patrick Henry at the Virginia Convention. He threw his hands in the air and turned his face to the skies. Sleepers and hoodlums alike seated nearby looked up groggily, flummoxed. What were they to do with this great fulminating vision in front of them, this avalanche of friendly and deafening vehemence?

"HE'S NOT GONNA STOP WORKING, UNTIL HE FEELS LIKE STOPPING WORKING!"

"Uh huh, he likes to work?" My normal voice sounded like a puny pipsqueak compared to his.

"HE'S OVER SIXTY-FIVE YEARS OLD! I WANNA BE LIKE THAT." Who else says *wanna* as such a deliberate, deliciously enunciated slow-motion detonation? "I MAY NOT MAKE IT, BUT I'M NOT GONNA GIVE UP." *Goh-nnuh.*

"Don't give up!"

"I COULD GIVE UP, BUT I'M NOT GONNA!"

Personally, I find something beautiful in his complete lack of irony. In an age when everything needs to have a layer of hipper-than-thou ennui, he is sincere: He wants to follow in the footsteps of his father and says so. With unremitting gusto.

Shortly thereafter he deboarded, but just because the bus was driving away, and he was no longer nearby didn't mean I couldn't still hear him perfectly. His reverberating half-a-block-away barrage read now as an ordinary voice right beside me. It said, "I aspire to my father."

I was reminded of the great Novalis quote, where he writes, "I am always going home, always to my father's house."

My philosophical reverie was shaken by further Hau Ling. He had other pertinent information he needed to share. I was all ears.

"I PUT ON COLOGNE!" he screamed, with the urgency of an untamed drill sergeant. "A LITTLE DAB HERE, AND A LITTLE DAB THERE!"

WHAT COUNTS FOR A PASS

10/16/19

A middle-aged man dressed in working-class exhausted, baseball cap and fishing rod and dirty T-shirt, sat up front watching me drive. We were headed north on Broadway. After a while he piped up.

"Does this turn into the 7?"

"Goin' the other way, yeah. I just came up from Rainier Beach."

"Aw yeah." He looked out the window for a spell before saying, "They get a little rough down there."

"Sometimes. I like it though. It's good people everywhere."

"I ain't been out that way in a while."

"Yeah it's changing even down there. Columbia City—"

"Once you get down past Othello though, it get kinda rough. 'Specially after a certain hour, mang, those folks be kinda *tough*."

"Yeah, you kinda gotta know somebody."

He replied, in a tone of mock proclamation: "If you don't have no ghetto pass . . . it'a be yo ass!"

I laughed. "Ha! You got that right!"

"Right about now, 8:45, when them streetlights starts comin' on, that's when I go home! Remember how like your momma said, when them streetlights come on, it be time to go back inside?"

My world *is* the world of the streetlights. Someone's got to be out here for the people who have to be, and if doing so makes me as happy as it does, well, I feel lucky.

He's right, there are some tough characters. It may not come across in my writing, because I tend not to describe them that way.

But these folks are the guys you cross the street for, not because they're Black or White, but because there's a look in their eyes you're smart enough to figure out.

It isn't supposed to involve you.

These are the guys I hear other passengers complain about nervously after they get off, because they managed to avoid a fight. Towering and humorless, tougher round the caustic edges, masters of the face that feels nothing; these are the men that teens and musical personalities pretend to be. The fact that even these souls recognize and respond to my acknowledgment, my respect, reveals something I find humanizing: They can value kindness too. Because there is no They. Don't you too value kindness, enjoy the sensation of being respected?

To all you "rough characters," or whatever it is people call you, what I have to say is: Thank you. For appreciating compassion. For valuing generosity of spirit to the point that it apparently qualifies me for a "ghetto pass."

Because I don't have anything else.

THE ANTIDOTE

1/26/22

I've just taken over my E Line in Pioneer Square from the previous operator and am preparing it to my liking: setting the mirrors, taping up my big yellow smiley face to the driver shield. Smiley faces are important.

I can hear two men outside talking on the Main Street bridge. One is well-spoken and articulate. They're having a pleasant conversation as they watch the freight trains below. Highlights I can recall: The articulate fellow saying, "I try to bring positivity and joy to people's days. I can make anyone feel better in three minutes. I'm great for three minutes. After minute 4:20, I'm gone though." To two women walking by: "Have a positive day." One didn't respond, the other turned and quietly said, "Thank you," as her friend continued talking. Him to his friend, later: "I tend to prefer doing meth alone." "Some people think I'm conceited, but I'm just being confident." He seemed easily approachable, small-framed and Midwestern scruffy—thin but with a movie-star face, like if Warren Oates had softer lines.

I called over to them, "Have a good day, gentlemen!" and we talked briefly about bus driving, about how it's the best job ever if you like people. He said he'd find it intimidating, the size of the vehicle, but the people would be fine, he's good around people. "I can tell," I said.

I'd inspected the bus interior before starting the trip. Toward the back on a seat was a pizza box with half a pepperoni pizza, and a huge maroon sleeping bag right next to it stuffed kind of beneath, but not under, a seat. It was very visible. It was so large I initially mistook it for a person. I opted to leave both as found. I hoped the bag's owner would return to recover it. It was a good sleeping bag. Incredibly, a full trip passed by in which no one touched either the bag or the pizza! On the return trip, a tall ruddy fellow intrepidly ate a slice and promptly fell asleep.

Subsequent trips happened with no pizza bravery (nor perhaps pizza desire), despite, well, everything you might imagine that would compel one to eat pizza on a bus: hunger, boredom, free food, ease of access . . . go figure.

More bizarre to me was the fact that no one touched the sleeping bag. I asked a dozing form at a bus stop in Aurora Village if he was awake, with a thought of giving him the sleeping bag plus pizza. He didn't respond. What a lottery he passed up! I didn't push it with him nor with other potential sleeping bag winners because I wanted to leave open the possibility of the bag's original (or last) owner returning for it. I left the pizza onboard too, as I'd prefer happy, pizza-fed people on my bus rather than elsewhere.

Six hours later, just before my last trip, I went back to the bag and inspected it. There was still a slice of pizza left. "You guys need to get better at eating pizza," I said to the empty interior, possibly aloud. The bag was in great shape, meaning: it had no needles in it. I took it with me and stepped out at 4th and Main, walking toward a gaggle of men on the BNSF railway overpass.

"Gentlemen," I called out confidently, "How's it goin'. Any of you guys know someone wants a sleeping bag? This is a good one. It's been on my bus six hours . . ."

The fellow from earlier, the friendlier Warren Oates, came forward. I hadn't noticed he was still here. "Hey, you're the guy from earlier!" We greeted each other like friends.

"Wow, this *is* a good one," he observed. He asked my name. We shook hands. The worst of COVID was winding down; I hadn't shaken a man's hand in two years. His grip was like mine: one firm shake, nothing more or less. His name was Major.

"That's an awesome name," I said. "Way cooler than mine."

He rebounded with a compliment I forget.

"I make do! Workin' with what I got," I laughed, looking at another fellow nearby, who was chuckling. I greeted him.

"This is LaVaughn," Major said.

"LaVaughn?! Man, everyone's got cooler names than me!"

Others sauntered over, but it was mainly the three of us doing the talking. We lit up the rain-speckled night. We forgot about the wind on the bridge. We forgot people have differences. We talked about Hollywood, where Major and I have both lived. LaVaughn was holding an ab roller. He'd dropped it on the downhill and gracefully picked it up again, nimbly circling to catch it on the downside. "Okay LaVaughn, I gotta ask you what that thing with the wheel is. I don't know what that is."

"It's an ab roller," he explained. That somehow led to LaVaughn revealing plastic black garbage bags under his sweater.

"Stayin' warm? Stayin' waterproof?" I asked.

"Naw, I'm sweatin' it off. I'm losin' weight."

Major said, "How much d'you weigh?"

LaVaughn: "Three."

"Three hundred pounds?" I said, "I don't believe that! What?"

"Three," LaVaughn nodded, sagely.

"Well, you wear it well. I never woulda guessed."

"I sat in jail for six months, put on fifty pounds, came out here to this shelter, put on fifty more pounds . . ."

We were the club of making each other feel better. They'd complimented my name when I'd praised their cool names. I said, "Well, this is the time of everyone puttin' on weight, it bein' COVID and all. Whether they're sittin' at home or sittin' in the office or sittin' somewhere else, they're all puttin' on the pounds."

We talked about bus driver weight gain, about bodybuilders who move stiffly because they forget to stretch, the need to be watchful of such things, complimenting him on his ab-rolling, his sweating, his commitment. I couldn't let it go. I said, "Hang on, LaVaughn. I weigh one *forty-eight*. There's no way you weigh two of me."

"Okay, I did some roundin'," he smiled.

"I knew it! I knew it!"

What else did we talk about? There were so many asides, quips, and laughs, the laughs you laugh with your whole body because the sidewalk is big enough and the sky is high above you. Because Major is major, and LaVaughn is on his way. They're in a recovery program that sounded killer. By luck or will, they'd landed in one that would help them with job placement and mental health counseling, that would provide room and board even after they got their job for another year, "So even if you're flippin' burgers, you're still gonna save some serious coin!" These two had been mistreated by the world and they had the nerve not to take it personally, summoning instead the monumental self-discipline necessary to help themselves, to keep on keepin' on.

"I gotta go drive," I eventually told them. I walked away faring each man well by name, gesturing thank you, gesturing love. There was so much I liked about the glowing space we'd together made. We men did not, as men all too often do, waste air performing assertions of dominance. We did not boast or talk about money. We spoke not in answers but questions, asking and learning about life, about each other, talking as adults at their best do. Polite. Open. We mirrored our best selves and rose higher and higher into the sky. I was nearly giddy as I got in my seat and started up the coach. They watched me make the turn onto northbound 4th, driving the behemoth away. Their joy poured out through me onto the people during this, my last trip of the night, and I noticed something different.

There had been a poison in the air of late, generally; something beyond COVID and harder to name, but just as insidious. A fear that drives people apart and makes them forget we're social animals, that we feel better when we connect. Antisocial behavior is hardest to find in working-class and low-income communities, but it had found even us, on the E line, which I've been away from long enough for the crowd to completely forget me. This was a new crowd, and they seemed unsure how to respond to my behavior. My goodwill had been striking them as foreign, and the best response they could muster was indifference.

But not tonight. There is something in me, infused in me from the earlier street conversation. Love instills confidence. Respect instills momentum. I'm full, rich, overflowing now. I'm motivated by the Glow, the radiance we'd built on the street corner. When that's inside you it's so much easier to disregard what others might think of you.

"Nice work!" yelled an unstable man who'd been watching me, at the end of his ride. The others waved in response to my yelled thank-yous, more than they normally do. They could somehow read the genuineness in my actions, feel it, and they responded in kind. How did they know? What was the giveaway, the tell, that my confident joy was unaffected? That above all I *wanted* to be there with them? What beauty there was in their now-uncharacteristic responsiveness.

Can the future please involve this?

FUNNYTRAGICSCARY-ENDEARING

11/7/16

There he is. By now I'd had several encounters, thankfully only the first of which involved Lukas and myself dragging him bodily off my bus.

"Mister Nathan!"

I love that he remembers my name. I love how he slurs out the formal designation 'mister,' in the perfect conflation of respectful address and garbled colloquialism. We're about the same height, perhaps even the same age. A Somalian accent, clipped, somehow always short of breath; he staggers forward on sea legs today, though we're on the dry land of Fifth and Jackson. I'm on the curb waiting for my bus and a friend is waiting with me when he shuffles forward. I reply to his call. "Abdirahim, hey!"

He corrects me. "ABdi-raHIM!"

"ABdiraHIM, how are you?"

"Mister Nathan, I lost one of my eyes!"

"Abdirahim, I'm so sorry! This is very serious!"

"Yes it's very serious!" He shows me, removing his aviator shades. The left side is swollen, stitched, caked with blood, the eyeball in its socket but barely visible, a clouded slit clearly blind. It still moves though. It appears to be looking at me.

"What happened?"

"I fell down some stairs."

I've heard that one before. But I'm more concerned about next steps. "Did you go to the hospital?"

"Yes." He says something confusing about medication; I think he didn't want to take it.

"Abdirahim, this is serious. You want to have both eyes. I mean I'm glad you still have the other eye leftover, but you really wanna have two eyes." I resist the impulse to share about dimensional and binocular vision, misjudging curves and so on . . . and instead just say, "It's important to go to the doctor. Did you go to the doctor?"

"Yes, I went to the hospital. Is it going to be okay?"

I could tell my assessment mattered to him. I felt out of my league. Where's Mother Teresa when you need her? He says again, "I just want to know, Mister Nathan, is it going to be okay?"

Give him the comfort he wants. Rise to the occasion. "Yes, but you gotta do what the doctor says. I know sometimes we don't want to go, but this time, your eyes are important, they are fragile." I'm genuinely concerned. He's far too hard on his body. "Be careful these days, go slow, get sleep, it's very important to take care of yourself."

Endearingly: "Nathan my whole face is very swollen."

"Yes, I can see that. It's not good now, but it's gonna get better. This is the bad time. It'll get better."

"Thank you, Mister Nathan. That is what I wanted to know! How are you?" Pointing to my friend, adding, "Who is she?"

"This is my friend, Mary!"

"Mary. Nice to meet you. You are . . ."

Mary says, "I'm his cousin!"

Just run with it. "Yeah," I say. I don't know why she said that. We're not cousins. We're friends. But family connections are easier to explain on the street than friendships, especially between genders. If you're not family, everyone thinks you're married, or you need to get married.

"Nathan, what is your, where is your family from?"

"Korea. But she is from the other side of my family."

"Yeah," nods Mary.

He says, "What is the other side? Europe?"

"They are from Hungary, yes," I reply. "Far back."

"Hungary. Europe! You know Josef Stalin?"

"Who?"

He pronounced it with a Y, like the Norwegian Jan, or the Spanish Jessica. "Yosef Stalin, you know Yosef Stalin?"

"Um, yeah. A little."

"He is from Europe too."

"I guess he is."

Abdirahim looks at Mary. There is a tightrope tensing; street conversations can take turns you never dreamed of, in a flash. He says to her, "You look like. You look like, Hillary Clinton!"

"Um," says Mary. Not all fifty-year olds like being compared to seventy-year-olds.

"Must be the hair," I quip.

"Yeah, must be the hair," said Mary.

"Hillary Clinton," says Abdirahim. "It is nice to meet you." The clouded slit of an eye, expressionless, peering out. Abdirahim's a sweetheart, but he doesn't leave quickly. "Mary, it is nice to meet you. If you don't mind." He says the last phrase, finishing off the pleasantry, but it comes out ominously. A one-eyed man bleeding from his other eye socket holding a bottle of Evian water filled with liquor can add to that. Mary is confused, and he repeats himself.

"If you don't mind."

"Uh," she says.

Me: "He's just saying it's nice to meet you if you don't mind."

"If you don't mind," he says again. You know when you're speaking a second language, and you can't explain it any other way but to say the exact same thing all over?

"Oh, I don't mind at all, it's very nice to meet you too!"

"Thank you. I'm sorry to interrupt. Mister Nathan, thank you. It is good to see you, my brother."

"Good to see you too!"

"Thank you for telling me it's good. Is it going to be okay?"

"Yes. Everything is going to be okay."

"Thank you, Mister Nathan."

Aw. He's a big teddy bear. Clinton comparisons and Stalin

non-sequiturs notwithstanding, he deserves binocular vision as much as anyone. I hope my words offered some measure of comfort and grace. I hope they helped, but I don't think he needed them desperately. There's something about how he conducts himself, even in the lowest of times, that I appreciate. The guy's newly missing a functioning eye, and he's making sure to say the right pleasantries. A little bit of dignity, or a lot; you can always carry it with you, though you may lose all else.

BOTH WAYS

11/21/15

I've always felt it a welcome surprise to return in one piece from international travel, while simultaneously finding the thought a bit silly; after all, driving a bus is more dangerous than going on vacation, and driving a car is more dangerous than driving a bus. But such logic stands feebly in light of my recent experiences.

I recall nights standing on Wilshire Boulevard in LA, waiting for the bus home, and witnessing a lot of car accidents. I remember thinking, it is such an unimaginable stroke of fortune that *nearly every single one* of the twelve million people living here will make it home tonight through all this madness, *completely unscathed.* One person not making it is still a tragedy, but that many people getting home safely in this madhouse is definitely a miracle.

What do we do? Do we shut ourselves off from everything? Do we stay indoors, avoiding the slippery bathtub, never turning on the oven, never going out . . . it's impossible. We have to continue, taking cues from what the universe seems to suggest, putting some trust in it, aware but not afraid. This is the beauty of the human organism, that we keep getting up. It's how we step outside of fear.

The most surprising thing about Paris for me was the tidal wave of concern for my whereabouts during the three days I was listed as missing and presumed dead. I never imagined so many people would give my absence much thought or take such effort to find me. How did they make the search for me trending on Twitter? How was there so much concern that an announcement was made on all the buses in King County? To return home to hundreds, upon hundreds more, of messages, emails, calls. To hear the lengths taken by my friends and family, many of them working together for the first time, involving the US Embassy, French Police, CNN and other news networks, and much more . . . it humbles me beyond words.

They stood in long lines waiting to look at the list of names of the dead. What did they think when they saw my name there?

They made phone calls, awakening old contacts in newspapers and television and international security. I had told no one of my plans or location, and that plus my penchant for traveling without electronics made the networking they did to find me both impressive and deeply moving. I don't know how they did it. I don't need to know. It's the fact that they *cared*. I'm almost jealous; when my friends have been pronounced dead they really were dead. Here, disbelief actually paid off for once.

Would that each of us could somehow experience our own false death (minus the trauma for all involved!) and learn how mightily we are cared for. You'd be surprised. I was. Paris was a wake-up call not only to appreciate—that is, love—the fullness of existence while I have access to it, but also to recognize how much appreciation—that is, love—is sent in my direction, every day.

It goes both ways.

The lesson began for me as merely a sleepy interruption in the wee hours, the hostel night clerk waking me up from the bottom bunk in a dark room on the third floor of a nondescript building off of Rue d'Atlas. The clerk was apologetic, saying they don't allow strangers to call their guests; he was terribly sorry to interrupt, but this caller was being insistent. I remember the clerk's face looking at me, confused, as though wondering: *Who is this kid? They care this much about their bus drivers in America?* And then the reporter's voice on the phone from CNN explaining things to me as I wriggled out of grogginess, asking me questions to confirm I was alive, that I was indeed myself.

I had no idea that moment was built out of such a mass of friends and entities working together, or that my sleepy mutterings of a response would mean so much to so many. Any words of thanks I summon now will fall woefully short of how I felt then, and today. We are, all of us, appreciated more than we realize.

TENDING TO THE LIVING

12/11/19

We were talking about everything and nothing, Tyrell and I, when he hit me with the news. Tyrell was a much-loved face on Rainier Avenue, a comedian by trade and friend to all in his off-hours. He had the trademark oversized jeans and massive basketball jersey, like many other men out here, but the amiable twinkle in his eyes was a reminder that big clothes and sagging pants are not inherently oppositional.

I'd been commenting on how cold it gets in Minneapolis, where I'd recently visited. "And they got a homeless situation there just like we do," I was saying. "Which I don't understand. Forty below? Where do these guys *go* at night? How do they *live*?"

"Well, you probably gotta look at the death toll over there."

"That's no joke."

Then he remembered. "Oh, you probably don't know, if you was gone last week. The window washer died. You know that guy, he always had the window washing gear, real tall?"

"Yeah." I paused, recalling his name. "Silas."

"That's the one, Silas."

"What? Are you serious? *Silas*, dead?"

"Yeah man, he got hit by a car."

"Hold up, I need to think about that for a second." I pulled over. Empty bus, after hours. You can do this at nighttime.

I could feel my brain—*slowing down* is the first impulse to describe it as, but it was really an expansion, my mind reeling out to take in the massive size of death, the eternal reminder that almost everything we normally think on is so much smaller.

Silas. The lanky and lovable neighbor, whom we knew as a character because he *wasn't* a character, just a reliably decent man, who'd dress crisply in a variety of styles, somehow able to elicit admiration from youngsters and old-timers alike. He was a man from the generation that will always exist in spirit, but sparsely: the reflective sort, your friend who thought before they spoke, who really did treat others as they'd wish for in return. Who covered their mouth when they yawned.

I couldn't believe it. I stared at Tyrell, and he looked back at me. We knew each other's silences then, the twin sensation of a world on pause; something was missing, and in its place was merely negative space. But Tyrell had more to share.

"Bro," I said. "Tyrell, you got me in a state of shock. *Silas?* I love that man! I picked him up last—two weeks ago!"

"Two weeks ago, that's right. I'm tellin' you. And check this out. Lemme tell you what happened, 'cause this is crazy."

I pulled back into traffic. He cleared his throat.

"So this car hits him. He's jaywalking, it's dark. It's right by the tree, by the store. You know. And the White lady drivin' the car sees what happened and pulls over, over there by the laundromat."

"By the laundromat okay yeah."

"I was already there, I was trying to perform CPR on him, but it was over. Wasn't nothin' you could do. Wasn't nothin' *there*, man." He gestured to his stomach and said it again. "Wasn't nothin' *there*."

"Man, that guy was the picture uh health," I mused. "He was always dressin' sharp, clean-cut dude always with a good word. Everyone loved Silas."

"His funeral was today."

"I woulda gone if I'd known. Love that guy."

"It was *big*, man. It was a whole lotta people there. He had twelve brothers 'n sisters."

"I bet it was big. *Twelve?* Gosh."

Tyrell continued. "So get this though. The White lady pulls over, she gets out her car. I'm trying to do CPR on Silas, but ain't nothin' happening. And then all of a sudden Nathan, instantly, all these African guys come running from everywhere. And they *pissed.* They be pointing they finger at her, like 'She killed him she killed him, the White lady killed him.' They's trying to *kill* this lady. And I had to make a decision, bro. I stepped in and said, 'Oh hell no. All y'all need to get the fuck on.'"

"Man, thank you. On behalf of humanity, thank you. 'Cause it ain't like she meant it."

"Exactly."

"She just made a mistake."

"Naw, not even that. She didn't do nothin' wrong. *He* jaywalked. He's wearin' black, it's nighttime. There wasn't nothin' she could do. And the African guys is trying to run up on her—and by the way, I don't know where the fuck these guys came from. There was a ton of them, I mean lots. And I'm out here all the time. You're out here too—you know. There ain't never a whole crowd like that."

"Yeah there never is. I don't see big groups of dudes anymore on Rainier."

"But I was like, 'Stay back, fools. It ain't like that.'" He snorted. "Trying to make it a race thing, shit."

"Tyrell, seriously. Thank you. Because that lady probably woulda gotten killed, which wouldn't have helped *anything.*"

"Exactly, man! I tried to help him, but he was gone. So I made a decision. I can't help him, so I'm gon' help her. I had a decision to make. It's good it was me. Everybody knows me, but they were still pissed."

"And when it's a mob like that, that's when people get killed. You know, the mob mentality, makin' people crazy."

"Right. I had a decision to make, man."

"I'm so glad you were there. You know she ain't ever gonna forget you!"

"I was there when chief John Williams got hit, remember that, the Native American dude got hit by the Black guy driving a car? It was in the paper. I gave John CPR!"

"You're a guardian angel, Tyrell. You know that, right?"

"I'm the 'hood doctor!"

"Ha!"

I tried to help him, but he was gone. So I made a decision. I can't help him, so I'm gon' help her. The endless wisdom of those lines. Tyrell just wanted to help, to further life, never mind who's who. In a split second he was able to enact what many of us take years to grasp: Tend to the living. What's past is past. The living are the only ones left, and they need tending to.

Yes, there will be the pain of Silas's family, the pain of his friends. There will also be my own confusion and deep sadness at driving on Rainier without ever seeing one of my favorite passengers again. No one was like Silas. He was expert at what I *try* to do—making you feel comfortable and appreciated, like you were special; knowing people by name, and always a kind word for me. You couldn't tell if it was his workday or weekend, because he was equally and consistently happy on both: a fifty-something man who looked thirty-five, with strong defined features and ageless dark skin, plus that irresistibly wide grin.

I'll mourn for Silas later. I get the feeling he'd prefer I just remember his best traits. What I found myself instead returning to that night, amid thoughts of my missing friend, was the car driver.

I thought about what she must be feeling. The guilt she'll carry for the rest of her life. The possible manslaughter charges, legal fees, and even jail time; but worse, the gnawing question that she might've destroyed a family's belief in a just universe, and that on her lowest days she may term herself a murderer. Be kind to yourself, fellow human. Silas would. In a decade of knowing the man I never heard him raise his voice and saw him calm down quite a few irascible souls.

I realized also that she would be forever affected in a positive way. Tyrell may not think she made a mistake, but I know *she* thinks she did. In her mind that night, she'd just made the mistake of her life, and every witness but one wanted her blood. She was at the mercy of an angry mob on the wrong side of town, and *who* saved her?

She will always remember who saved her.

A Black American man in the 'hood, who saw her for her core, the common humanity they both share, who understood her. Who helped her in a time of tremendous need, gladly and significantly risking his safety to do so. A Black American man who walked, talked, and dressed just like any number of movie villains we've grown up with, hard-fronting media figures the youth so baldly try to emulate, and real-world criminals I happen to know.

She will always stick up for a certain type of person now, give them the benefit of the doubt, more so than before, no matter what her views were to begin with. She will have a comprehension of how wide love can run in a way even her closest friends may never comprehend.

I was down, she may think. I was hated by the mob, by God, by myself.

But not by Tyrell.

OUR LADY OF MIRACLES

6/15/20

There she was, again! The same niqab and stroller, but most recognizably the immediacy of those smiling eyes, and the ebullient voice from behind the cloth.

"You came back!" I exclaimed.

"Yes, I came back!"

The last time I'd seen her I wished her well in my heart, appreciating her audacity but not optimistic about her hopes. I see far more people with plans than people who return to tell me their success stories. I was worried at how badly it might have gone and considered not bringing it up at all. You remember: she had traveled across the country to recover a daughter she wasn't sure she could find, who might not even want to see her, with hostile family members and officials thrown into the mix for good measure. Just the thought of how awful it could go would be enough to make me consider not even trying at all. What had those eyes seen?

I had to ask.

"How was Minnesota?"

"I had a great time. The hotel was nice, the people are nice. But it's so hot!"

It was summertime. "Yeah it is."

"You've felt it too?"

"Yeah, a different type of heat than here, huh?"

"Yeah I don't like the heat," she said. "But I like the people. And it's cleaner than here, yeah?"

"Yeah. Yeah, I was thinking about you, wondering . . . um. Did everything work out okay?"

"Yeah! Everything worked out!"

Just go for it. Just ask. In the good mood she's in, how badly could it have gone? I cleared my throat. "Did you find your daughter?"

"Yes, I found her! We made up, now she calls me every day!"

"Wow! My *friend*! Congratulations!!"

"Yes I talked to the police. I could not find her so I said to the police to find my daughter. I explained my situation."

"And they have to listen to you, you're the mother."

"Yes they found her. It took them five days."

"I'm so glad they helped!"

"Yeah. She opened the door and saw me and she cried."

I made a mental note: Don't be such a pessimist! Miracles happen more often in life than in stories, and here was yet another. A daughter receiving a tremendous act of love from her mother, a woman who risked much after years of hardship. Who must have felt such shuddering relief at things working out better than anyone could dream of. What a wave of peace must have coursed through her soul!

"I'm so glad she understood, she understands," I said. "That you're her mother and you love her."

"That's right!"

And how.

After she stepped out I grabbed a transfer and began writing. Thank goodness the light at Henderson takes forever. Following an extended bout of scribbling, I settled into a reflective silence. Carla the impassioned Christian operator crossed my mind again, the fearless young lady who marched to a drumbeat that worked for her. I slowed for a turn, softly, and began ascending a hill.

Somewhere along 62nd Avenue I realized it: Carla isn't going out there assuming everything will go well. She's going out there trusting she has the *tools* to handle whatever comes her way.

What tools do I have?

Of course Cause and Effect are real. What was I thinking? Actions have consequences. Haven't you seen the smile you cause to bloom on someone else when you smile at them? The dancing shifts of mood you bring as people respond to your tempo, whether it's thoughtful, kind, or cruel? The most powerful tools are not weapons or laws, but ideas, and the emotions that galvanize them. The *emotional* response to respect, kindness, patience. Maybe these things have more influence than we realize. How could it not help, to lean toward the glow?

You can feel the accumulative effect of goodness coming back around. I see it about me gently, like a mirror refracting light. Sure, it doesn't happen all the time. Sure, things happen that don't make sense. There are always mysteries.

But who am I to assume that because I don't see order, it must therefore not exist? Don't we find echoes of the sublime all around us? Tell me you don't see something incalculably true when dappled rays of sunshine spill through trees. When the stark and welcome beauty of the clouds stops you in your tracks, whispering to you in a language beyond words:

"There's more than you know."

CONVERSING WITH MY COLLEAGUES: II

11/21/19

"I think he's getting worse," I said.

"It couldn't get any worse than this," Don snorted. "After this, there's just being dead!"

We were talking about Pawel, a colleague of ours. I don't spite my coworker friends who have terrible attitudes. I did judge them when I first started, because I was unintelligent. But two decades on, I can understand how easy it is to get caught in the undertow of life's wrongs. I'm no longer mystified by the pull of frustration and dejection, the urge toward jadedness as a survival mechanism. It's okay to be unhappy as a bus driver. It's okay to be unhappy walking down the street. I get it.

But even if we do that, why would we want to? Life is short, and modern life is the act of editing. In the ocean of stimuli we nowadays wade through, what do we cut out? Which attitudes will we favor? It's hard to disagree with the Dalai Lama's quip: "Choose optimism. It feels better!"

Don was shaking his head. "The guy ages ten years every . . . *month*. I'm worried he's driving around wishing he was dead. Which is not, you know . . ."

"Yeah, not good!" I voiced what I've often wondered while listening to Pawel's diatribes: "What I don't understand is, I mean, why doesn't he *do* anything? If there's something in your life you don't like, you change it, and if you can't do that you rewire your brain so you're okay with whatever it is. Right?"

"Right!"

"He hates it here. Great. Why doesn't he leave? I mean okay I know it's complicated."

"It is. His wife and kids . . . here's what happened." Don went into the convoluted details, concluding, "Basically, he's got dual citizenship here and there, and he owns a—an apartment building? A home? On the actual island."

"Oh my gosh this guy! Dual citizenship between here and that country is impressive. I've never heard of that. He's got money, he's got property. What the heck's he still doing here? Does he *like* complaining about every second of every day of his life?"

Don cleared his throat. He was beyond complaining about complaining. "So I've been listening to this guy, Hicks. And his whole thing is frequencies and energies and whatever other bullshit. But the point of it is, I really believe that if you search out the positive stuff, hang onto the positive, dismiss the negative stuff, better things end up happening to you."

It was the kind of statement your cynic voice would tear apart. Nothing dismantles optimism like trauma. Paris loomed. *Maud was probably a positive person.* But when does sorrow lose proportion and become unproductive wallowing? We have to start somewhere, and what Don said made sense. Different behavior will result in different outcomes, and if people believe the world is a good place (whether or not it is), they'll act in ways that make it more so. I found myself replying with a vigor that surprised me: "Thank you! Exactly! The circumstantial evidence is overwhelming!"

"And whenever I listen to it, I think of you because you're the fucking poster child for this shit. If you just flow with life instead of fervently wishing for what you want, because that's really just you thinking about how much you *don't* have wherever it is . . . if you, like, disconnect yourself from an outcome and just put it out into the world, your good energy, your positive energy—"

"It totally comes back around!" I paused, trying to gather my growing excitement into words. These were the thoughts that seem like contraband, ideas you don't share aloud except with certain people. Don was one of them.

"Stop me if I've told you this already. But I remember reading this study, okay.* They got two groups of people, a group of people who consider themselves lucky in life, and a group that considers themselves unlucky."

"Okay. Lucky and unlucky."

"Yeah. And they had each person, individually, walk down a sidewalk upon which a $20 bill had been placed."

"Uh huh."

"And each of the people who thought they were lucky walked down the sidewalk, noticed the $20 bill, picked it up, and felt great about it."

"Sure."

"And then each of the people who thought they were unlucky walked down the sidewalk, and none of them even *noticed* the $20 bill. Not one!"

"Because they're not looking for it! They're not looking for anything except their own favorite negative bullshit. You can't expect to find great stuff if you're too busy blocking it out and looking at only the stuff you think is there!"

"Just going with the flow, gently down the stream kind of thing. Whether driving the bus or in life. Aren't buses just the perfect metaphor for life?"

"Ha!"

I don't want to put a value judgment on which outlook is better. People have their methods for getting through the day, and I find that impressive enough. All of us face certain, impending, incontrovertible decay, gut-wrenching loss, and annihilation. There's no way around it. On top of that the dispassionate heavens above drift slowly by, regarding all that is beautiful and awful transpiring below, confounding in their refusal to answer the questions we so ache to hear responses to. They force us to generate our own truths, making what music we can in the face of unending silence.

Isn't there something poetic about dancing toward the light, nevertheless? Laughing together, smiling, joining hands? Goodness is the tool we have for resisting death. It won't work on our last day, but for right now, this afternoon . . . it does.

Because it makes us feel whole.

---

* For more, refer to *The Luck Factor*, by Dr. Richard Wiseman.

POKER FACE PRACTICE

1/23/16

"You know, I find this job oddly relaxing," I told a man with a box of cupcakes. "I basically tool around for eight hours talking to people. You never know what's going to happen, it keeps you sharp . . ."

That was earlier in the night. Now we're going up Pine Street, working our way through Capitol Hill. A fellow about my age stares vacantly at me from the sidewalk.

"I'll just go one stop," he says.

"Sure yeah, come on in. How ya doin'?"

"Good." Pause. Then, not quite slurred: "How's your night going?"

He keeps staring, as if directly through my head, listing a little in the sway of bus movement. Slightly heavier, a collection of tan and olive, his shirt riding up on his navel.

I reply to his query with, "It's been cool! Yeah, it's been very pleasant." *Pleasant* really has been the operative word tonight. Not sure why. A young couple steps out the back doors, blowing me kisses. But I want to do something about this unnerving intra-cranial staring that's happening up front. To distract myself I keep talking to him.

"So are you goin' home for the night? Or uh, just getting started?"

"More like uh. Just getting started."

"Makin' the most of Thursday night. Thursday's the new Friday, right?"

"Yeah it is." Gazing ever still.

"You know," I continue, "ten minutes ago, this guy was on the bus giving out free cupcakes!"

Cupcakes have a way of waking people up. "NO FUCKIN' WAY," he screamed, as though I were suddenly fifty feet away.

"Yeah, true story! He works at a bakery. You shoulda been here."

"Did he give you one?"

"He did!"

"Good."

"Yeah, it was pretty amazing, I have to say." The cupcake is on my left, by the door release handle. "Actually, I have a half-eaten cupcake over here that, I'm not gonna eat it. I'd offer you a half-eaten cupcake, but I imagine you probably don't want a half-eaten . . ."

He thought about it and said in a reasonable tone, "Only if I can lick it off your balls."

I love this job. Where else can you practice responding to completely absurd comments with a straight face? With just your matter-of-fact let's-talk-about-the-grocery-list voice? Who knows why doing so is so much fun. You never know what's going to happen, indeed!

Missing only a small beat (give me time; I don't hear this one every day) I replied, "You know, that's nice of you to say, but uh, what I have to offer is simply. The cupcake."

"Well . . . ," he said. Decisions, decisions, as he weighed the pros and cons of cupcake sans scrotum. He looked genuinely conflicted.

I needed to get rid of this cupcake and stay healthy. It was salted caramel, and far too delectable. "Do you want it? 'Cause it's good!"

"Really?"

"I'm not sick, I don't have germs, I promise. Yeah, it's good."

"Thank you. Oh, I don't care." He took a bite. "OH MY GOD," he roared. Then, sheepishly: "I'm sorry for that vulgar-ass comment. Earlier."

Vulgar-ass! How perfectly self-reflexive and postmodern! We could write papers about this . . .

I sensed he was embarrassed, and thankful I hadn't railroaded over his appeal for romance. I've been known to use slightly different language in my own pursuits, but I can understand a bit of his vulnerability. We become a child again in those moments, as much as we pretend otherwise, and how we interpret the responses can prove formative in ways that last lifetimes.

"Oh, that's fine," I assured him. "We're on Broadway. This would be the place to say it!"

"Thanks. I'ma check this out," he said, noticing a crowd of youngsters laid out on the cement by the former Castle Megastore adult sex shop. "Later!"

"Okay! Goodnight!"

VERN: I

5/28/20

His name is Vern. Why does this Norman surname, which means "alder," seem so appropriate? For me the title calls to mind *verdant*, as in burgeoning green growth, and *verve*, as in Vern's beautiful toothless grin every time he steps on. He's the friendly neighborhood stalwart, the fifty-something Black American face with a grubby beard and a kind word for everyone.

I particularly enjoy how unkempt his appearance is. His good humor offsets it, upending expectations and lighting up the other passengers with newfound knowledge of what's possible. He makes you look differently at every soul with holes in their threadbare coat, tattered sagging jeans, uneven fingernails, and shoes worn down past the heels. With Silas you expected geniality, and you got it; but Vern's the one who taught me to give guys like Chosen a second chance.

"Hey, Vern!"

Someone behind me muttered, "Aw you know Vern?? Das wassup!!"

"How you been doin'?" I asked.

"Aw, I'm . . ." He trailed off, unable to give a pat answer. He was pushing a walker, which I'd never seen before. He'd been a cane man or less up until now. I tried to cheer him up. "Good to see you're still hangin' in there."

"Yeah. They got me in this walker though."

"I hope it helps a little."

"Yeah, it do."

"It's always good to see you man, still goin' strong. You always have a smile. Any man that could smile in this modern life—that's beautiful, dude! I respect that so much!"

"Thanks man! Ah could still smile 'cause a friends like you!"

"Aw, thanks, man!"

Ideas are best countered with other ideas, and emotions best conquered with other emotions. He seemed a touch demoralized, reduced by the vagaries of old age. We know it's coming, but we somehow imagine it'll never reach us . . . until it does. One day you and I will struggle to stand from sitting, will soil ourselves, will be slow to speak and remember. We will be lucky to live to such an age and will hopefully be better equipped than now at putting pride aside.

I endeavored to restore his mood tonight as he has so countlessly done mine over the years. I like to think we got somewhere together, turning our feelings around in the space of a few words, gifting each other with a new slant; a reminder of our mutual respect and appreciation.

Love. It is the name underneath all good things.

JUST THE TWO OF US, GRUFFLY

6/14/19

It was one of the best conversations I've had, and I don't know why. As ever in the summer of 2019, I was seated on the concrete in front of a CenturyLink office building, leaning against the warm brick wall and waiting for my 120 to pull around the corner.

He, a stranger to me, ambled up with a bicycle rolling alongside, forty-five and suntanned, clad in construction-spattered garb with a ponytail and bandanna. I nodded a hello.

He began.

"Man, I try to offer my seat to a lady standing on the bus, I forget how she said it, but she was like, get away from me! And I'm like whoa, lady, I wasn't tryin' to do nothin'. People think you're trying to take something, but sometimes it's—"

I knew exactly what he meant. "Ain't no agenda!"

"Right! I was taught to hold the door open for people."

So was I, but he abruptly changed course. I leaned forward.

"My girlfriend she works for FedEx. She's private contractor, she gotta load her own stuff. The FedEx Express guys, they just stand there. Them boxes now, used to be 70, now they're 120 pounds, I don't even know. I tell her she should get a DDL."

"CDL?"

"CDL yeah. She has a perfect record, could get retirement, everything, but she says no. She complains. She always be holdin' it in, every car that goes by she has to cut in front of that car. Cussin' people out. I'm getting tired of hearing it, bro."

The tone infusing his frustration was that of reasonableness, perplexity. He was only exasperated in the sense that he should be taking action in some way, but how? I could see the concerns were pressing to him. The seat on the bus was forgotten; these were deeper notions, heavy on the mind. He fumbled with his bicycle. Sometimes you just need someone to talk to.

I said, "That stuff's dangerous man, 'cause the five people around us . . . we end up becoming most like the five people we hang around the most, you know?"

He became animated: "Dude. Dude."

"It's dangerous to be around all that negative energy. You might start to—"

"You're *right*! 'Cause I notice myself starting to bitch about stuff that never used to bother me. She gambles like crazy too."

"Oh, man. Money's too hard to get."

"That's what I'm saying!"

He paused. We were in the realm society tells men they can't go, but we didn't care. We were talking out our emotions, through them, trying to reach clearer understandings of our mental health and why we cherish what we do. These are the conversations I usually have with my female friends. To be with a man discussing this—especially a bearded he-man in macho construction wear—was intoxicating. We were talking about sensitivity and matters of the heart. Is anything else more worthy of reflection? This is how I wish all men were willing to be.

"I don't know what to do. I care about her but I'll be honest with you bro, I don't love her. She's good person though."

"I'm sure it ain't all bad," I said. "I'm sure there's parts about her that are great."

"Oh hell yeah."

"But you got to take care a yourself. *Protect* yourself. If you can't be yourself in the relationship, that ain't healthy. And it's so hard to see straight when you're inside the relationship."

He said his next words aloud as immediately as he realized they were true: "I gotta cut loose of her."

I let the pause afterwards live a little. Was it because we were strangers this was going so well? Are the channels of intimate communication only open with either closest confidants or complete strangers, and no one in between?

"That type uh negative stress is like a disease in the mind, I think. It's tough to get that out, especially if she's around all the time."

"I don't know what to *say* to her. Man it's so good to talk about this," he mused. "I can't be tellin' my friends, they'll just tell her and tell her all wrong. I don't know how to say it, you know?"

"Maybe just be like, here's some stuff that's been on my mind. But you ain't got nothing to feel guilty about."

"She probably gonna react emotional, like what are you trying to say, you tryin' to break up with me, what are you saying."

"But just be like I ain't trying to have no argument, I'm just lettin' you know here's some stuff that's important to me that I been thinking about. You ain't responsible for her emotions."

"Hmm."

"You know the thing that always happens to me? Is six months later, I get torn up and regret leaving whoever it is." His eyes lit up in recognition as I continued: "But that ain't true. It's just emotions, 'cause they're still them and you're still you and it's gonna be all the same problems all over again if you get back together."

"Bro. Totally. Man, this is so good to talk to strangers. I could never talk to anyone I know about this. My name's Williams."

"I'm Nathan! Best of luck, I'll see you around!"

"Hey, anyone ever tell you look seventeen?"

"Ha! Only every day!"

"That's alright though, keep bein' you!"

"You too!"

You could smell the ocean of relief within him. He exuded a newfound calm, a sense of belonging in the world. I'm convinced this belonging was only half to do with decisions for his future; it was as much the bodied satisfaction of talking things over with a companionable ear. Of being *heard*, whether or not anything we discussed would actually prove useful later.

The difference these things can make.

SAINT GLADNESS

6/6/18

We're on Aurora, just about to turn off and go burrowing west into the quiet residential tracts. He boards in true Aurora Avenue garb—grey carpenters and a white T-shirt dirty from work or play, jailhouse tats emblazoned on his arms, once pale but now tan and coarse. A stubble-faced traveler edging out his fourth decade, tough but friendly, companionable even, with the bass-heavy grit of life's long road in his voice. He knows how to meet you on your turf.

"I think my transfer ran out," he says. "Gimme a second with these bills."

"Oh, just some coins is cool."

"Points?"

"Coins, just some coins, yeah. You're all right."

"Oh. Thanks, man." He's taken aback. I often feel I've seen more beautiful things with more regularity at this job than anywhere else: Look at the world in his eyes now, the realization that he's in a safe space, accepted. Among friends.

"Hey," he adds. "You know what? You're all right."

"Thanks, man!"

"Listen, I bet you hear a lot of stories but lemme tell you. Years ago, I made a mistake."

"Okay—"

"And I'm gonna to see my mom and wife right now for the first time in six years, we're gonna have dinner."

"Wow!"

"Then tomorrow I'm going on a thirty-eight-month sabbatical. But I've got today, and I'm gonna have a great time."

"Oh man! Okay that's fantastic."

"Yeah I, well I made a mistake."

"Okay."

A quick speaker. "I used to run with . . . you know, I was just Downtown makin' a couple rounds. I wanted to say thank you to some of the guys down there. I used to hang out around you know UGM, Rainier Beach—I mean these are not guys you would introduce to your grandma, lemme tell you. But I wanted to thank them for being part of my life and my journey, right? Now my mom wouldn't appreciate them at all. But here's th' deal, I shook their hand I said, 'You treated me with integrity in my journey but I'm never gonna see you again, 'cause if I see you again then I'm 'onna cause trouble, make a bad mistake.' But I shook their hand. You know what they said? They pretty much said the same thing they said, 'Pleasure seeing you. You go take care your business and you go get your family.' And these guys. These guys . . . and so I keep makin' these runs right, on the E Line, I started hitting this *wave* of grumpy people, and I jus' got through with this one guy . . . I mean I was like I should just take this guy and throw him off the rails but I'm like no no no. He got me all riled up, and then I get here and now all of a sudden for some reason I'm at *peace* again, and to have you say that, I'm like you know what?"

"Dude,"

"Just so I'm tellin' ya—"

"That means a lot—"

"Little things like that—"

"—the details."

"—go a loooong way."

"What an awesome journey, man, first time in *six* years. And okay, thirty-eight-month sab*bat*ical—"

"Yeah well what happens is I made a mistake nine years ago and . . . okay I made a poor choice, thought it was quick fast, thought I was a gangster. So what I gotta go do is go back to face a first-degree armed robbery charge?"

"Okay—"

“And what happened was I got out, left DOC and got a job and got all this—but I left the County after nine months. I took a three-day violation and turned it into thirty-eight months, but you know what? I’m here.”

It was a sabbatical. More jail time—and jail time for paltry reasons from the sound of it, pertaining to no new crime towards others . . . no one would fault him for being furious at the world, or hopeless, and yet . . . He called it a sabbatical. Would that I had a fraction of his temperance and perspective. He had one day with his family after six years, with another three away in front of him, and he wasn’t dismayed in the slightest. He talked about it like it was time to think and grow.

Part of me wondered what had kept him extending the traveling violation. Love, perhaps? It must have been something worthwhile. There was no fear in him now, nor energy expended on any other negative emotion, no matter how expected—disappointment, frustration, disillusionment. I’ve met monks that aren’t this good. Did he read the Stoics during his time inside? Or did he and Epictetus simply reflect and conclude similarly, never mind the millennia separating them?

Take life as it comes, and make the best of it.

He waved back at me, one last time, clearly invigorated by the evening that lay ahead, his gladness at our exchange, for what today meant. Here was a man who knew how to enjoy the present.

PART V

HARD TIMES

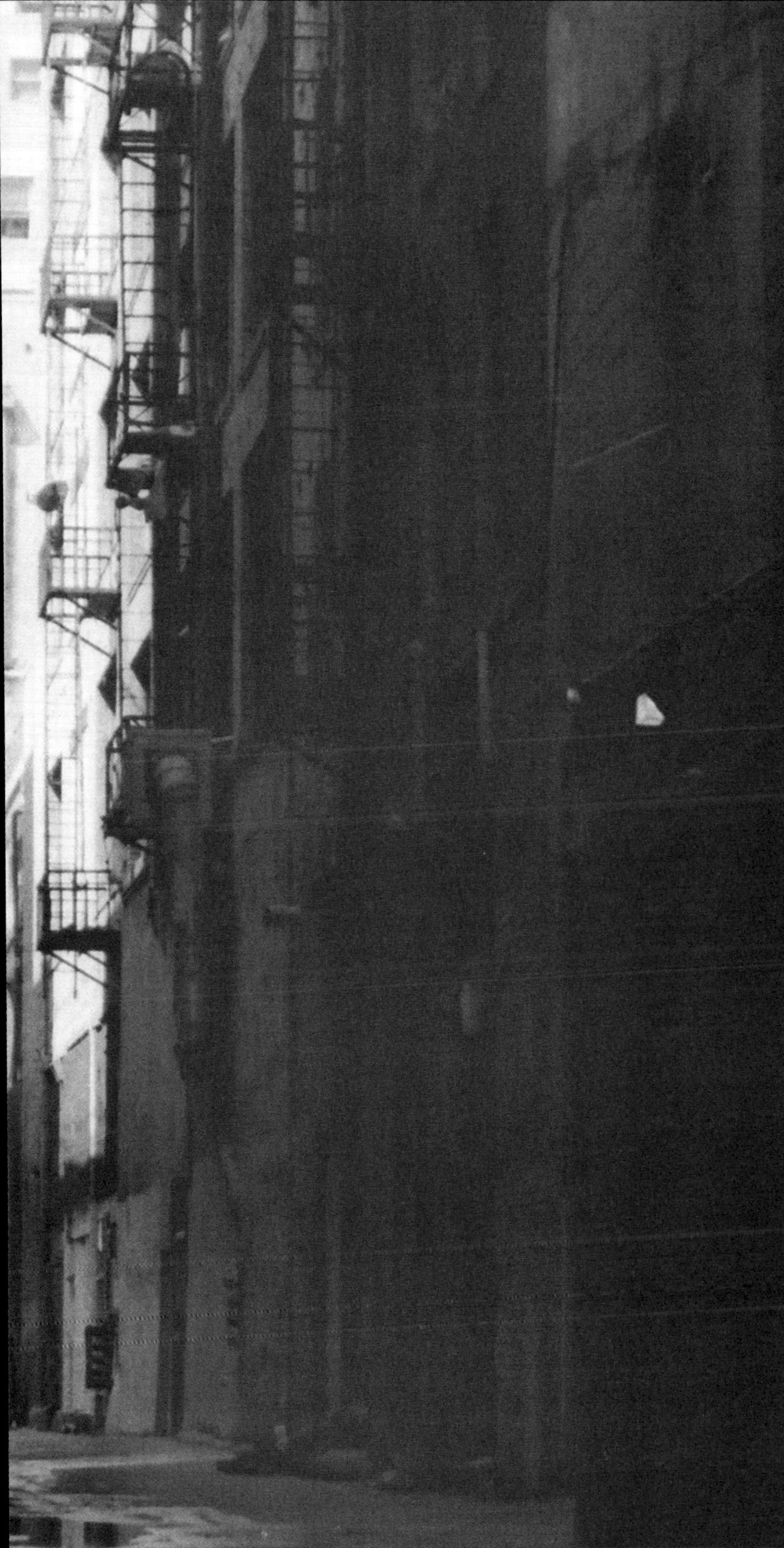

POEM FOR THE WALKING DEAD

12/16/23

They slobber past you with their bodies, at once aimless and committed, a sort of slow-motion resolve in that stumbling post-COVID gait we now know so well. Never before have they existed in such casual profusion. There were more closed doors back then, places to hide, institutions to rely on. Now things are different. As long as drugs are more accessible than solutions, people will medicate their problems with the former.

You can kill yourself at Third and Pike now for eighty-eight cents.

It is easy for we the sober-minded to laugh, to marvel at the stupidity of strangers. Look at them, sagging their pants below the knees, fishing through litter, pawing at the cement not for scraps of food but for the smallest, most unlikely hint of a fix. Here is one sitting in a pool of his own excrement, another huffing down stolen ice cream to rebalance his blood sugar, snot glazing across his mustache and lips, feeding into blood from open sores. "They pay money to look like that," a rumpled but drug-free passenger on my bus chuckled as he watched them outside, incredulously. "They actually pay money to fall asleep! Idiots. Dumbasses!"

Look at their muscles collapsing from the hips up, a new generation that stands with head and knees at equal height, legs bent and bending lower, reaching blindly for the earth's opposite horizon. The nigh-comical walk and Dickensian squalor of their clothes and skin, practically a dress code by this point; we call them lost, these haphazard solipsists, slinking ever onward in their knock-kneed gait. They are so easy to ridicule.

However.

There is always a however, and never more so than here. We the Sober can involve the future in our decision-making. We can consider others. The addicted brain does not. Its comprehension of the future only extends as far as acquiring its next fix: an hour maybe, or less than that. Life is measured in blinkered minutes. Only in such a tunnel can the decisions I see out here begin to make sense.

Do you know what an accomplishment it is, to resist a pill? To flush your supply down the toilet, say no, ask for help? These are actions harder and more worthy of our praise than winning the Nobel Prize. The trepidatious tender courage needed moves me more than those who win elections or run companies, more than lofty resumes or mantles stuffed with trophies. Is an achievement somehow less because it goes unrecorded? Particularly with what we know about addiction's effect on brain chemistry, I bow to the person who finds it in themselves to refuse a drink, pill, straw, needle, powder, patch.

These are the silent accomplishments. Imagine regarding your strung-out self in a bathroom mirror (in a gas station, in a high-rise) and seeing those gaunt eyes staring back, as you remember who you thought you could one day be. *This can't be how it ends.* You remember you can still start over.

That is the battle these people are trying to win. It is a shameful and humiliating battle, but they fight it in public, ignominiously, while the rest of us shake our heads and judge. These people deserve pity, not ridicule.

"They" were all you and me once, like Darlene, like our friend on the 12 with the cancerous growths, children with dreams and ideas that made them excited and sad and hopeful. They did not know they would one day start fights over nothing, soil themselves in public, walk into the road not caring if they live or die.

They did not know the halfway point of their lives when it blasted right past them.

I attended elementary and junior high school with a girl named Alana. Being the same age, we shared many classes, sitting next to each other in Math and Language Arts, and again in Social Studies. She was friendly and smart enough. Many years later she'd board my 3/4 with her Shih Tzu in tow, surprised when I remembered her full name. We trundled down Third Avenue in good spirits. She was searching her cluttered bags for her phone, thrilled when it began ringing. "Bye, Nathan Vass!" she called out as she left.

Everything seemed fine.

Then I would see her intermittently, across several years. A decline was underway. I began seeing her in the unforgiving back alleys of the city, too much makeup now, a puffy jacket and flip-flops in cold weather; with different men each time. Shame crept into her gaze, and then the rest. The only constant was her smile to me and the dog, always her faithful Shih Tzu accompanying her.

"I'm glad he's always at your side," I'd say.

"We've been through a lot together," she'd reply.

Alana would die before either of us reached twenty-five. Alana McCrawley from Math class and Language Arts, who remembered my full name. Her dog would end up outliving her.

What was her final thought?

I stop for the people at 12th and Jackson. I don't pass them up, and they know that. I want them to know that. At night somebody there will always wave if they want me, almost frantically, because they're so used to being passed up. I respond with my own wave. Some of my favorite passengers out here. "Aw, it's Nathan," one said recently, with happy relief. "He's not gonna mess with us!" I want them to know my bus is a little different. *This is the guy who cares, who doesn't look down on us.* I doubt I pull that off every day, but that's what I'm aiming for.

Some of them will make it out and live to tell me about it. Others of us don't know that we'll unravel, a paycheck or an injury away from Western society's most slippery slope. Maybe it'll be us stumbling about one day, another slipshod pants-sagging drifter in search of joy, meaning, conscience, belonging . . . wondering where it all went, baffled by how elusive those things are now. Who among them used to have it easy? Who among them once snickered, looking outside, really believing themselves as they laughed, *that'll never be me.*

Do not be too quick to sneer. The story is not over yet.

SHE'S ON FIRE

10/4/19

She looked agitated. She was.

"How you doin'," I asked in a calming voice.

"Those fat bitches," she replied, exasperated. "If you'll excuse my language." She was looking down the sidewalk at a trio of ladies walking away from the bus. "They left they baby all the way over there in the alley." When one of the women turned back to her—our friend the speaker was still halfway stepping onto my bus—she yelled, "Yeah you *better* walk away before I call CPS on your dumb ass! You wanna bring your three aunties out on the town you still can't even hire no babysitter . . . all y'all dumb bitches oughta be ashamed of yo'selves!"

A scruffy young man in an entirely different headspace stepped aboard after her.

"Hi, how you doin'," he said to her.

"What?"

"I said how you doin', sister."

Clearly still incensed but knowing to be polite to this unrelated figure: "Fine thanks for asking."

I smiled. She was mirroring my initial words to her, and so was he; I'd just exchanged a how's it going and thanks for asking with him in earshot of her. Kindness can be infectious. But so can the lingering aftereffects of anger.

"Hey," he said again.

This time she reacted as many a woman might wish to when a man unduly bothers her, exploding with careless abandon: "*Ah already spoke to you so what are you still doing in mah face*!?? A person don't have to talk to every single person the whole goddamn night when they tryna go home!"

The expectation of sensibility latent in her outburst prevented the air from becoming threatening. Respect was still floating about. He blew her a kiss, unfazed but acquiescent.

She said, "I apologize bus driver, I'ma be quiet now."

"Okay, but it's all better now . . ."

"Ah just don't know how I'm gonna make it to mah destination with all these people bothering me!"

"Well, let's see what happens!" After a pause I added, "I admire your integrity. I respect how you're standing up for yourself."

Everyone's got a different strategy. Hers was of the stripe that can lay down the law with an authority that still feels respectful, that somehow doesn't strike one as judgmental.

I'm not good at that. I'm so busy thinking of the angles that the clarity needed to invent such forceful statements on the spot without fearing their outcome eludes me. I tend to think a few chess moves ahead, considering how I can get along with whoever it is.

But I'm glad folks like her exist. Those ladies needed to be told off for abandoning their baby in an alley, and she was just the one to do it. The too-friendly guy needed a boundary drawn for him, and she cast it down with iron and fire. She has skills I don't have.

It takes multitudes, this life does. We all have our role to play.

SOMETHING EARLY

11/23/21

No child is born taciturn. What makes some men so? What wrongs have they suffered, what kindness of theirs thwarted, scorned, ridiculed? Fragility is what drives the urge to present a deadened exterior, and no creature is more fragile than the human male. How tantalizing it is to embody invincibility, especially in the spaces which all but demand it: armies, sports, prisons. The street. You do it long enough, and you might even begin to believe your facade. *So rough, so tough.* You speak no longer in sentences, but pronouncements. You dominate. It is at this point, the last part of your soul's capacity for love drifts off, and its final slumbering thought is, *Well, at least this is easier.*

But is it worth losing your ability to feel? What is living if not feeling? Are not the harder thing, and the right thing, usually the same?

He was a master of the callous front, and I wasn't about to criticize him for it. You get your heart railroaded enough times and the animal urge to protect yourself makes the decision for you. Shut down time. This man's face said Closed for Business, with one difference: he still looked people in the eye. The principal contrast between street smarts and book smarts is the former demands direct engagement with one's immediate present. He may have been taciturn, but he responded to me at least half the time, stalking quickly past me after putting his bicycle on the rack.

Me, giving the upward nod: "How's it goin'?"

Him, gruffly: "'Sup."

Me, calling out as he zipped past me to get his bicycle: "Thanks man."

The deep voice: "Yup."

The other times he'd just stare balefully. At least it read as baleful. I don't think it was. It was his way of confronting the world: fearless and direct. He wasn't trying to leave an impression, but for me he did; a noncommittal, gangster quiet. Was that a teardrop tattoo? I couldn't be sure. Those with the most interesting pasts keep them hidden.

He was taller than me, slightly, also a mixed-race Asian man. Always the dark blue hood pulled close round his head. Even if you're a quiet person, which he was, you have to talk to the driver if you're a bicyclist who uses buses. He found the least affable way to do so, yelling "Bike!!!" as he jumped out the rear door and scurried up to the front.

And then one night, as there inevitably is in life, there is change. An event. Here is a furtive young White man, ratlike in movement, dressed in a grey hoodie and black pants, hiding within his too-large clothes, muttering and hunched over as he picks about at the bus's scrap-laden floor. No bus interior gets dirtier than the nighttime E Line.

I'm at a zone with the ramp out, helping two passengers and their bulky wheelchair. It's taking a minute. All three doors are open. Taciturn Gangster is seated in the back area like he prefers, with his bicycle mounted up front.

Now the furtive ratlike fellow, slinking out the middle doors and up to Taciturn Gangster's bike. Look at him sniffing at it. Caressing the handlebars. He looks around, looks at me looking at him, my attention divided. He starts to fiddle with the securing mount . . .

I'm on the mic, and loud. "*Dude with the bike. Someone's trying to take your bike. Come on up and get it.*"

Taciturn Gangster's response is instant, almost military in its alacrity. He stands and sees and is instantly at the front outside the bus, covering the ground alongside in something smaller than seconds.

Here is a backhand smack across the face, with words to match.

In life most punches make little sound. What you hear is the rustle of clothing. But the young grey man stands as if unsmacked, impervious. He stares with no expression. Rain begins to fall.

"Why you touchin' my bike? That's not yours! Get away from there!"

Others are jumping out to watch, to support. For once, everyone around Taciturn Gangster supports him. They silently advocate for him. When did he last experience this sensation? There is no danger now. No question that the bicycle will stay. But the ratlike grey man sees differently, like he's breathing air from a distant someplace else. He doesn't realize he needs to stop. He gazes over at the Krispy Kreme doughnut shop, and back again. His face is pink and grey with stubble.

I'm distracted with the wheelchair. I look out again and he's drifting back to the bicycle once more, like maybe none of these people will notice if he steals it slowly? He looks at me.

I shake my finger at him with a grin, my index finger wagging back and forth: "No-no-no you don't," a preschool teacher's gesture echoing from long ago, stored in time for just this moment.

Taciturn is beside himself. He's a logical man, and Grey Man isn't. I hear spittle in Taciturn's voice as he tries to understand. "Wha—? What are you DOING?!? That's not your bike! Tha's *my* bike! Don't touch it! Man, get the fuck away from here—"

Sometimes a push is all you need.

Grey Man somehow doesn't fall down. He slinks away, first maybe toward the doughnut place, then no, maybe I'll go across the street or something. He drifts across Aurora Avenue's seven-lane expanse with gentle composure, never mind the honking cars, never mind the oppositional cluster of men behind him. A rat who lives to fight another day.

Taciturn returns to his chair, and everyone reboards. Time has returned to itself. He was exactly who he needed to be, in that moment. He had the confident forward propulsion of a person unafraid to act, who doesn't question themselves. The universe presented this problem to the person best equipped for handling it. Critically, he was also, like me, a person who never wears headphones in public. Had he been so, he wouldn't have heard my announcement and would have lost a bicycle.

He yelled up toward me from his seat after a moment of reflection, cupping his hand like a megaphone to project his voice, the better to ensure I heard him: "Thank you bus driver!"

I was still with my wheelchair-related companions when his exhortation cut through the public silence, traveling through them and up to me. It took a moment to recognize his words; they were unexpected.

"Anytime, anytime!" I replied, my open hand raised in the air, a stationary wave.

When he eventually deboarded, he scurried up to his bicycle alongside of the bus as per his usual, from the back doors and past my open front door, at which point I called out: "Have a good night!"

He paused. He stopped. He came back, leaning around the open door. "Ey. Thanks for doin' that. Thank you, mang."

Sometimes people speak to you with their eyes. The voice is an afterthought, a supplement. Look at his eyes, the dead-dog seriousness of his face now benevolent. Now *receiving*.

"Happy to help," I said.

"For real though." He wanted me to know he felt it.

"Always," I replied, my hands in supplicating prayer-gratitude mode, a gesture I've learned from the street and made my own over the years, then my hand on my heart, for truth. He put his fist to his heart also, mirroring me. I watched him grab his bicycle, an effortless economy of motion separate from his thoughts. He flashed the 'Westside' fingers as he walked off. I had earned my way into his respect.

But more importantly, I remembered his eyes. How they both contrasted and melded with the stillness of his deep and present voice. Something soft was in there. Something early, from childhood. It felt like a long-lost thought, reawakened: *sometimes people are good to each other, for no reason at all.*

I saw him have that reflection, stilled by its gentle surprise. The world includes *this*, too. Amongst the selfish, solitary, broken Now, there are also people who care, and who demonstrate that through action. It doesn't matter that it was me. Another driver would've done the same. I was thinking about *him*, feeling the moment from his eyes. *If this is possible, then what else is too?*

There are things we believed in childhood, that we no longer believe, that may still be true.

TRUTHFULNESS, THE FINAL CURRENCY

7/23/16

"That's a nice flower," I said. She held in her hand a single long stem rose, light pink.

"Thanks!" she answered, cheerful and animated. I remember large brown eyes and flowing auburn hair. "A stranger gave it to me!"

"Oh! That's kind of excellent!"

"Would you like it?"

"That's so nice of you! Thank you!"

I set it on the dashboard, draped over the dials and toggle switches. What a perfect addition to the driver area. What made people ever stop designing with such aesthetic embellishments? Why are there no *fleur-de-lis* and gargoyles on this bus? I grinned inside myself, feeling new and warm and validated. A short while later another young woman came forward, a student here at UW, with rippled blond hair and an Eastern European accent.

I asked, "How are you?"

Ask it brightly. Watch a smile form on their face, as you mirror each other's best side.

"Good!" she said, suppressing a laugh at my enthusiasm. "I like your flower," she said.

"Thank you! A passenger gave it to me!"

"Aw!"

"Do you want it? You should have it!"

"Me?"

"Yeah, yeah. Happy, uh, Tuesday!"

"Ha! Thanks!"

I asked about her day. We talked of school and work and work-study. She tossed her hair back. She was in the sciences. I asked what she liked most about her field. I like hearing people expound on their passions. Don't ask her name, I told myself. Don't say, *I hope I see you again*. I wanted her to know the flower was real. That it came with no agenda. This is about strangers being lovely to each other and paying warmth forward. I'm sure her conception of individuals whom she knows is positive; but I wanted to be part of her positive conception of *strangers*.

My mind returned to a note I was once given. A woman about my age handed me a folded square of paper. I didn't catch her face; too busy trying to stay on the trolley wire. I caught only a glimpse of cigarette pants and long black hair dashing into the twilight. I put her note in my breast pocket and continued along the route. At the terminal I unfolded it. It said endearing and adorable things. It also had no contact information of any kind.

Which is how I knew it was completely genuine.

DAWIT

7/13/14

You can guess the degree to which I like talking to people, but we all have our quiet moments. There are certain cloudy days which have an indescribable and almost comforting air of melancholy. You want to withdraw, accountable to no one for now, just you walking under that grey Seattle sky, enjoying the green leaves and open roads in your periphery.

It was in such a headspace that I once boarded a 41, dressed incognito, on a day off: black sweatshirt sized small, dark blue jeans, and scuffed dress shoes. Walking about Downtown I inevitably run into people I know, which is delightful, but today I wanted solitude. As much as our culture celebrates the active over the passive, there is value in taking time simply to reflect. I leave my phone in my pocket, trying not to retreat into the cozy confines of distraction, that addictive place where I don't have to confront my own thoughts. Let me rather take the dive, that I might feel something real. Creativity requires boredom to exist.

I sat down next to an African man, first generation, neatly shaved and dressed. Leaning back into the seat, I enjoyed that wonderful sensation operators feel when they board a bus they're not driving: *this bus is moving, and I'm not responsible*!

"You're not working today?"

It was the gentleman next to me. Time to turn back on.

"Hey! You recognized me!" I said. Must be a passenger I don't remember. His good-natured smile brought me back to the excitement of dialogue. How was his day going? How did he recognize me, though I was in my elaborate Nathan disguise? He responded by describing how memorable it is when I'm driving, and how could he forget such an experience? Naw, I said, trying not to blush. Yes, he replied, laughing. Don't be silly! He shared a few more compliments but most of all wanted to emphasize his appreciation that I was kind to immigrants. It's a big deal, he stressed, for people who are new here, because it's hard to get around, confusing, and sometimes you need someone who won't judge you, who will give you a few extra moments, as it can make all the difference in the world in feeling welcomed.

This led to me mentioning my own background, coming from parents who immigrated here and growing up speaking multiple languages at home. It only seems natural to be kind to such folks; I see echoes of those dear to me in their questioning eyes.

His name was Dawit. Language is important, we agreed, and I mentioned an Ethiopian friend of mine, Abebe, whose three young sons were already studying their native language as well as English, French, and Spanish.

"Does he live in Bellevue?" Dawit asked.

"Oh my goodness!" Who could've guessed we had a mutual friend? Abebe is one of the great bus drivers, one of those people whose every word you hang onto, because you know they think before they speak. The quiet voice, eyes twinkling with verve and wisdom. We've shared many a meaningful conversation.

"Yes, language is important," Dawit said. At this point he began telling me a story, and the longer he spoke, the more rapt with attention I grew.

Many years before he sat next to me on a 41 in Seattle, Dawit lived in a village in rural Ethiopia. He spoke four languages: Amharic, two local dialects more specific to his village, and a fourth language nobody used, but which he knew anyway. Being multilingual was not unusual, but not too many neighbors knew that fourth language. It was a remnant from his ancestry, relatives he hardly kept in touch with.

In the mornings, Dawit would rise early and walk alone on the dirt path to a nearby bridge. This bridge was special, because from it you could see the most spectacular sunrises. Never anyone else around. When you're raising a family, time alone gains a different and specific value. Watching the predawn light come to blazing life was Dawit's way of carving out space for himself.

Word had gotten out from nearby villages that invaders were on the loose. A nomadic tribe was moving from here to there, killing the village residents as they went. Panic settled in: Were they near? Were they far? Were they rumor?

They were real. There they were now, suddenly, black figures against the dirt path one morning, weapons on view, blocking the way to the bridge. The sky was just starting to lighten when the leader of the bandit tribe spoke.

"Where are you going?"

It was the fourth language, the one nobody ever used.

Dawit responded fluently, in the same tongue: "I'm going to watch the sunrise from a bridge that I like."

"How do you know our language?" Confused and surprised. It's from my relatives, Dawit explained. An uncle, something, the details of ancestry hazy but undeniable. There was a political figure of some repute Dawit knew, whom the nomads knew too. Through further conversation Dawit was able to prove it.

The leader stood there for a minute. Dawit waited under the lightening sky. Life, and nothing less, was what hung in the balance.

"Okay," the bandit said finally. "Because you know our language and because you know this man, we won't kill you right now. Today you can watch the sunrise. But you cannot come back again. If you are here tomorrow, we will kill you."

Dawit recounted the man's words as being spoken plainly, matter-of-factly, with the deadened flatness and ugly apathy you hear in truly violent men. After that Dawit never walked that path again.

I looked at him seated next to me, struck like a thunderbolt by how little of this world I know. I was looking upon the same being who one morning wasn't sure if he had seconds left to live, couldn't be sure if his family would ever know him again.

"Wow," I said, at a stunned loss for words. "Wow. It is *so great* you knew that language, or else I would not be sitting next to you listening to this story on the bus right now!" He smiled. "I am so glad," I continued, thrilled that he chose to speak to me. "That you knew that fourth language."

"Yeah, it's important," he said.

ON TERROR AND OTHER THINGS

10/3/17

On the morning of September 11, 2001, I was a high school student riding the Metro bus to school. There were no cell phones, and the internet hadn't taken over yet. Those were the years of calling the movie theatre for showtimes or looking them up in a newspaper; of finding a payphone to call that classmate you had a crush on. You had to call their home *landline* and suffer the embarrassment of speaking with their mother first. Remember that?

I noticed the other passengers, all adults, were talking about a disaster movie in serious tones. It sounded almost real, the way they somberly detailed explosions and collapsing buildings. What were they saying?

September 11th was probably the last major historical event to be understood slowly. It took hours of watching news networks just to comprehend the most elementary basics of what had happened, and most of us wouldn't be aware of the full scope of the event until the following morning's paper, with further details illuminated only later, throughout the rest of the week.

Paris 2015 approximated this sensation on the ground, because of the multiple attack sites. While they were underway, no one knew how many there were. Everything was happening at once, and the sensation of an entire city under siege was convincing. With all transportation shut down, you were stuck wherever you happened to be. The gradually revealed nature of the perpetrators' identities and their captures also elongated the experience.

Today's massacres take place in a different landscape. It's the same globe now as 2001, with the same goals, desires, and emotions, but they express themselves through different concerns and at a different speed. What took a week or more to understand in 2001, we already know overnight about the latest incident. We had videos online from the crowd being shot at in October 2017 Las Vegas mere minutes after the event. We had recordings of the police response and a clear, eyewitness-like understanding of the intolerably continuous duration of a shooting that killed or injured 473 people. The horror is that much closer to us—and that much more fleeting. Who among us reading these words now even remembers which shooting I'm referring to? And yet, fleeting or not, quickly delineated or not, the underlying question beneath the questions remains unaltered:

How should we react to such incidents?

On that fateful Tuesday in 2001, the TV was on in our AP English classroom, but only for the start of class. Professor Keable was a Vietnam vet, and for him, a man who had seen a lot of death—year after year of young, poor, tired men killing each other at the behest of their respective governments—the best way to deal with this atrocity was to get on with the business of living. At some point we just have to, he said.

Other teachers in the building reacted differently. They left the TV on all day, they talked and hugged their students, or they went home.

What is the right way to deal with something like this?

Massacres are always tragic, but the October 1st incident in Las Vegas, being the largest individual mass shooting in US history and the only one to remotely approach Paris's numbers, was the first to truly remind me what November 2015 felt like. It rattled me further because, unlike Paris, it had no motive. We know radical ideologies are no excuse for mass murders in major western cities, but we recognize the explanation: they thought this, so they decided to do that. Terrorism may be the worst form of communication in existence, but it's still communication, an attempt to shift thinking through fear.

Las Vegas lacked even that. The meaninglessness of October 1st represents a yawning void much larger to me, more bewildering than similar events. We don't even know if this guy hated the crowd he shot at. Perhaps he was bored. Maybe he found it amusing.

Once again, I recalled the night a group of teenage girls pepper-sprayed Chosen at eye-blank range, while he'd been minding his own business. I found the event so ugly because it had no meaning. Was the Vegas gunman's motive simply a bloated, amplified exacerbation of the same apathetic impulse? The Great Universe never explains itself.

Kameron, a passenger, would ride my bus a few nights later in October. "You a good man though," he said, after a discussion about his term papers back in college. He was excited about Metro's hiring campaign posters of me. "You steady doin' commercials, and I'm steady lookin' for 'em! When I see you on the side of the bus I say heeyy, that's my guy, that's my friend!"

I chuckled. "Can't get away from that dude!"

"Just like that!"

"Thank you so much. I'm so thankful—"

"Man. If you stay thankful and humble—"

"That's the key right there. It allows us to be so much more happy through life, right?"

"If you stay thankful and humble, you'll always prosper, bro."

"Keeps our perspective in the right place, lookin' the right direction."

"Just like that!"

I then finished my shift and caught fellow driver Grady on our walk to the parking garage. Grady spun around happily.

"How was your evening, good sir?"

"It was particularly fabulous," I exclaimed, returning his beaming persona. "Some really wonderful people out there."

"I echo the sentiment!"

"We're really living the dream out here."

"It's so true. We really are. I feel so fortunate."

"Humble and thankful," he said. "Humble and thankful. That's the theme!"

I hid my surprise at hearing the words again, and so soon. "It so is!"

"Humble and thankful. If we can do that, everything will fall into place. Everything."

"I'm gonna put that in my pocket!"

Grady doesn't know Kameron. They have no idea of each other's existence. Their only commonality is they've each Been Through Some Stuff. And this is what they had come up with. Does the Universe really never show its cards?

There is no right way to react to incidents like these. But I can't help but think these two strangers are on to something.

ANGRYNICE, AGAIN

7/7/16

I'd never seen her at Fifth and Jackson before. Iris's squat profile was instantly recognizable, her silver hair backlit by the storefronts opposite.

"Hey, Iris," I said, looking through the gloom at her stroller.

"Hey, Nate," she replied, hobbling a step forward. Quickly, knowing I've turned her away before, she said, "I got a new stroller but it has broke wheels too."

Maybe she couldn't see my face in the darkness from out there, but I smiled with my voice. "That's okay, thanks for getting a new one. That's what counts."

"It still has a problem."

"That's okay."

Iris stepped in keeping pace with the glaciers of old, cursing the nerve pain which shot through her swollen legs at each step. She still demanded the front seats be lifted in a particular fashion I can never remember. I really ought to write it down. Tonight, a young male passenger—don't say the youth never help their elders!—assisted her for me.

I couldn't see her as we carried on our way but heard her just behind me. Snatches of another life drifted within earshot; I strained for the details. She was ready to go home, she sighed. "I got up at four A.M . . . 'cause when people are in pain they make a lot of noise. He's been in a lot of pain." She kept saying "he," and I never got an answer to who *he* was; only that he was a veteran and someone special. I said that's a hard life, being a vet, and she didn't disagree. He went in for surgery, she said, but he's okay now.

"I'm glad he's okay."

"I'm gonna take care of him," she remarked. "He's not gonna do anything to me."

"That's good."

The briefest sentences, and the lifetimes behind them.

"You can sit down! It's safer to sit down!" she hollered at an Asian man, trying to be nice. I caught a glimpse of her craggy face in the mirror, her grey-blue eyes still blazing in late age. I'm sure she fit most people's definition of pretty at some point in her life. Does she reflect on her past, as I do, when the pain is not as strong? Sleepless in the wee morning hours, lying in repose, a reverie between the ceiling and ourselves. It's a solitary act, and something we all share. I hope there are good memories.

"Getting operated on . . ." she was saying something about medical procedures. Then a thought on housing, how they're gonna tear her house down, putting up condos instead; I can understand that frustration. "They need to be more kind to me." Her grumbles mingled with the gentle hum of the electric trolley. Then I heard her, and heard her again. She said it more than once: "Everybody just needs to be loved."

We Americans are a vocal sort. We wear our emotions, our opinions, anger, ignorance—loudly—on our sleeves. But there are things even we don't bray out into the world.

I believe loneliness is the premier element of the human condition. It doesn't matter how popular you are. We are individuals who process things within our own minds, and that is always and ever a singular act; how many millions of thoughts will you never share, because they were too trivial, private, hard to contextualize? We brush our teeth, tie our shoes, and hang up our clothes alone. We crave acceptance and love from others in an effort to combat it. Loneliness is not quite up there with the fact of death, as the motivating engine for all human action, but it's close.

And we never talk about it.

We wax and wane around it, hinting at it with all our talk of relationships, psychology, and desire. "Everybody needs to be loved" is a valid statement on its own, but it's also code for something else, deeper and more personal. I heard it in her plaintive voice.

As she left: "Nate, I'm glad I got to see you tonight." She apologized she couldn't ride further, explaining that she really did need to go home. That's fine, I said. She took forever. Then she hollered into the wind, her cry reaching through the closing doors, me turning the wheel to pull back into traffic. She was yelling more nice things. So nice, perhaps it's good I didn't hear them.

Some days later, Iris was at the Andover Street stop. She was surrounded amongst her things in the bus shelter, camped out for an afternoon siesta of sorts. She didn't want the bus but waved upon recognizing me. I was busy with other incoming passengers. They had questions and concerns of their own; there was shuffling and rustling and general confusion. Iris called out, feebly, struggling repeatedly to reach my distracted airs: "Thank you Nathan, thank you! Thanks for being my friend!"

Of every noise I heard that night, every song, yell, and murmur, hers was the most meaningful. You could see that her speaking up took effort, but some sounds cut right through the clutter. I had the image of a newborn bird, or the fragile "I love you" a spouse says after being yelled at: a lack of armor which stops you in your tracks. It was a bald and delicate sentiment she needed to express, naked though it was. Because on the street you never know when, or if, you'll see someone again.

More crucial than any other concern was making sure she knew I heard her. "You too, Iris, good to see you," I loudly exclaimed, leaning forward, practically shouting through the people who were in the way. They can be confused. I called after her with urgency, yelling in love.

I hope she heard me.

TO THRIVE, MEANWHILE

6/24/20

"Hey, it's my guy!" I called out, with pleasant surprise. I only see him down south on the 7, on his way to the 107. What was he doing up here in the U-District? He explained about a new job, a different restaurant; Ivar's, if I recall.

"Does this mean you're no longer at Jimmy John's?"

"No way!"

"Ha! Feels good to be outta there?"

He was a mixed-race man my age, of Latino heritage; stocky, with long frizz-wavy jet-black hair, the sort that wouldn't be out of place on the front of a romance novel. He spoke the chaotic vernacular of 21st-century America but exuded a radiant kindness, that generosity of goodwill you sense in certain people even when they're not doing anything. I felt like my people were near when he and his ladyfriend would get on late at night on Rainier.

"Yeah, and I'm 'bout to be a prep cook, they're gonna pay me sixteen an hour."

"Awesome! You know I was just thinking about you the other day, 'cause I was in that Jimmy John's. I thought okay, he musta found something else . . ."

"Yup. And we're living in Bothell now." Standing at the front by me, excited.

The 'burbs? The *far-out* 'burbs? I said, "*What*?"

"Yeah, and—hey, did I . . . ? Lemme show you. I'm a father now."

"Whoa, congratulations!"

"Yeah, it's a daughter."

"When, how old is she, when did this happen?"

"She's five months. Here, hang on."

"Yeah yeah, lemme find a red light. Oh she's beautiful."

I let the big news sink in. "Man, being a father, they say it transforms your mental, your headspace, you know?"

"You're not a father?"

"No, but I hear people talk about like, on a fundamental level—"

"Yeah. It changes your whole . . ."

"Perspective, priorities?"

"Yeah, what's important, your priorities. 'Cause even if my girl and I aren't always together, I know I'm always gonna raise this kid."

"That's beautiful. Man five months old, that must be some real 24-hour type stuff."

"Yeah. 'Cause I take class in the day, go to work at night—"

"Oh what type a class? Like parenting stuff?"

"Yeah parenting stuff, and also uh, some drug stuff, 'cause I had some run-ins with the law when I was younger."

"Right on. We all do. I feel like the two hardest things to do in life are, gettin' offa hard drugs, and raising a child."

"Yeah."

"And man, you're doin' both!"

"Thanks, dude!"

The conversation could've taken either fork in the road: lighthearted and fun, or truthful. He was feeling truthful. After a moment of reflection watching me work, he said, "You really love this job, I could tell."

I smiled. Most people stick to talking about themselves. He was open to the world beyond his needs, taking in the experience even of strangers like me. Soon I would know why.

"Yeah man," I said. "I'm thankful to have the job, but I'm also thankful that I *like* it, you know?"

His mind was on a larger plane. His forthright urge fulfilled itself, spilling out unbidden, in the manner possible only when you know you're in a safe space: "Actually," he said, "I just found out I have diabetes."

It was the kind of statement which makes you replay the entire conversation in your head. New jobs, fatherhood, self-improvement . . . the connecting tissue revealed itself. We were talking about mortality, and all the ways us tiny humans try to stand up and face it. When you've been diagnosed with the seventh-leading killer of Americans today and the number one cause of kidney failure, adult blindness, and lower-limb amputations . . .

Photographs of your daughter need to be shown to strangers. Proof of life. Proof of cyclical recurring goodness and existence. The drug class, the efforts toward being one's best self. When the Void shows you its face, a new urgency courses through you, makes you better than you ever were before. My solution has been a headlong rush of creating, as heedlessly best as I know how—films, books, the desire to generate complete and finished entities, things made. His solution wasn't so different: creating, growing, nurturing. It is what we do.

"What??? I am so sorry."

"Yeah man," he said.

"Oh," I said.

Our pauses weren't awkward. They were fraught with recognition, silent comforts. You go through your pain so you know how to listen to someone else, someday, when they go through theirs.

"Yeah dude," he said. "I got diagnosed earlier today. I mean I kinda knew I had it though."

"Bro. Check out this documentary, it's called *What the Health*."

"Dude, I seen that! That's my favorite type a thing, stuff like that. I watch all them shows, like *Food, Inc* . . ."

"Chicken, sugar, hospitals, it's so interesting!"

"I'ma watch that one one more time and take notes!"

Diabetes, today. The weight of it, to look about yourself and know everything will have the slant of *this* changing things. You pretend it isn't a big deal, and in many ways it isn't. You downplay it so you don't have to stare into the gaping void.

Why did I live?

An asterisk would now follow him, trailing his decisions; shaping differently what he called freedom. The diagnosis must have been overflowing his mind. I'm glad he let it out. We do what we can in this short life, humbled ever further by age and time.

But I know if he read this he would laugh at my heaviness. "Ease up, bro!" I can hear him saying, with a grin. And I would admire him for it because that cavalier optimism is exactly what we need mixed into our sorrows if we are to flourish. Laughter is magic precisely because it lacks logic; it is beyond reason. I will smile now, regardless of my futures. The void can wait. This is what is real and true, right now, and it is fabulous:

Making friends on the bus ride home.

THE DAWN OF TIME

4/11/18

I was sitting one table away. A food court in an Asian market, two middle-aged men from somewhere far away, dark-skinned with accents I couldn't begin to place. The bigger fellow listened; across from him sat his friend, a spry man in black, his collared coat covering a service uniform. They were chewing on their chicken, but appetite was giving way to a different voice now, a somber tone amongst their leisure.

"I'm worried about my kid. My son. He started acting bad. He beat my wife. His friends. I try to follow him; see where he go. They call me at my work, and I get worried, because it's the work number. My boss says your wife is calling you. And she explains what's happening. And I say let me talk to my son. And he swears. At me! Says F word. 'I don't give a fuck,' on the phone. Hurts my feelings." Gruff but sincere. His body leaning forward, hands spread apart. He had the poetry of an unrehearsed lament. "Because I work hard. For them. For him." He paused before continuing.

"So I took them and sat them all down. My wife, my son, my daughter. And we pray. To all religions. I say if this Christian religion, Jesus, if exist, please. Please! Take him down. Take my son and help him. And I say to the Muslim religion, Allah. If he exists, Mohammed. Please, take him down. This is my son. He was good child, good in school. Good grades. Everything good, until now. I don't know what happened."

At first his friend had kept eating, chewing on thinly sliced meat; you could tell he was trying to hide his enjoyment of it, but he had stopped by now. They were the units of conflict and audience—

human drama—at their most elemental, with a purity of truth so many operas, films, symphonies, and literature could never hope to capture. Two men at a table. His pronunciation of *Allah* was perfect, the accent you can't fake: emphasis on the first syllable, and a thick rendering of the double L.

His companion did the most friends can sometimes do: listen. These were the queries that bruise the soul, with hardly an answer in sight. It was a question parents have asked for thousands of millennia. Odds are high that child will one day grow up and ask similar questions about his own wayward son.

Perhaps at a table, with a considerate friend.

JESSICA LEE

2/19/20

Broadway and Pine, inbound, in Seattle's thriving Capitol Hill neighborhood. Every city has a stop like this.

It's one of my favorite zones because, like Fourth and Pike, there's usually a mob waiting for you. In the suburbs, crowds at bus stops form into orderly lines; here in the city center, disorganized mobs are the going thing. I'll take either. It's the pleasure of a big group entering your space and getting a quick second to greet every individual stepping aboard. These were the days of front-door only boarding, which created a safer and more communal environment within. The opportunity to 'check in' with each incoming passenger worked wonders. On top of that, I simply had to marvel at so much Life, rushing at me in such short sequence. Can you believe each is the center of their own vast and detailed journey, with joys and sorrows just like yours?

Here's a man my generation but stockier, Latino, fluent in the language of the street. He was clad in beanie and sweatshirt and collapsing pants, slightly unshaved with piercing brown eyes, a spirit at ease with itself. Not all boarding passengers look at me; he did. People comfortable with street life usually do.

"I need to get your autograph, bro!"

I smiled. "Aw naw, I'm not that good!"

"For real though. I read your story in the paper when I was in prison. It brought tears to my eyes, dogg."

Then he was gone, walking down the aisle and already replaced in my field of vision by the next face. But the comment stuck. I was moved, and at a loss for words. The article in question was a *Seattle*

Times front-page feature covering my enthusiasm for Metro's least desirable routes and the people who ride them.

Over two years later, at an unrelated stop in a different neighborhood, I greeted another face: "You wanted the 7, right?"

"Yeah, just going 'round the corner," he said. "'Round the corner and down the street I guess."

"Cool, just checking. Most folks here want the 70."

"'Preciate you stopping. Last dude just rode on past! You ain't like the others, man. I done rode wit' you a few times now, you always be respecting the people, whether they got the cash or no."

He was sprawled out on the front seats, thin and older with glasses, owning the space, his arm around the seat next to him. He observed as I acquiesced to a passenger's request to ride for just partial payment. "See, just like that, how you let him on. Lil' thing like that could make somebody's night. In fact, I may as well tell you, I was in prison not too long ago."

"Okay."

"And I read that article about choo."

"You found the article!"

"Yeah, it was the *Times*, man. Front page. And I ain't gon' lie, man, readin' that paper, about you, how you is with the people out here at night—that brought tears to mah eyes, man. You got no idea the impact you be having on folks that's down on they luck, that's going through some real shit. People need that light. Tears to mah eyes."

The fact that I'm the person in the article is the least interesting part of this story. I share the above not because of that, but because I am the only person able to tell you the piece meant something to these two individuals. Neither is aware, in all likelihood, of the other's existence.

I briefly wondered if they knew each other. Did they share a cell, or a block? Or were they, far more likely, two lonely souls in similar rooms dozens or hundreds of miles apart, reading and feeling the same restorative hope? Who had no idea their loneliness was shared by a stranger far away, also in captivity? Who was also moved to silence by the same words, the same glinting reminder that compassion is out there, and is directed from time to time at faces like ours?

We are all rather less alone than we imagine. Every emotion others display is something you too have felt the seeds of. And the universal human sensation, loneliness, is felt by all, and by extension its antidote is longed for with similar potency.

Let me live up to the words in that article. You both read it and believed, were inspired; in times like these, the world would have us feel otherwise.

Being human, I'll let you down, as I have myself. But I can keep trying.

SADDEST MUSIC IN THE WORLD

9/11/16

Upon arriving at the 36 terminal in Othello, I looked in the interior rear-view and noticed a large body sprawled out on the floor of the rear lounge. I walked back there. He was big—not fat, you understand, but tall, well-built, a forty-something Black American man not having his best day. His clothes were larger than he was, dark expanses of stone-washed denim and thick cotton, in keeping with styles of men half his age. He lay on his stomach, crumpled, a leg or two bent out underneath his torso, his cheek resting on the soiled, lint-covered floor. I couldn't tell if he was conscious.

Don't yell at people who are sleeping; speak in a normal voice and clap loudly if you have to. A yelled human voice at close quarters is too confrontational. I spoke in easygoing tones, code-switching unconsciously as I often do; a result of my time in LA and South Seattle, spaces which teach you that dialect is less racially than regionally specific, and the neighborhood's various residents meet somewhere halfway, united in speaking something that's limited to, specific to, celebrated by—the working class. It's cringeworthy when adopted by outsiders, but a badge of togetherness otherwise, though I've discovered over time it's less necessary for connection than I once assumed.

"Hey man, you okay? Bro, can you hear me? Can you hear me all right?"

He stirred.

"How's it goin', big boss? Doin' okay?" He grumbled incoherently, and I worried he'd fallen due to my stopping quickly. "I didn't know you was back there, bro, I'm sorry. I gotta ask you to hop out though, man, it's the last stop." I was rambling. Nothing was happening, so I kept rambling. "Give you a couple minutes to get settled, but I gotta ask you to jump out, alright? Thank you. 'Preciate you."

We're slowly losing the first syllable of *appreciate*, out here in the urban vernacular. I hear the word used often to indicate genuine thanks, but nobody bothers with the first syllable. Maybe they know it's not a real alpha privative construction.

He spoke slurringly, into the floor, at my boots. "I'm a veteran, in this country you get nowhere. Federally, you know?"

"Thank you for serving."

"I'm a private, now, now, niggers they don't talk. They get shot in the back, they don't count."

The words brought me to where he was, and I now saw he was nearly in tears. I heard his helpless anger, the multitude of horrors those bloodshot eyes had witnessed and continued to relive again. I didn't know what to say. From his position he couldn't see my face.

"They don't count, man! They colored! Nigger's life don't mean shit. Nigger's life don't mean shit, nowhere, no way!"

His voice was the pain of an observation so awful you can hardly believe it's true. It was exclamation and dismay all at once, the dying breath of his belief in a just universe. The intimation of self-worthlessness stunned me most.

He twisted his body now, such that he could see me. I was squatting down, reflecting on his words, moved by the candor of his despondency. We met eyes. I remember exactly what I was thinking: *You do count. I think you count.*

But I didn't know how to say it.

It's such a given to me that every life has value, that regressing to a place where it has to be verbalized feels foreign to me. I was moments away from tears myself, imagining his words from his perspective. *Of course I think you count.* The crushing sadness of everything that could lead to such a state . . . I looked at him. He held my gaze for a moment, reading my thoughts. I guess it was probably pretty easy, looking at my face, to gather where I stood.

His voice was practically apologetic. Sheepishly: "Alright brother, I'ma get up, man. Sorry 'bout that, I'm, I'm . . ."

"Take my hand, take my hand. Then we'll get up, alright?"

We struggled a little— "You got it, yup, there we go—alright, big boss—"

"Yup, I'ma get up—"

"Yeah yeah, happy to help, happy to help."

We were a hulking Bernini statue, two intertwining forms rising from the floor, a collection of strong limbs and boots, thick and draping fabric, dirty uniform, shoes squeaking on the floor . . . the two of us grunting with exertion as we ascended, living marble, to an upright position.

He coughed, phlegm sticking in his throat. "I was in [unintelligible], man."

"Alright, you got me? There you go."

"Where we at?"

"This' Beacon Hill. We're at, this' Othello."

"Okay okay thank you. Sorry 'bout that, man."

"It's cool."

"Gettin' old, man."

"No worries, you still got it!"

"Thank you, bro."

I watched him walk away, shaken. His words from the floor were a knife cutting through me still. I was inside my bus and he was out there, in slanting afternoon sunlight. I stared. A few elderly Chinese women selling their goods on the sidewalk frowned as he approached them, regarding him warily. I thought about him as a young man, perhaps a teen signing up because he thought it would make a difference, supporting a country that had slighted him and wanting to protect it anyway. All those hopes, the ideas for betterment, bitter self-loathing, trauma, and powerlessness, were now collected in this empty-shocked shell of a man, lost on a sidewalk.

Part of his soul was still inside.

THIS, TOO, HAPPENS

6/10/20

I'm aware that many operator assaults can be causally traced back to the driver's attitude, choice of words, or tone of voice. Nobody deserves to be assaulted, but you understand what I'm saying here. It generally takes two to tango. We mirror each other, and disrespecting someone, even in a way you think is small, can beget further disrespect. People can *smell* when you're condescending to them, and it stings. Doesn't it sting? Don't you resent squirming under the thumb of a belittling authority figure? That's how they feel in that moment. It takes two. However.

Sometimes it only takes one to tango.

I've had moments in my past where I know my tone contributed to how things went down. Where I should've bit my tongue or been more patient. This wasn't one of those times. This was absolutely and incontrovertibly *not* one of those times.

I'm inbound at Broadway and Pine. The last passenger, a young White woman who smiles a *thank you* to me from the back door, deboards. As she is stepping out a young Black man about her age—mid-twenties—of stocky build and, by the condition of his skin and attire, decidedly less comfortable in life—hops in. Blue hoodie sweatshirt, grey sweatpants, just barely unkempt. He waits briefly for her to step out. He enters the empty bus.

He stalks up to the front.

It's COVID season, and like all other buses in service, a Velcro strap currently separates the front ADA seating area from the rest of the coach interior. He sits as near to the front as possible without crossing that barrier. In my head I think, *interesting choice, coming all the way up here from the back door*. Maybe he's unsure of his destination and wants to sit close to the front. He hums quietly to himself.

Since there's only one passenger, I don't call out the stops, except to say as we approach Fifth that I can't stop at Third and Pine because we're turning into a route 7. Not exactly confrontational.

He ducks under the strap and comes forward.

Again I think, *interesting*. I wonder what sort of headspace would think that's the thing to do. But I don't say anything about that. I say, gesturing to the bus stop at Fifth, "D'you want this one right here?"

He says, "Yeah."

I feel a need to break the ice, make friends. Let him know I don't look down on him. I say, "How's it goin'?"

"Good."

"Cool."

Do you know how many *thousands* of times doing that has worked wonders for me? Solved problems before they even began? Do you know how many thousands of times that has *continued* to work for me, afterwards?

Innumerable thousands, that's how many.

Except this time.

We get to the zone. I open the doors and say, "Thanks, man."

Then he morphs into another person and explodes. He is spitting on my face four or five times, cursing in furious anger, now quickly exiting, stalking toward Westlake Park, looking back to see if I am following.

For myself, I was so utterly shocked I didn't respond at all. Events like this have a duration of seconds; the only way to get good at responding to them is to experience them regularly, which I don't. I said "Whoa, whoa," trying to calm him, but I couldn't form words to speak. Maybe that was for the best. What would I say now, if anything?

I might try, *What was that?* Or just, *Talk to me*. These lines would have the effect of humanizing him, forcing him to engage emotionally. Which pissed-off dudes don't like because they can no longer merely be angry anymore. *Why are you mad?* They have to go back to being human, which means no longer spitting in people's faces.

I believe this was premeditated on his part.

Why else would he come sit at the front? Duck under the strap? He wanted to get back at an authority figure. He was coming from the occupied protest zone on Capitol Hill and was likely seething with anti-authoritarian anger. He wanted to fight the world. I had nothing to do with it.

Why do those in pain want others to feel pain? Why does someone who feels hated want to hate others? These are questions that answer themselves. He was a young Black man who probably felt scared, hated by the broad spectrum of an uncaring society, and who was definitely unstable. Not a great mix. Like me, he seeks balance, and felt this would right the wrongs of society. He assumed I was part of the problem because many people are.

This has happened to me before. I remember an operator telling me afterwards, "I told the other guys in the bullpen, and we all just sat there dumbfounded, like: If this can happen to Nathan, we're *definitely* screwed! You're *fuckin' nice*!"

Don't think that, friends. I'm grateful for the implicit compliment, but I believe it's still constructive to go out of your way in being kind. Respectful. Patient. Compassionate, without expecting thanks, without expecting good treatment. Remember, *passion*, for most of the existence of the word, meant suffering. *Compassion* means to suffer together. Life is supposed to be a struggle, and we're supposed to love each other. In 1871, George Eliot wrote, "What do we live for, if it is not to make life less difficult for each other?" Her words are still true today.

This would be easier if I had been a jerk. Because now I would know what to do next time: don't be a jerk. Easy. But I didn't do a *thing* to invite this one. This was a solo tango *par excellence*, and he had no dance partner at all. What, then, do I do next time? Should I let this alter my approach?

Absolutely not.

Don't sit there devastated, thinking there's no point to being nice. *Your strategy doesn't have to work every time to be worthwhile.* No strategy works every time. My method works 999 times out of a thousand. It's not the only way to do things, but it's a heck of a batting average, if I may say so. I will not allow him to make me forget that.

I will instead allow him to be small.

A pebble in the roadway, not a roadblock. You can go through the worst hate, and survive—that means you're More Than It. If you can thrive in spite of your traumas, you can do anything.

You've heard the idea in philosophy: we humans are relational beings. What does that mean? We define things by their relation to another thing. Night, as the absence of day. Light, as the opposite of darkness. Have you noticed how often dictionary definitions only tell you what a thing is by describing another thing?

The implication is that there are opposites, contrasting degrees of existence, and that this is inextricably woven into the fabric of life. Because there is heat, there must be cold. What goes up must come down.

I exist, and therefore my opposite must also exist.

Who is my opposite? Or, more accurately (and in accordance with how we think of things like day and night and hot and cold as balanced) as two sides of the same coin: who is my *equal*?

I think I just met him.

I love people without reason. I don't know why I'm nice. I just am. Am I crazy? Sure. So is he, who hates people with apparently the same fervor, and also without reason. I have met my equal, and I will force the tragedy of the encounter into a learning experience. I will gain something from this, some insight that brings me closer to peace. I will not let it dominate me with thoughts of spite and revenge.

You never need to worry about revenge.

The world does that for you. If he's cruel to you, he's also cruel to others, and he's going to meet someone who's not as nice as you, who has nothing to lose by biting back. Let them do the hard work for you. Don't worry about it. Worry instead about how to let this *not* take you over. How you can become stronger. Because:

Losing is when you learn.

You don't learn much from winning. Suffering is when you have a chance to bind yourself to something higher. How will you strengthen your worldview *without* resorting to bitterness? Bitterness is easy. How will you accept the existence of hate as you continue going about your life, stopping its spread, and giving love instead? Doing your small part, and never mind what you can't control?

PART VI

SOFTLY, WHILE WE STILL CAN

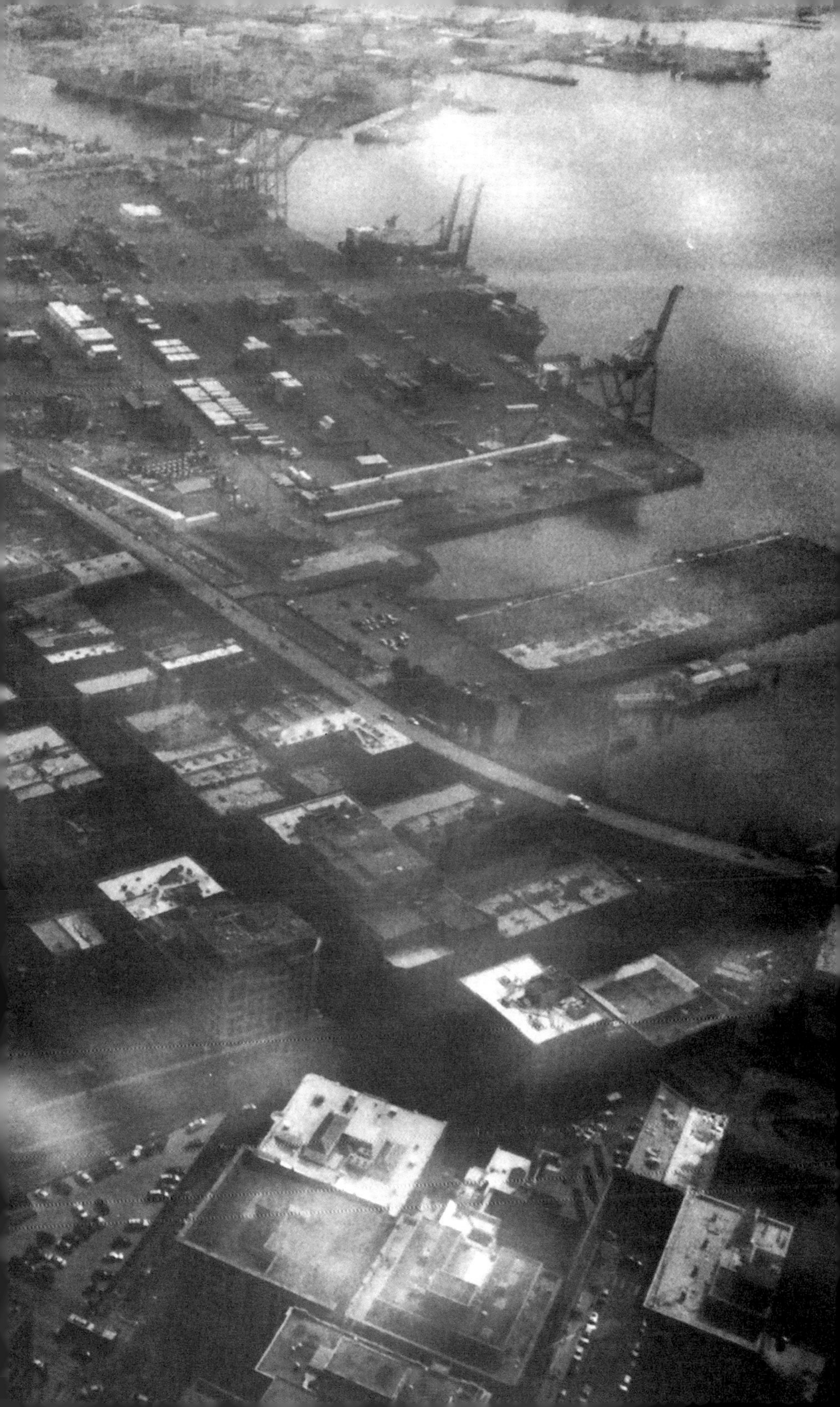

KINDNESS IN THE DAYS OF AFTER

7/22/18

We knew each other once, intimately. The trim figure, the vivacious brown eyes and half-smile that just about screams vitality, even when silent. Many people merely repeat the headlines they've read; Svetlana was different. She could give a reason for every word she blurted, no matter how unconsidered they appeared. She had complete ownership of her thoughts.

I'll refrain from describing her appearance further except to say the boys always had a word and a glance for her, and she knew exactly what to say to every last one. Street smart and book smart, spirit strong with a lot left over.

Here she is tonight, wrapping up her swing shift, a figure in the dark ready to go home. I tilt my head in a smile. We've drifted apart in the intervening years, sure, but it's been amiable. That takes two, and I'm thankful for her maturity and graciousness. You take care of the people who were dear to you, never mind that they're no longer part of your life; if they're still kind, that is enough.

"Why is it every time I have a shitty day, I'm visited by an angel?" she asks rhetorically, opening a smile for me. She's explaining her groan of a response to my pleasantries. Tough day for her. I extend my arms out for a hug, reminded of a night two Novembers prior:

The 2016 presidential election had just been lost, and Seattle was devastated. People were hugging each other in the streets, sobbing in the arms of strangers, clusters of disbelief. That November 8th,

Svetlana and I barely knew each other. I saw her walking home alone, crossing the street in front of me. Like many of us inside the bus and out that night, she was crying. Ours was the mood of the city, the collectives who'd become accustomed to tolerance, stunned by such support for its opposite.

Our society is structured to minimize the ability for individual citizens to effect widespread change. That's not to say it isn't possible, but even more importantly: isn't the most potent impact we can have on others always and only ever the personal, the one on one?

I tapped the horn lightly, opening the doors where she was. We looked at each other. I'd never hugged her before.

I asked, "Do you need a hug?"

Red lights were made for this.

We embraced tightly, searching for words of comfort. Loss, failure, triumph; these are the things that make us one. "I'm so glad I ran into you tonight," Svetlana said, a wan smile beneath her mascara-streaked cheeks.

Tonight, lifetimes later, she has hardships once again, but of a more private nature: family troubles. She's waiting for an important phone call and fills me in during the interim. I've seen her only in passing for ages now. Somehow, we've managed to bypass the awkward stage, the post-mortem of hurt and clawing insecurities. There is just the easy comfort of a person who once cared and still does, in a healthier way.

Eventually her important phone call came, and she withdrew for the remainder of the ride, relaxed, safe in my space, the mobile Nathan Living Room.

She rose to exit, still on her phone. Into it she said, "Hang on. Lemme say bye to the bus driver. He's a good friend of mine."

I sighed with gratitude and hugged her tightly, again. She'll never know how much those lines meant to me. Kindness after a concluded relationship has no agenda. It is simply kindness, genuine, given for its own sake, because it is consistent with who we are.

Is there a bigger relief than still being accepted, after everything is over, by someone who knows your every weak point?

The answer to despair is never reason. We do what we can to help each other, to get by.

WHY SO SERIOUS

6/29/20

Sure, why not, I thought. There's no one else out here.

I stopped in the middle of the block to let two runners into my empty bus. It was the end of the evening, my last trip on another late night heading down Broadway.

"I 'preeeeeciate that," said the first man.

The second looked up. "Thanks bro—oh, hold up! Yo, this guy is famous."

"Aw yeah!"

"He's the friendliest, most incredible—"

At this point I had to interject: "Nawww!"

"Bro, I'm for real! Shit, no wonder he stopped for us, that's why. 'Cause he's the hella cool famous guy. Check it, this guy, man. He don't never lose his cool, always good to people, relaaaxed."

His friend said, "I bet he got people fightin' for him."

"He be like, come on in. You got two dollars or two pennies, don't make no difference, he still gon' be nice to you. Listen to me, my dude. You're doin' God's work."

"Thank you!" I said.

"For real. 'Cause it'a be some bus drivers you try to pay yo fare, I seen this one guy he had a dollar forty and he ask the driver for a transfer, he done already put money in the thing and the driver say no! What that guy supposed to do? He don't have no money left!"

"He shoulda just walked right past him," the other fellow remarked.

"Drivers pulling that type a shit, it ain't no wonder people walk right past!"

I sympathized, but I had to clarify a point: "I appreciate it when people ask me though, 'cause they *know* they could just walk right past and I'm not gonna do anything, but they ask anyway. Which I love, 'cause it's outta respect. They don't have to pay, and they know they don't have to say anything. But I love it when they say hey."

"You know that's true," he reflected. "Yeah it's cool when they actually say something. Not like them dudes that be steppin' on like they *own* the motherfucker. Walking all up in here like the bus *belongs* to they ass! Some a these guys makes me laugh, bro. Hey, like this like this."

He stood and began pantomiming what Tom Wolfe calls the pimp roll, the expressionless swagger we would chuckle at more often if it wasn't always carried out with such desperate earnestness.

I was laughing. We all were. How great to see someone sending up the self-serious obsessiveness of certain street attitudes. A relief. Particularly because these two men, dressed as they were, speaking in the vernacular that they were, of the race and socioeconomic class they were—came cloaked in expectation whether they liked it or not. They were the sort you expected to be doing the swaggering, not calling it out.

But the world is more complex than any stereotype could ever dream of.

I said, "You know exactly how it is!"

"These niggas be rollin' on with this fuckin' stone-faced killer bullshit like the world *owes* them a mothafuckin' ride! Like the rest of us is *working* for they punk ass! I pay my shit every month. I put my shit in the mail. But these dudes, oooh no. They be swaggerin' on in without a word like they *built* this fuckin' city! Shit is hilarious, dogg! Yeah you right, those fools could at least say hey."

"Some kinda connection, human to human!"

"Yeah, it's disrespectful. It makes me mad, but it makes me laugh. You got to laugh. And then they be like, 'I'm old, I'ma need you to get the fuck up outta them front seats! Yeeeah. I'm a need a seat right here, nigga, what choo gon' do?' Steppin' at me like this.

Walking in like this, and then like, 'you need to get the fuck up.'"

Reader, how can I convey how hilarious this was? I've never laughed so hard at one in the morning. He was mock-behaving the role as he described it, acting it out in the most exaggerated manner possible. The narrow, hypermasculine template of existence embodied by certain young Black men is notable—like all modes of hypermasculinity—in taking itself almost absurdly gravely, and each of us was so well acquainted with such solemnity as to make his parody of it absolutely hysterical. His version of a self-serious teenager swaggered so hard it bumped into the stanchions, and his guttural verbalizations ("*Sup.*") were an outsized riot. He cocked his head back so far while trying to maintain a forward gaze he was practically looking at the ceiling.

"'You need to get the fuck up, so I can sit my important ass down,'" he was saying, by way of illustration. In his own voice he added, "and I get up. 'Cause it's what you do as a reasonable person. You get up. People get up. Shit like that ain't worth bothering with. It's stupid bullshit but it's funny as hell too. You gotta laugh. Anyways. We appreciate you drivin' the bus how you do."

"Young man makin' money," his friend said. "Keep it up!"

"I never get to see this cat anymore. This nigga here," the first said, shaking his head toward me in admiration.

I had finally calmed down from laughing. "You guys were the *highlight*! It was a beautiful day in the neighborhood, but you guys were the highlight! Thanks for stoppin' in!"

"Always!"

'Cause it's what you do as a reasonable person. I appreciated hearing that. Some attitudes can drive you up the wall. They're designed to. Don't give in, because like he said, it ain't worth bothering with.

If the interaction is in passing, I consider giving them what they're doing a terrible job of asking for: respect. That's the only reason people pull such ridiculous behavior. They're not getting respected, or acknowledged, or loved, or all three. And so they try to demand it. They don't know what you already know, and what will get them into trouble later: merely acting like a king won't get you treated like one.

But giving them what they have no clue how to ask for might soften them a little, keep them from needing to shove their bravado in your face so much. Respond like reeds blowing in the wind, bending instead of breaking.

Maybe one day, they'll learn they can bend too.

SHE DID IT ON A MONDAY

2/28/15

I pause at inbound Henderson, waiting for an indecisive runner. Why am I irritated by his vacillation? What is this rushing stress which infrequently bubbles inside of me, rearing its head like a stranger within? Something to work on.

"How's it goin'," I ask him as he pauses outside the front doors, staring into the middle distance. He decides to step aboard, a White fellow in middle age, thin and very cold, underdressed on this February night. His bowl-cut hairdo, parted in the middle, has the precision of a machine.

"Hey," he asks. "Are you going towards Garfield?"

"Yeah I am, yeah. Come on in. How you doin' tonight?" Sometimes when I'm feeling less than stellar, I'll force myself to reach out further, asking about people's days or complimenting their hats. You can use the people to bring you back up, get yourself out of your head.

"Oh, not so good," he responds with a companionable sigh.

"I'm sorry to hear it. I appreciate the truthful answer, but I'm sorry to hear." That's becoming a go-to line of mine.

"Well, it is what it is. We're here."

"And that's a good thing. We're alive, we've got our health—"

"Hey, there you go—"

"Lot to be thankful for." Reminding myself as much as anything else.

"You got that right. Hey, you go up towards South Edmunds?"

We sort out the geography. His name is Marlow. I can tell he knows the terrain, but perhaps hasn't been out here for a while. He asks how my night is going, and I mention how much I love driving the 7. "It's a favorite of mine."

"How come?"

"It stays interesting out here. High energy, a lot going on, lot of color—"

"Man, *you're* positive."

I laugh. Marlow notes that he most recently saw me on the 49, and I mention how the two routes are interlinked at nighttime.

"Yeah," he says, "my girlfriend and I, we were together about ten years—"

"Oh wow—"

"Yeah she lived at the end of the 49 line, and I lived halfway down the 7 line."

"Oh excellent. Sounds like a pretty perfect setup."

"Yeah, it was a perfect setup. She was great."

Marlow pauses.

"You know, she actually ended up killing herself."

"Whoaaaa. Oh, no. Oh, no." Suicide guts me on a level other violence doesn't come close to.

"Yeah," he said. "Yeah."

"Oh." A heavy exhalation of air, the fitful attempt to release a burden.

"And it was totally unexpected, she was a positive person. She just . . ."

"Oh, my goodness."

"She was just, sometimes she would get real down."

"Was it like a clinical depression thing?"

"No, it was more of a bipolar type thing. She would have these moods, I don't know. She had a head injury way back, and ever since then—"

"Okay—"

"Yeah, it affected her mood, affected everything—"

"Like a chemical imbalance—"

"Yeah. She did it on a Monday, man." Silence. "She knew I was always busy running around on Mondays, and she chose a Monday when I was just payin' some bills."

"Oh, my goodness. That's heavy. That's, wow." I mention some incidents which took place when I was a child, and he tells me similar events happened amongst his acquaintances as well.

"So yeah, it just gets to me," Marlow says. "And the thing is, it's not really her, but that chemical imbalance, the injury."

"Yeah, can't blame her."

"Can't blame her. It feels strange to say it, that she's gone."

"When' this happen?"

"Three months ago."

"Oh my goodness. Oh, man." We drive in silence for a short bit. Here's Othello Street. Here's Frontenac, here's Graham.

Me again: "But you know, I'm glad you guys got to have those ten years together."

"Oh yeah."

"I mean, that's huge. She's always gonna be part of your character—"

"Ooh yeah—"

"And that's good. Ten years, man. I admire that. You know, somebody said once, 'We're gonna lose *everything* we love in this life—'"

"Yeah, yeah." Nodding.

"'—And all we can do is just figure out how to, uh, enjoy it while we have it.' Like, a relationship's not all bad just because it ends, right?"

"Yeah. Yeah. Well, so, uh, hey, how've you been?"

Marlow and I laugh together, the pent-up sorrow belching out into something more familiar. We bring back the conversation, discussing such banalities as the number of round trips I have and how there's hardly anyone out tonight. We cling to the ladder rungs of the ordinary, speaking and sharing our way out of the depths, rising slowly, such that we might feel all of life's colors, and not just the thudding, aching blows.

WITH WHAT TIME WE HAVE

November 2015

An evening in Paris, alone, a weeknight in the 12th just north of le Parc de Bercy. I'd just taken the route 27 out there, having developed as much of an affinity for Paris's world-class bus system as their world-class metro. I preferred the buses because you could look outside. They linked the city in ways the subways couldn't.

Was this days before the attacks, or right after? I'm surprised I no longer know. Paris has always been a city whose silences contain the multitudes of history, where the present is always in danger of being engulfed by its voluminous past. The bombings and shootings of that week bewilder my understanding not only of the empty days afterward but also the lost innocence just prior.

Enough time had elapsed since January 2015's Charlie Hebdo catastrophe that the city went about with mostly untroubled ease, the freewheeling gumption of confident youth; we seem to alternate through life, oscillating between 1) periods of perspective better described as youthful enthusiasm, regardless of age, and 2) a certain sober melancholy. Large cities pendulate similarly, and the transitions are instigated by moments of seismic comedy or tragedy.

Melancholy, Hugo wrote,* is the happiness of being sad. It is impossible for me to recall the days leading up to the attacks in any other light. They may have been days of careless ease and youthful abandon, but I will never remember them that way, unless it is to remember the frailty of happiness before the fall, before it knows how hard it needs to work to stay alive.

The Cinémathèque française was doing a retrospective on Martin Scorsese, showing all his work at their vaunted theatre, and most of it projected on film. Naturally I was there almost every night.

This evening, I was at a Chinese restaurant just north of the Cinémathèque. Though I've been to China, the best Chinese food I've had was actually in Paris. They have some killer spots there. This wasn't one of them. It was the Parisian equivalent of strip-mall teriyaki, if there can be such a thing, but I didn't care.

Doesn't getting dinner alone before a movie carry a sense of urgency? By yourself, in love with cinema, about to see a classic film you'll never see in a theatre again, and you want to be fully awake for it, fully present. You need food. You got there too late for a decent meal because you're cheap and you took the bus, and you don't care what food it is as long as it isn't McDonald's. This Chinese hole in the wall was just the ticket.

I ordered in clumsy French. You have to speak French in France. It doesn't matter if you're awful at it; you respect them more by *trying* their language than by continuing a mastery of your own. Contrary to the stereotype, no person in Paris was rude to tourist me, and I'm convinced it was because I always tried. I ordered *à emporter* because I wanted to eat outside. I asked them which meal could be made the fastest, and the middle-aged woman at the counter was accommodating as I embarrassed myself linguistically.

Unlike the boisterous crowd of the restaurant Yi-Syuan and I went to, only one other party was dining in: two thirty- or forty-something men seated near the door, close to me. As much as Parisians can be, they were unglamorous, genuine in their plain attire and unshowy character. I couldn't divine their relationship. Friends perhaps, or lovers, or colleagues; in any event definitely long acquainted, comfortable with sharing silence. You only go to cheap Chinese with someone you know well.

When my meal came, I asked in my clumsy French if she had chopsticks. Who am I, Korean American that I am, to eat noodles with a fork? It'd just be wrong. I had to ask. She obliged.

They could hear me, the two men. They heard my terrible French when I came in, they listened as I blundered through ordering, and now they ate silently as I mangled my request for chopsticks. *Vous avez des baguettes?*

Then the one fellow said quietly, amiably, to his partner:

"Élégant!"

They'll never know they made my night. I smiled to myself. They didn't care about my language abilities at all. They saw me rather for what I did. I needed to eat with chopsticks, and that struck them for some reason. The last thing I felt in there was elegant. They made me feel better.

Was it before the attacks, or after? Years later this is the question I get stuck on. They say what you lose first of memory is timelines. Perhaps it doesn't matter. Perhaps melancholy encapsulates the whole of existence. Whether those two men were enjoying each other's company on a night before the fall, or in the tough days of after, there is something endearing to me about their unsophisticated and quiet affection for a simple night out. Unpretentious food, together shared and enjoyed. There's not enough time to make fun of people; only to appreciate them.

Life is not easy. They were both old enough to know.

You do the best you can.

---

* "La mélancolie, c'est le bonheur d'être triste." From his 1866 *Les Travailleurs de la Mer*, translated into English as *Toilers of the Sea* in 1888.

DESERVE, THE CONCEPT AND THE SONG

9/18/17

I was telling a supervisor friend about an assault—not the aforementioned 2020 incident but an earlier, similar one. I avoid recounting unpleasant bus episodes, the better to keep them out of memory, but they happen. No matter how nice you are there will be a few days out of the year that are spectacularly awful, and this encounter was one of them.

Three months after the fact, my colleague listened, and as she listened, she grew appalled. She was visibly upset, flooded with concern for me and flabbergasted such an event could transpire. What was most appalling wasn't the passenger, but the lack of response on the part of Metro and King County Sheriffs, which I have to admit was as much my fault as theirs.

"Still," she said. "You deserve better than this."

She meant I as an employee deserve a timely police response. But I took the statement as something larger, more philosophically expansive. *I deserve better*. I deserve to be treated humanely.

I walked to my shift with these thoughts in mind, realizing the perspective felt new. Maybe I as a human really *did* deserve respect, acknowledgment, fairness . . . all the time. And since I deserved all this, I could expect to receive it from the universe. The sensation was akin to letting something go, dropping into a cocoon under someone else's control, where I didn't have to take care of everything on my own; I could trust and expect to be treated fairly by everyone, from individuals to institutions.

How nice.

I started my route. The previous driver gave me his bus, thrilled to be done, and I hopped in, excited as usual. I trundled up and down Third Avenue like I always do, lollygagging up Jackson like any other day, drifting down Rainier as per the norm . . . with one small difference. I was expecting people to treat me nicely.

It was one of the worst afternoons I could recall.

Nothing had changed except my frame of mind. People walked on without speaking, as they sometimes do; they asked for free rides and transfers; they asked for second chances; they didn't think about me, my needs, or that of others, but simply their own. In their struggle to survive they didn't think about giving back to society. They had agenda items more urgent than being polite, more pressing than altruism and making me feel respected. The notion of deserve implies the notion of justice, and the sheer amount of *injustice* visible disturbed me. I desperately wanted to do something about it. This person shouldn't get a free ride through life while these others pay through the nose for it, and so on. It was terribly frustrating. I thought I, and everyone else, deserved fair treatment. I wasn't getting it, and neither were they. I was shocked to find myself arguing with customers. What was happening?

Normally, I wouldn't even *notice* most of the above. It'd be business as usual, and I would work on my two tasks: be nice, and don't crash into anything. I believe in the concept of 'What Goes Around Comes Around.' To me the anecdotal evidence of this truism is incontestable, even if we all know it doesn't happen immediately. Those wheels of justice . . .

But as a bus driver, I don't get to participate in What Goes Around Comes Around. I see massive injustices all day, and I don't get to do anything about them. I have to trust the universe to work things out and meanwhile be a positive influence toward my fellow peeps—not an enforcer, not even a teacher, just a friend. But today I wanted justice to come around instantly.

What does it mean to deserve?

To deserve is to be entitled. I was driving the 7 with a sense of entitlement. Should I really be surprised that didn't turn out so well?

"Don't expect people to be reasonable or do things that make sense," I remember telling Albert. "That way, you won't be disappointed when they don't." It was time for me to follow my own advice. Some of the behaviors I see just aren't worth dwelling on. When some guy who's high as a kite urinates on a garbage can while reciting the Ten Commandments in reverse order, well . . . it's just not my department, and I don't have the context to understand it anyway.

Deserving comes down to a question of expectations. A line from a favorite passenger, the late Shoeshiner Tim, came to mind. He'd seen his share of hardships. Halfway through my shift I recalled Tim's jovial, gravelly voice:

"The world don't owe you nothin'."

He was explaining why he respects everyone as much as he can, and why there's no value in blaming the world for your problems. "The world don't owe nobody nothin'. You just try to do right by the person nex' to you. You coul' be the evilest person on earth, but I'll try t' put a smile on your face, you know?"

"You're a gentleman," I'd said.

My night started getting better immediately.

As an operator, you do deserve a timely police response. In relationships, you do deserve kindness and respect. Of course. We have societal concepts of rights that should be preserved and expanded. But those are still small. I'm talking about fundamentals here. As another passenger once told me, "Kindness is not a right. It's a privilege. A privilege to receive."

We don't do it for brownie points. We just do it, so other people can feel what it's like to be loved.

GO FORTH

5/5/19

He was smiling so hard I had to laugh.

It was infectious. I'm guessing he was older than he looked; the sort who humbly attributes their looks to genes, but you know it's as much their beaming attitude as anything else. Confident happiness is more attractive than the sharpest cheekbone. He was a balding Black American man in nondescript jeans, stocky, warm jacket over a thick sweatshirt, and he was happier than lil' bus driving me was—which is to say, he was ecstatic.

"How's your day been?" I asked, matching his grin without realizing it. "It's *gotta* be a good one!"

"Oh man, it's been so great. You're the first bus I stepped onto after they let me outta jail."

"Well, I'm glad you chose my bus!"

"Ha! Thank you for your attitude!"

"You got it goin' on too, I could feel that positive energy! I'm glad you're out!"

"Oh you got no idea. The *food* in there. Check this out. They give you one boiled egg. The yolk is black. The white is green."

"Uuugggh! That's like something right outta Dr. Seuss!"

He guffawed with his whole body. We laughed together, sub-guttural happy, joined in unstoppable goodness. We couldn't stop. His relief, reader! The welcoming sensation of an equal plane, shared and free of judgment! The music in his barrel-chested laugh. We were equal, respected, seen, here on this tiny bus in the corner of a small American city.

We were huge.

The ridiculous image of the eggs, now forever consigned to the past, had just become a symbol that conclusively collapsed his entire inmate experience into a chuckle, a thing one has conquered and now successfully pushed aside.

Go forth, my friend. The world is yours again.

21ST-CENTURY MAN

8/30/19

Something about the hard shadows gave the proceedings a quality of immediacy. You know, like the old westerns: standoffs beneath an unblinking desert sun.

I first knew him as a sullen teen sitting in the back of today's largely empty 120. He pimp-rolled to the back lounge, a high-schooler swaggering to an audience of no one, preening like a sage grouse on an empty prairie. It takes a lot of effort to look like you're putting in no effort, as many a teenage boy knows, but the few passengers I had—an East African grandmother here, a Latina mom and toddler there—couldn't care less.

He sprawled out on the back bench and lifted up his shirt to expose his chest, revealing sculpted muscles and smooth, dark skin. Glancing in my rear-view mirror, I stifled a chuckle; who exactly was he trying to impress? Was he aware how silly it looked to 'accidentally' lift your shirt up to your neck and leave it there? No one does that. But hey, to each his own. It's not like he was bothering anyone.

He got off on Ambaum at 124th, sashaying up to the front door, silently ambling out into the hot noonday light. Someone else was putting a bicycle on the bike rack, and thus I remained stopped.

He moved to cross in front of the bus.

Collisions put you in a different modus of processing time. It's a strange and terrifying mixture of everything happening both much too fast, and sickeningly slowly. The car that flew down my left side seemed unstoppable.

He moved to cross in front of the bus.

Ambaum Boulevard is four lanes. My bus was southbound,

alongside the curb. Lane one. Lane two was invisible to him, because my bus was blocking his view. That's why there's a sign inside every bus that says, "Do not cross in front of the bus." He was breaking into a jog now, crossing in front of me, oblivious. It was still today for him, regular unremarkable today.

I've seen people get killed doing this.

I remember a man's body spiraling in the air after contacting a car he didn't see—because he ran in front of the bus. I was a passenger, route 16 at Fifth and Northgate Way. I remember him talking on the bus two seconds prior: "Thanks, driver . . ." And now, somersaulting against his will off a speeding car hood, smashing onto the ground and hard, the base of his skull the first point of contact.

That man died instantly.

I remember everyone from all directions dropping their concerns and running over—sprinting over, even if it was too late. In the mid-nineties people didn't wear earbuds; we all heard the snapping report of separating bone. I saw the car that did it speeding off as fast as it could, the only thing moving away from the body. I recall a man in dress shirt and slacks, dashing over from across the street; something about his concern remains an image stuck in my memory, the kind of thing that makes you want to be a good person.

That's what I thought about now. I thought too about my operator friend Paul, who years ago taught me to avoid laying on the horn—unless it is to save a life. He's saved someone that way, and I have too. Did I honk now? I actually can't remember. I want to say I did, and I may have, but the *speed* of existence sometimes . . .

He is turning his head.

He is turning his head to the left, looking up the street, looking for cars. Smart. But this car is *flying*. Flying, down lane two, passing by me on my left. I'd looked in my left side mirrors and seen it also. I'm always looking at my mirrors.

It happened both very fast, and at exactly the speed it needed to. Here's three young kids in a middle-class white Volvo, probably their parents' car. It's a total mom car. Practical. Three Asian teenagers cruising down lane two on Ambaum, not slowing down because why would you, it's midday in the suburbs with no traffic, and sure we're passing the bus but what's the big deal.

Kid from before, in lane two now. He's standing right in front of them. This is life measured in fractions of a second. You have to be up for it, or else.

A minute ago, I'd thought he was a lanky show-off, swagger-splaying his body out in the back of the bus like that. The kind of insufferable self-absorbed haughty machismo that the hidebound definitions of masculinity within hip-hop culture too often celebrate—in short, the Black kid I see other Black kids rolling their eyes at.

All that vanished from my mind. Isn't braggadocio just another form of insecurity? Boys who are lost take themselves too seriously, as the saying goes; but wouldn't we be serious if we were lost and confused, and what is adolescence if not an overwhelming period of confusion? It is the time of going too far, testing out what this strange life is, the better to figure out what suits you, as you settle into something mellower later on. That's all he was doing. I saw him in the moment of his imminent death as the child that I also am, that we all are. The universal human child, living life for the first time, searching in the dark for answers.

I desperately wanted him to live.

The kids in the sedan slamming on their brakes. The antilock mechanism preventing a skid. They are stopping fast; but they will still hit him at this rate of speed. The air is pregnant with heat and silence, only the sound of the car really, the top-down noonday shadows striking everything with an evenly graphic visual drama, clear-tinted yellow, contrasty.

He has registered the car's zooming approach. With half a second to spare he jumps straight into the air, directly up, up, up, lifting his knees.

He is jumping into the air as the car drives beneath him.

He is landing on the hood—balance, almost—wobbly—scrambling up the windshield and toward the roof because the car hasn't stopped yet. Responding by reflex and momentum now, still moving to counter the car's continuing roll beneath him.

The car halts just then, as he makes it to the roof. He has sort of run up the windshield glass, and is standing on the roof now, teetering, arms out for balance. I think to myself:

Whoa.

Now everything is silent. All eyes are on him—me, the kids in the car processing what just happened, a pedestrian here and across the way, somebody on a balcony, the guy with his bicycle on the rack. Our youngster is still standing up there, spread-eagled and balanced like da Vinci's Vitruvian Man. It's a shock to the system how fast that happened, to me, to all of us, and to him too. It's catching up to him, the present is. And something else, manifesting now on his face: *I just pulled that off. I am still alive, and there isn't a scratch on me.*

We didn't run to him because we collectively perceived we didn't need to. Every eye on him now had an element of admiration. The agility, the sheer *speed* . . . when things move so fast your reflexes do the talking for you, you better hope you've lived a certain way. He had to have been athletically inclined. The entire thing was over in under three seconds, and his every move was perfect. Sublime. The first time I saw someone cross in front, all those years ago, they died. But he, because of his inclination towards track or basketball or soccer or jogging or whatever it was—he lived. *Because of who he was*, he lived.

Life can give you no better compliment than that.

He sat down on the car roof over the driver's seat, his legs dangling down over the driver's side window. He leaned his head way down, to look downside up at the driver, who was rolling open his window. I wonder what they said to each other. Neither his bearing nor the driver's gave any indication. Our Vitruvian Man spoke briefly and strode away. The rest of us together watched him finish crossing the street, still processing what had just happened. It didn't matter how haughty he was, who he was, or how he acted. None of that mattered. He was a young man in the 21st century. I wanted him to live.

And he did.

VERN: II

5/28/20

His friend was scrambling about his pockets for loose change when the first young man yelled with gleeful abandon, "*Dis nigga don't care*!!"

Meaning, *this driver is sympathetic to your cause and prioritizes larger concerns*!

The speaker looked exactly like Mos Def. The two of them sat together before the friend dipped out at Othello Street; Sir Def remained, a young man at the end of the evening, headed home on an empty bus and with only his thoughts for company. Not everyone stares at their phone on this side of town.

As we passed Graham, I peered across the street to see if Vern was panhandling at the gas station. He was. I double-tapped my horn in a friendly honk, getting his attention and waving large. Vern lit up on recognizing me and returned the wave.

"Is that Vern?" Mos Def asked.

"Yup! Cool guy."

He grinned. "I think you're the only bus driver who does that."

At first I was going to disagree, out of humility, but then I had to admit it: Who else is going to wave at Vern? And who's going to take the trouble of honking the horn to do so?

I smiled. "Probably, yeah!" After a pause, I said, "I'm too nice, I can't help myself!"

It was an admission of kindness, vulnerability. If Mos had still been with his friend, I don't know that I would've said anything. But on solo terms, you can go a little further. Sensitivity can blossom a bit more. He grinned in understanding.

"Naw, you just part of the neighborhood!" he said, appreciatively. He settled further into his seat and looked out the window.

Thank you, world, for making room for someone like me. For letting me exist, even thrive, from time to time. I'm just the skinny Asian kid with a tucked-in shirt and glasses. I used to think fitting in was the way to survive. Learning the opposite is closer to the truth has given me great peace. You go out there as your best self for long enough, and you begin to notice Like attracting Like. You bring out your qualities in others. Not every time, sure, but often enough to make it worth it.

I wave at Vern because waving at Vern makes me feel good, even if he doesn't notice.

But I won't deny it's a cherry on top that he saw me tonight.

THE PROBLEM WE ALL LIVE WITH

12/25/14

She was fifty, with a cute and approachable face. Her glasses were a touch foggy and may have been broken, and her brown sweatshirt was frayed and lived in, with the moisture a fleece accumulates after continuous long hours outside. I didn't read her cardboard sign as I walked past, in a hurry like the rest of the urban human race, but I noted her presence. Fourth and Pine, northwest corner, under the overhang. She was sitting with her back against the diagonal corner wall of the Macy's building, in front of a window display modeling clothes and Christmas presents.

I had about ten minutes before my 49 showed up. As a rule, I give out food but not money (Iris notwithstanding), and today I had no food on hand. I had a few bills but hesitated to part with them as I'd just cleaned out my bank accounts preparing an upcoming trip to Paris . . . in my own world, I was poor. I'll watch and wait, I decided, before doing anything. It's Christmas season. Maybe all these passing crowds were relishing the giving spirit of the holiday, handing off pastries and coffee and loose change like nobody's business.

Part of my basis for thinking so was a recent memory of driving around (in my car) on Thanksgiving night. I'd just had a massive 'Friendsgiving' and was tooling around Downtown before going home, equipped with copious leftovers, and searching for folks in need. Incredibly, however, everyone already had food! I couldn't believe it. Here was a city of street corners chomping on turkey and ham with pineapple. A couple of men underneath I-5 at Cherry Street topped it all off—I approached them trying to get the attention of one who was urinating behind a pillar, but before they heard me I noticed their plates of food, which were complete with well-done *steak* and potatoes that still had gravy! These guys had better-looking leftovers than I did!

The generous had already passed through town, and I continued home amused and pleasantly surprised. I did manage to part with stuffing and macaroni—a man at I-5 and Madison got excited when I walked toward him in the dark yelling, "Do you like stuffing?"—but that was all.

Additionally, I recently bought a coffee for a character at Third and Cherry, only to have two others walk across the street to supply her with coffee at exactly the same time. Worse things have happened, we concluded. Maybe this woman at Fourth and Pine had similarly been helped. I tarried, taking up a post just outside her periphery by some newspaper bins, and settled in to watch things play out.

I was very wrong. Thanksgiving at midnight must summon an urge for sharing that the pre-Christmas shopping crush simply doesn't possess. I watched the hordes at Westlake walk past, and walk past, and walk past, decked out in finery and stress, without a care beyond their own in the world. It was a cacophony of shopping bags and heels, watches and plush sweaters, skin daubed up with cream. There's a man who sometimes carries a sign which reads, "I feel invisible," and that sentiment certainly applied here. Watching with her in mind, the affluence nearly felt like it was being rubbed in her face consciously. A well-dressed young man, completely oblivious, walked in front her as he arranged large bills in a money clip.

After seven minutes of sentry duty I decided action was necessary. I stepped across to Starbucks, immediately stepping back out upon seeing the long line. Not enough time to buy anything; forget the food rule. I'll just have to give her one of the two fives I was carrying.

"Hey," I said, entering her field of vision. "How's it going."

"Not too good."

Don't tell anyone I gave her two bus tickets as well. "Here. This is for now, and this is for later."

"Oh, thank you."

"And I'm gonna give you one of these fives, I need the other one to buy lunch—"

"Oh thank you."

"I've been watching you, and I can't believe that no one has stopped!"

"I know. No one's given me anything for three hours."

Wow, I thought. "Okay, you need to have the rest of this," I said, handing her the remaining five. "My name's Nathan."

"Jennifer."

Handshake. "You can ride my bus anytime, any day."

"Thanks."

"Be safe today." As I began walking away, I added, "Treat yourself to something nice."

Upon hearing that she immediately burst into tears. That wasn't the effect I intended the line to have. Her shoulders shook from crying.

I should've stayed with her longer.

A GIVEN THING

12/25/17

People will surprise you. They'll prove themselves toward a worthiness you may not have thought them capable of. It doesn't happen all the time, but it happens often enough for a pattern to emerge: give somebody time, respect—or space—and they'll reveal volumes, qualities they haven't had occasion to show before.

I was wrapping up my break at the U-District terminal. A still night, empty, where each word meant a little more. Marcel tapped on my door just as I opened it.

"Nathan, can I please get on early. It's cold out here and I'm feelin' sick, man."

"Oh hey Marcel. Sure thing."

"Thanks." He swaggered in, tall, a brown hooded jacket over another brown hooded jacket, the heavy outdoor gear, big backpack, and garbage bags a contrast to his wire-frame spectacles and gruffly companionable self. He had the affable calm that comes with middle age. "Hey, what do you do for sickness? What's the Asian remedy, Nate? I got to know."

"Uh," I said. "Water's good."

"Cain't do that, makes ya pee."

"You got a cold or something, the flu?"

"I don't know what I got. People coughin'—"

"Yeah, don't know what's goin' around. A number of folks I know got colds, it might just be a bad cold."

"It is. I can't handle it though," he said, in a rare moment of masculine frailty. "My body's achin', my legs—"

"That's awful, man! I'm tellin' you, water, it's good for the joints, flushes out the system . . ."

"Gotta drink a whole lotta that. Hey Nathan, take your time gettin' down there. 'Cause I wanna catch the 1:08 5. Don't wanna sit out there forever."

"Man, I love that! No one tells me to take my time, they're always saying hurry yourself up!"

"Ha!"

"I will happily take my sweet time."

"Stop and get a Dick's burger." He reached in his bag and said, "Here."

The knit cap still had the price tag on it, and rested factory-flat in my hand. I took the proffered item, saying, "Are you giving me this hat? This thing's brand new!"

He reached in again and handed me a bag of new wool socks.

"Marcel, are you sure? I got socks . . ."

"That's alright, I got 'em too. I tell you what, pick my bag up."

It was the size of a small child and weighed more. I hoisted it with a burst of energy. "That's a beast!"

"That's all clothes."

"Marcel, you are hooked *up*!"

"Yeah, I'm hooked up. And I'm tired. Tired and sick . . ."

"I'll take the hat."

"Naw, take the socks too."

"You serious? Thanks, man! I wish I had food or something for ya tonight—"

"Don't worry 'bout that. I got that too."

"Okay."

He spoke a little more about how important socks can be, how fresh a new pair feels if your shoes are wet. In certain countries the gesture of gifted food is important, and you accept it whether you're hungry or not. You don't turn down that goodwill. I imagine Marcel knows I already have socks and hats aplenty. But he needed to express his gratitude, and his pragmatic demeanor didn't allow for that to happen in words. His love spoke through the language of gift-giving, and I wanted him to know I heard him. We carried on at the leisurely pace he specified, my favorite. I left the interior lights off; just he and I drifting through an abandoned city.

"Merry Christmas," I said after a while. I'd almost forgotten what day it was.

"Merry Christmas," he replied, a softer voice now, distant and pleasant in the land of partial slumber.

PART VII

YOU WON'T ALWAYS BE AROUND

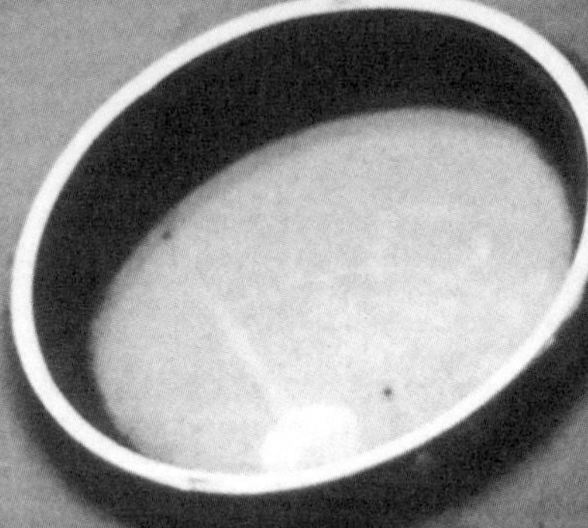

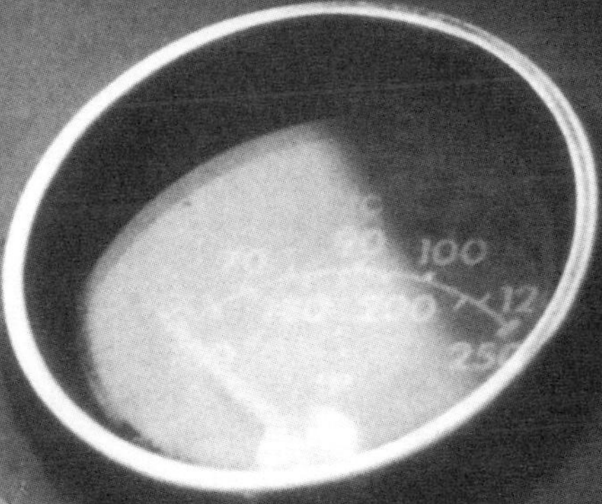
ENGINE
TEMP
KIEPE POLES

DETAILS ON A DAY OFF

2/8/17

Paris has continued sinking in, and the result isn't quite what I'd expected. We've mentioned bitterness as one response to tragedy, and I don't begrudge the choice. But I can't settle for that. I turn the acrid memory over in my mind, searching for another slant, hoping for a prismatic beam of understanding. We are lucky in that Time, the great equalizer, does some of this heavy lifting for us.

I find myself settling deeper into an almost unhinged thankfulness. Everything is cause for celebration. The paralysis of grief and its accompanying confusion sometimes give way to the realization that we are deeply fortunate, that we must recognize this, and we must pass on this burgeoning well-being to those around us. To appreciate what I still have while sharing it around; is that not what those lost souls would have me do, those ghosts I so unfairly survive?

I walk out the door and get on the 41. I'm going to class. Who's driving? David's driving. "Hey, stranger," he says affably. We talk about how they're changing the shifts at North Base next pick, how they're cutting down on bonus time and overtime. Neither of us likes this one bit, but we both know we'll live. Inwardly I marvel at how he, a fairly senior operator, has sustained such good cheer for so long.

I get off by the Asian market. Rain sprinkles from the sky like we're all plants in Priapus's mythic garden. What a silly idea when you think about it—water falling from the sky? Who came up with that one? I don't use drugs, but thoughts like this are why friends think I'm high all the time.

I'm eating as I walk. I'm eating leftover curry chicken with rice and roasted veggies. It's downright delectable, a gift from Maya, the darling regular passenger; she got me a little extra somethin' on her PCC run. Thank you, world. Walking in the wind with a plastic fork, hair going crazy, black nylon wool jacket flapping in the wind, ironed grey dress shirt rippling underneath. Dressing inappropriately for the weather while at work is something I've basically co-opted in the last several years, but I still yield to reason in my off hours. (The Nathan Bus Outfit has slowly set itself in stone, and jackets, overcoats, or cardigans would all make too much sense! Find me in: dress shoes, navy blue slacks, and an ironed, tucked-in long-sleeved oxford, with the sleeves rolled up, as in, "Let's get down to business." Yeah, baby. The anachronism of wearing borderline formal dress to do service work on the city's worst bus routes excites me.)

I'm done with the food, striding through the market now, calling out *hellooo* to the woman at the Hawaiian restaurant stand. I don't know why we started doing that, or when. At some point in our daily crossings I think it dawned on both of us that there's no reason not to say hi. I buy gimbap and mochi for my Korean teacher and classmates. On the route 5 up to class, I chat with the driver.

Arriving early at the University, classmate Jean-Paul and I amiably go over the homework. We talk about suffix particles and when to apply them. Why do some sentences contain the 에 location marker while others don't? Why indeed. I haven't been in school since graduating UW almost nine years earlier. It's humbling and demanding and wonderful.

After class I consider catching the bus home. I know who the driver will be, and last week we had a lovely conversation onboard with a new transplant from the East Coast. What was her name? On impulse I change course. It's not yet time to go home.

My friend Jamar's having an art opening, and I realize I'll be disappointed if I don't go. Friends support other friends and their art. What's the most valuable gift I can give, after all, besides time?

I'm happy to devote part of this precious night off to being there. I walk over to the 8. Who's driving? Wendosun is driving. I sheepishly have to ask his name after he so easily remembers mine. How does he remember a conversation we had two weeks ago? He "wakes up" upon seeing me, his regular workaday shift enlivened, made new by a friend stopping in. Wendosun. Fresh, sharp, quick to smile, not afraid to think. My kind of guy.

He asks about my class, and I ask about his route. Earlier today there were huge accidents and blockages, but Wendosun ("Call me Wen") is in bubbly spirits. He's only got one trip left. Sitting in the back for part of the ride, I look at the tech commuters around me, reflecting: most every young person *thinks* they're unattractive, but are in fact beautiful. It's about more than surfaces. Look at these vibrant lovelies. I hope you all know you're worth it. I step off Wen's bus in a spirit of happy inclusion, traipsing through Cal Anderson park, headed now to Vermillion Art Gallery & Bar. I nod at somebody in the park. He looks confused and avoids eye contact. That's okay.

On 11th Avenue, I walk in the roadway instead of on the sidewalk. I used to wonder why people did that, until I went to East Asia and discovered it's the norm on side streets there. The sidewalks are narrower and usually blocked with items. I do it tonight in honor of the Seoul sidewalk. I realize this makes no sense.

For a long time, I was terrified of going to events alone. Especially hobnobbing events. At first I didn't even attend my own art openings. Oh, hobnobbing. Isn't it the worst? It is if you go in thinking that. Don't try to "network." Just say hello to the friendly faces. There are good people everywhere, and half of them are as diffident as you. Put on your best clothes and walk in like you own the place, nodding and smiling as if these people are actually supposed to know you.

Before I even enter Vermillion, a face calls out my name. I haven't seen Bobbie in years. Here's her companion, Eva. What a delightful couple. We chat away. Why are we talking about Postmates? It's about the camaraderie beneath the words, the shimmering acceptance. I get excited as I explain "how completely awesome" I find the job-related side of the restaurant industry.

Finally I wander inside. A few faces see me but don't approach; they're trying to place me. Where have they seen that face before? Why is it smiling at them? But here's Jamar. What a guy. I see him before he sees me, as he works the change machine. "You're all set for laundry money," I say. Handshake, handshake, and man hug.

Look at the genuine thankful thrill in his eyes, in his voice, as he expresses his gratitude for my being there. Here is everything good about our generation, and it is significant, generous, and true. I know how hard it is to make time to talk to one person when you're the center of attention, as he is tonight, but he takes time to give me his tour of the work. Truly one of a kind, that Jamar. A bouncer, painter, rapper, comic book enthusiast, as simultaneously book-smart and street-smart as they come. I've known him since we both took darkroom photography in 2005. He was in high school and I was in college. We haven't spent enough time together.

I look around at the walls. The show consists of proposed land use signs, all recut in the shape of coffins, with various art—photography, paint, spray paint, ink, and more emblazoned over them. It's a funerary cry for the vanishing Seattle. Jamar shows me his contribution to the show, and knows all the other pieces too, clearly passionate about the work of his artist friends. I want to congratulate one of the artists on her photographs, but she's a little too into her boyfriend at the moment. We'll let them have their space.

"Listen, I gotta go to work," Jamar says, meaning hobnobbing. Forget handshakes; he hugs me tightly.

DETAILS, CONTINUED

2/8/17

As I walk out of Vermillion—there's Trent! Drink in hand, ice cubes with lime, head cocked to one side. What a splendid fellow. I join him and his friend Elena in conversation. We're talking succession politics. I mostly listen. Don't you love listening? I already know what *I'm* going to say, after all! Trent makes the salient point that hereditary monarchies, imperfect as they are, were an attempt to offer an alternative to brute force regime changes. Something besides the physically strongest always taking the throne. A compelling argument, but I feel the call of Metro. Adieu, friends.

Avoiding the famously unreliable 11 (live loops will be the end of us all), I walk over to the 49 stop right as one rolls up. I realize that aside from the day of the week, it's my own piece of work I'm getting on! Am I really that nutty, riding my own shift on a day off? Such is the humor of the universe. There it is, big as life, turning the corner now. Is that what I look like? A Latina woman at the zone recognizes me. We exchange pleasantries.

"Your Spanish is good!" she exclaims.

"¡Un poquito! ¡Que tenga buena noche!"

"¡Igualmente!"

Stepping aboard, I look around, all grins. Who's driving? It's José! He exclaims, "You just can't get away from this, can you?"

"Ha! I love it that much!"

I sit down, smiling at the next man getting on, a scruffy rough-and-tumble character looking rather down on his luck.

"Oh, it's you," he says.

"Hey, how ya doin'?"

I explain it's my day off, and we talk about "hangin' in there." The best we can do. He asks if I know *Real Change*. Of course I do, I tell him, proclaiming it the best newspaper in Seattle. We talk about last week's issue. I commend him for the difficult work he does—selling a newspaper on street corners is only for the insanely self-motivated—and we start talking burger joints. He mentions the new Dick's Burgers in Edmonds, and we try to ascertain how many Dick's there are. Make him feel normal, not ignored. Human. Counting them off on our fingers: "Let's see, we got Ballard, Capitol Hill, uh huh Wallingford . . ."

A woman seated nearby whom I vaguely recognize is watching us, perhaps with surprise at what we must look like—the odd couple of all odd couples, talking up restaurants. What's going on here? Just two guys on a bus, thirty years apart, one with shiny dress shoes, LA jeans, and an ironed button-up, the other with tatters and grizzle and an indefatigable eye. His name is Michael Moore. "Like the filmmaker!"

I bid José farewell, calling out, "Say hi to all my people for me!" I can't stop smiling. I beam at the female passenger as I run past. She looks pleasantly confounded.

Racing down the steps to my next bus stop, and not more than five minutes later the 41 surfaces to take me home. How glorious. I peer through the windshield—it's David again! What are the odds? I recognize some passengers within, but chat with David while I can. He's retiring soon. We talk about Camino Island. He bought a house out there. We talk about the ferry system. Here's the thing, he says. Of course it'll be great to retire on Camino, but for his final two years working, his commute will be an absurd fifty-two miles each way! David bought a jalopy of a Honda for that purpose alone—a quick temporary purchase. Throw on a new set of tires and knock 90,000 miles into it, then retire. Not bad.

I'm about to walk home, but wait! There's Deborah the sweetheart, driving the 348. How does she manage to make a mullet look slick? Decades of experience, I suppose. I ride with her for one zone. She tells me about the nutty folks she encounters on her route. I quip, "Hang on. Is the 348 the new 358? Is that what you're tellin' me?"

It's a ridiculous comparison; the 358, precursor to the E Line and formerly Seattle's most notorious route (much loved by me) and the only one so stunningly—awful? awesome?—as to have its own Yelp page, complete with abysmal ratings, and the 348, a sleepy suburban shuttle. Deborah laughs. "It's gettin' that way!"

"'Cause if that's true, I might have to start picking it!"

"You really are crazy," Deborah snorts. When I mention I drive the 7/49 on all five of my work nights, she reminds me Metro offers free counseling and therapy services. She tells me about her exciting medical procedure, happening tomorrow. They're turning her into the Bionic woman—implanting a device in her body with actual buttons! "You know, like 'press this if you feel pain here,'" she explains.

"Gosh! I hope you like buttons!"

"I love 'em!"

How could I not be interested? Trent's monarchies, Jamar's coffins, Wendosun's traffic, Bobbie's Postmates, Michael Moore's burger joints, David's intentional jalopy, Deborah's mysteriously admirable mullet . . . it's like diving through pages of the densest tome there is, our swirling book of life. I'm just a student in this glorious and many-splendored racket, and I drink it all up. The encounters feel like they bring me closer to something, hinting at the shape of this mysterious journey we're all on.

Strolling through my door, I realize: I've just spent *the last seven hours* talking nonstop to acquaintances and former strangers. How did this happen? Aren't people—especially in this city, if reputations are to be believed—supposed to be apathetic, withdrawn, and self-centered? O, streets of Seattle, how I thank thee, for correcting my assumptions and taking me in your arms. You've taught me things I had only the slightest hope for were true.

Once inside, the framed photograph catches my eye. It always does. It's a multiple exposure I took in Paris during those shell-shocked days of after. High-contrast green, inky blacks with splashes of white and red; in the center, a ghost of a figure reflected in sunlight, a woman crossing the street. I welcome its centering weight, inhaling deeply, feeling its specter-like power counterbalance the still-echoing day. I keep the image framed front and center in my living room.

Death disorients us because it is enormous. It swallows our plots, ideas, beliefs, concepts of right and ordinary. It reminds us of our place and proves the existence of time.

We get up in the morning and throw ourselves into matters of varying importance. We continue the Great Search for happiness and meaning, the quest in which we do the dumbest and smartest of things, feeling our way in the dark towards the answers, answers we gradually realize will not be revealed in this life. But that is okay.

Because the fullest, most complete expression of existence is in this unfinished birthing we take part in every day. The small joys and details, successes we find along the way which are worth it, whether we live another hour, or for a hundred years.

THE CHILD

7/1/18

Ah, Fifth and Jackson. It's a plaza intersection with four very different and gradually changing corners. The northwest corner has been vacant of late. With the waterfront streetcar steps now chained off from access, there are still places to urinate, but nowhere to sit. Good thing there remain three other corners to choose from. The northwest edge beckons me today not for lavatorial reasons but because it's the corner I need to be on to start my evening shift. My bus will be here any minute.

The corner is deserted as usual for this time of day, save for one soul: the middle-aged Laotian man squatting back against a pillar. I've been saying hi to him for at least a half-decade. He taught me the traditional Laotian greeting years ago: hands together as in prayer, a head nod down, and the word, "Sabadi!"

I greet him just so, and he smiles in return. There are a few teeth left, and his silver-grey strands toss lightly about, almost as if underwater. His appearance is a medley of amenable grit and texture, jeans torn not from fashion but use, blemished surfaces, and split ends, that olive-skinned grin somehow sustaining through it all. What is he doing out here? The maxim of homeless Asian people being nonexistent isn't entirely true, but you'll agree there's a reason for the adage. It's rare. He mostly keeps to himself, a quiet sort who doesn't fit in with the intersection's obstreperous bawdiness. He has a gentle smile for me every time I see him.

Today though, I get more than a grin. He rises and walks toward me, one arm held out, trying to thrust three one-dollar bills into my hands. "Here, for you," he says.

"What? No, my friend, no way! You need that way more, I think!" I have to put some effort into turning his gift away. "Thank you though, that's really nice!"

He explains how his brother has just won the lottery, and that the whole family will share. He's thrilled and feeling generous. We confer over the details. I want to make certain his brother knows how to find him; really did win; and really will share.* It all seems to check out, but for now our friend is happy, and maybe that's the most important thing.

A family is approaching from across the street, coming closer now. European, dressed in relaxed casual, a mother with short hair pushing a stroller, with another toddler alongside holding daddy's hand. Perhaps they're tourists.

Our friend moves quickly toward the stroller. He extends a filthy loving hand as he did to me a moment ago, holding out the three dollars to the toddler inside. He is smiling, nodding: "Here! For you!" The mother is shaking her head, "No, no, no," confused, scared. For her, it is all happening quickly. The father doesn't notice; he's walking ahead. The baby doesn't understand what's happening either but accepts the proffered bills.

Giving. Why does it feel so much better than receiving? I knew the sort of high Mr. Sabadi was on. It didn't much matter to him how they responded. He just wanted to give and was searching for the most worthy recipient in sight. Of course it was the child.

Afterwards he turned back to me, laughing. He was utterly unswayed by the mother's attitude.

He said, "They do not know I am a good man!"

---

* Further confirmation is in the fact that I never saw him wandering Jackson Street, or anywhere else, after this date.

BETTER TO SUFFER HARDSHIP THAN CAUSE IT

12/22/21

It's near midnight. Isn't it always near midnight when the best stories happen? A figure is running over. I'm early, sitting here at Campus Parkway for an extra light cycle. No need to leave this fellow in the dust. I'm feeling generous. Why?

About twenty minutes ago, eggs were thrown at my bus, spew-cascading off my left side and mirrors. It took me a bit to piece together. First a flash more like sound, a scattered sparking flare on the asphalt; then I notice my left exterior mirror, newly hazy, slimy, the only time yellow is ever offensive. The car speeding off now makes sense. I'm more confused than hurt. What did this mean? What *can* it mean?

Seeing this running figure now, I didn't have the energy to be spiteful. He was a tall Black man wearing all black, American, hiking up the fabric of his jeans, the better to allow him to run. Urban fashion *du jour*—sagging pants, overheavy construction boots, unlaced basketball sneakers, loads of heavy cloth, layered jackets over hoodies . . . people who dress like this can't move quickly. But he put himself together as best he could, hustling briskly over. You do what you have to do.

"Man," he breathed. "I 'ppreciate you so much."

"Oh for sure! Always!"

"Seriously though. You changed my night. I'm so grateful." I could tell he meant it, too, out here in the late night. Not everyone out at this time is actually going anywhere. But for those with destinations, a desperation sets in as the buses become less frequent, each hour a little colder.

"Dude, for sure. Too long to wait for the next bus, you know?"

He grinned in the dark. "I *know*!"

As we pulled away, I added, "I ride the bus all the time, so I know how it feels."

"You already know. Man, there's times when I come runnin' up on the side of the bus, I got my hands together like this, begging. I'm *begging*! And he done just drives off."

"Ooohh! That's terrible! Why!"

"Or another time I'm tryna get the 49, it's 'bout two o'clock in the morning, right—"

"Yeah." I've driven that one. He had the storyteller's enthusiasm, and more. Look at his eyes glinting brightly, his pearly white teeth perfectly aligned, gleaming against the dim interior. I briefly wondered if he's had braces, like me. He continued.

"And I'm *begging*, bro!"

Anyone puts their hand on their heart, and I'm theirs. The gesture of an appeal to one's better angels gets to me. I said, "How could anyone say no to that?"

"Yeah! And he leaves me, but I run after him. And I make it down to the next one and *then* the next one and he lets me on. But that was after I chased him all the way down."

"Man, the *stress*! 'Specially that time of night. I'm so sorry. I try to make up for those guys."

"You *so* do. Man, *thank you*. You made my night. Now I got something to tell my wife. This was th' highlight of the whole day. What's your name?"

"Nathan."

"Nathan, my name's Jimmy."

"Good to meet you."

"You too."

Some people hide their enthusiastic verve because they're worried about being ridiculed. Not this guy. I decided to be honest about my feelings. Do you know the sensation when you realize you're among like company?

"Actually, dude, I'm glad you stepped in, 'cause right before you got on there was some folks in a car that was throwin' eggs at the bus."

"What? *Eggs*?"

"Yeah, just drivin' past. There's some on the outside of the bus." I gestured to my left.

He really heard me. He was slowing down now, a birthing seriousness. I could see him picturing the event. "Man, that's messed up."

"I was like, where's this coming from, why would they do that? Are these high school kids or something?" At what age do we learn that being spiteful, holding grudges—is a waste of time?

"*Eggs*? At a *bus*? Maaan," he said, incredulously. "I wish't I could a been there, I woulda hopped out and—"

"It's like, come on now! And it's not like I did anything to them, cut 'em off or something, they just came outta nowhere."

"Yeah, I see one on th' glass there." Referring to my left side mirror. "That's the world we live in though."

"Yeah, it's a funky time right now."

"TikTok and all that, people rather do that and go to jail. Man, why they wanna throw shit at a bus?"

"Doesn't make any sense!"

He said it suddenly, with urgency: "I wanna wash it off for you." I looked at him. The passion in his voice went straight to my heart. I didn't know what to say.

"I'll hop out really quick the next time you stop."

"Aw, it's cool," I said. "Thank you though, I appreciate you."

"Naw, man—"

"You don't have to do that."

He said, "Bro. We gotta take care of each other."

And with that Jimmy was out of the bus at Rainier Vista before I could say anything. I pulled the emergency brake. He grabbed a few masks from the dispenser as impromptu paper towels and scrambled over to my left side, scrubbing and wiping away. This man *cared*. He needed to balance out the world's hate. He wanted to show me my fragile goodness, my kind intentions, were appreciated. That they deserved more than trampling.

We gotta take care of each other.

I could have cried. He leapt back inside with alacrity, saying, "There, that's better. I hope that's better."

"You're amazing," I said, looking at him. "Seriously, thank you."

"*Got* to look out for our bus drivers!"

"Man, Jimmy, thank you so much." We were parked at a bus stop, and outside my still-open doors a young woman was watching us, waiting for another bus. I looked at her and yelled out, gesturing to Jimmy, "This is the man o' the year right here! *Man of the year*!" She smiled. He did too.

We were on our way.

"It's crazy, 'cause, I'm used to driving routes that are more . . . *intense* than this, like I drive the 7 and the E Line, but this never happened on those ones! And this' the 75, and nothing ever happens on the 75—"

"NOTHING!" Jimmy practically howled, in wild agreement. He knew the lay of the land.

"Totally! On those routes, people would sometimes step up to help me when somethin' was goin' down, and I always appreciated that. People helpin' each other out."

"Man, if this happened on those routes I bet some folks woulda stepped out the bus to take *care* of that car, no questions asked. *Eggs*? Seriously, who *is* these people?"

At some point you run out of air complaining, and life starts back up again. I said, "So you just gettin' offa work?"

"Yeah, I'm at the Gyro place on the Ave."

"I hope they give you a discount on the food."

"Yeah, family owned, so stop in!"

So that's why he was out here. His last words are how I remember him. He said them with unabashed enthusiasm:

"Man, I wish there was more I could do for you. You changed my night. Thank you!"

You remember Lukas the Angel of Broadway, helping me out when he didn't have to. I'm now christening this fellow Jimmy the Angel of Campus Parkway. Some guy running after the bus from across the street holding up his pants with one hand. Can you believe it? *That's* the nicest passenger of the night.

I'm so glad I gave him a chance.

I reflected as I drove away. I thought about him, but I couldn't help thinking about the eggs and eggers as well. You've been there, I think, mistreated; I'm sure our friend above has too, and I imagine that's at least partly what motivated his vigor in correcting the night's error. You've suffered, and afterwards the question has nagged you also: *Why do people sometimes hurt other people*?

We have to start by remembering two things. Firstly, as Rutger Bregman points out in his *Humankind: A Hopeful History*, humans only commit evil when it's disguised as good. When it achieves a balance or aim they deem worthy. Secondly, people often assume others think like them. A cynic will interpret your actions cynically; a pessimist will think you're pessimistic, or else not pessimistic enough. Crucially, a distrusting and deceitful person will imagine you are the same.

They will not perceive their slip-up in assuming this.

You may be gullible and friendly, like me; but they can still think you're manipulative and hateful, if that's their own modus through life. People don't see you. They see their *experience* of you, and that perception is based on *their* life experiences. Which have nothing to do with you, of course.

The angry mind searches for a release nonetheless, in harm done to others, attempts to assert power, the self hunting for itself in all the wrong places. Those poor souls don't have a clue. Will they one day discover what you and I already know, that hate never results in happiness?

In the long run, for the ease of your heart and the health of your soul, it is infinitely better to receive harm than to cause it. Nothing calcifies the spirit like pretending to yourself you are good when you know, deep down, that you aren't.

Those people had no idea why they egged my bus. But I know why. It was so I could be bathed in glowing goodness and love twenty minutes later. So I could know how that feels, how real and true the best sides of humanity are.

Thank you.

AH, VOLUME

5/29/18

Merriam-Webster defines *roar* as "to utter or emit a full loud prolonged sound" or "to sing or shout with full force."

And how.

I recognized his face and got excited. Time for a volume adjustment—lots of roaring for him, lots of listening by me. I was on the point of calling out his name when he beat me to the chase, bellowing: "HAU LING! HAU LING!"

He marched to the center of the bus. The nighttime silence began to envelope us again, slowly, returning to the norm of what 23:00 is supposed to sound like. Dead of night. The whirr of the electric motor, the intermittent blast of the heater.

From the thinly peopled interior came the deafening pronouncement: "HOW WAS YOUR DAY, BUS DRIVER?"

Hau Ling makes me quiet. I liked to match Darlene's boisterous volume, but Hau Ling's stentorian decrees are on another level entirely. You can't match him. Why bother? I feel duty-bound to balance him out with meek, reasonable sentences, like:

"Oh, pretty good. How 'bout you, are you headed home?"

"A GREAT PLACE TO GO TO," he screamed, with warlike enthusiasm, as though I'd just suggested something illegal.

"You got that right," I said. We work well together. With his glass-splitting howls and my innocuous volume working in counterpoint, we almost add up to a normal conversation. Almost.

"I JUST PAID MY RENT FOR FEBRUARY. COME MARCH, I'M GONNA PAY IT AGAIN."

I didn't know it was possible to combine equal parts gleefulness, belligerence, and gratitude into a single inflection, but he managed it with aplomb.

"GUESS WHAT I DID TODAY?"

Hau Ling makes the ordinary, elemental. He describes normalcy with the indomitable moxie of a new firmament, elevating us to the plane of larger-than-life. When you hear someone saying "*I went to the waterfront today*" at a level that nearly makes you cover your ears . . . well, let's just say it's better than the movies.

"Oh, cool," I exclaimed. "Was it nice?"

"YES."

"Was it cold?"

"COLD?" He roared slowly, rhetorically. Rhetorical roaring is hard. Try it sometime. "THIS ISN'T COLD. YOU WANT COLD?"

"I suppose—"

"ANCHORAGE, ALASKA," he boomed, a decorated general discovering a new planet and naming it for the first time. "THAT'S COLD."

"I bet it is!"

My quiet comments, intended for an audience of one, and his pronouncements, designed for a cast of thousands. Yes, a perfect pairing.

"HAVE YOU BEEN THERE?"

"I have not. Have you?"

This could almost be a regular discussion. But a rubber duck isn't a rubber duck anymore when it's six stories tall. His voice wasn't a voice: it was a three-dimensional living thing, an entity that used its vessel to express itself, rather than the other way around.

"I RECOMMEND GOING THERE IN THE SUMMER MORE THAN THE WINTER!" He laughed maniacally, perhaps imagining the mayhem of subzero temperatures, cackling as though his comment had an obvious and irresistible double entendre. "THE SUMMER OVER THE WINTER!"

After a moment he added, "THEY'RE TOUGH UP THERE,"

almost reflectively—as reflective as you can be when shattering glass.

“I bet they are.”

“IF THEY GET THE COMMON COLD, THEY STILL BUCK UP AND GO TO WORK. THEY STOCK UP ON CHICKEN NOODLE SOUP.”

Chiiicken noooodle soooup. He stretched it out, giving each syllable its proper time in the sun. He made it an art piece no less than Warhol, but with a grit, a truth, an innocence, and a complete lack of pretense Warhol could never hope to touch. It’s nice to be cultured, but there become certain things you can’t see anymore. Hau Ling’s admiration for hard work was uncomplicated, rooted in simpler truths, that rare and essential ability to wholly appreciate the ordinary. Biting the cold and putting good work in, on plain food—isn’t that something to admire?

And with that, he abruptly got up and raced to the back, leaping out the open back door. But I had learned the night’s lesson of sorts, just in time.

THE GLOW

6/6/19

Unrenovated Fred Meyers will always have a special place in my heart. Are there any left? I know of only one in Seattle, nestled in the Lake City neighborhood. The layout, font, aisles, and floors . . . these are the ingredients of my childhood, and they comfort me.

The American allergy to the past pains me because of its relish for erasure. We strenuously work to hide the existence of time, of history, because age reminds us of death. A new facade, a new logo; do-overs absolve us of the pain of preserving, because it is easier to replace than to treasure. But I want to feel the truths of an earlier time. I came of age in such spaces and find myself in a reflective state when in them, able to think in the language of decades.

It was while in such a headspace that I stood in line at the Lake City Fred Meyer, observing the beige background behind the Tuscan-red sans-serif lettering which denotes what lies down each aisle. “Chips. Cookies. Peanut Butter.” Sublime. “Bath Tissue. Cleaning Supplies.” Navigable and plain, echoes of a time with no need for stylish flash.

Don’t tell me you don’t secretly love this stuff.

The non-slip flooring, a collection of unglamorous off-white creams and tan streaks, the better to hide debris; shopping carts and crates and doors and railings with dents and scratches you know the histories of, shapes your childhood hands remember well. Does everyone find themselves so heartened by such details? The passage of time writ on a space is one of the few reminders of mortality that is pleasant: we take comfort knowing we, too, have similarly survived the vagaries of time.

I looked at the person standing in front of me in line. She was dressed in a white habesha kemis edged in blue trim, with a netela wrapped around her head. Her face was exposed but turned away from me.

Was it her? The bouncing ball of joy I used to drive to the Ethiopian church on the 36, who cleaned airplanes at Sea-Tac? Her ebullient character stuck in my mind for years after last seeing her. The sort who makes friends easily and is no doubt well-loved in her community. People love those who bring out the light.

"Hi," I said tentatively as she was half-turning to look at something. "It's Lulit, right?"

She needed no reminder, no clarification. Her eyes immediately went wide with animated recognition. "Hiiiiii!!"

Lulit outstretched her arms and before we knew it, we were hugging tight, the way acquaintances instantly become good friends when meeting on the other side of the world. I recalled now that she'd mentioned this Fred Meyer, but I had never seen her off the bus; here we were now, neighbors in life. She was thrilled. We asked about each other's jobs, where are you living now, do you still do this or that . . . but mainly we sang in the voice of community and belonging.

I found myself seeing the scene through the eyes of the cashier, who watched our merriment with delighted surprise. She was a young woman who wasn't expecting two such culturally contrasting customers to suddenly explode together with glee; a demure Ethiopian woman in traditional attire on the cusp of middle age, and some young westerner in boring clothes. What could they have in common?

The cashier's elated wonder only added to our jubilance. It became the three of us as I explained how we knew each other, and now we were a trio watched by the rest of the line, showing them what's possible.

At the center of it all was Lulit, a beacon who loved and felt loved in return, who lived in the easy burgeoning newness of a present she made. Such people are inspirations, especially when the world feels like it's collapsing around you, changing at a pace you can barely keep up with.

There will come a day when I won't recognize the interior of any Fred Meyer, or perhaps any store I enter. I will feel lost, as I sometimes already do, losing ground on a shrinking island as the world becomes less familiar. I hope then I'll still carry this memory. Maybe all that will remain of it will be her smile, preserved in something akin to a photograph: Lulit making the world glow.

I hope that's enough to remind myself that I don't have to be a product of my environment, but my environment can be a product of me.

ON ACING IT

6/9/24

Four years ago, I froze.

Nothing bothers me more than men harassing women, and that's exactly what was happening on my 49 one afternoon in Summer 2020. He was big and tall, lanky, with the youthful self-absorption that breeds the worst kind of entitlement. He sat next to a young woman and leered like a Disney villain, putting his arm around her in a way that was obviously invasive. I said, "Let's try not to touch the other passengers please, that ain't polite," to which he replied, "She's my girlfriend!"

The woman was silent, and I wondered if I'd misread the situation. We carried on.

Ten minutes later, he was sitting behind her now, reaching around to touch her in ways that will get you arrested. She froze. I froze too. I can't blame her for freezing, but I do blame myself. I froze just as I have the times others have assaulted me, frozen with confusion and disbelief, confronted by human behavior I forget is even possible, and am utterly unprepared to react to.

After a second I said, "Okay," in a tone of deep disappointment, and pulled over, opening the doors. But I didn't know what to say next, or how. He was bigger than me. He was looking at me. He had nothing to lose. I had a lot to lose. I was frozen. She stared at me while I sat there doing nothing. I'll never forget the look on her face.

Fortunately the female companion I'd been talking with up front wasn't frozen at all. She saw me look back, followed my gaze, and immediately shouted, "*Hey, what the fuck, man*!"

My friend could do what I couldn't; a woman intervening in situations like this tends to work better than a man doing the same. It creates a sisterly two-against-one dynamic that helps tip the scales in the right direction, rather than escalating manly confrontation. Her caustic comment worked beautifully. I mumbled something in support, and the offender exited one stop later. I closed the doors after he exited, but, stupidly, opened them up again for a thoroughly oblivious earphoned-in commuter who asked to get off there too. Now I would know to refuse his request and attempt to explain, but I was still frozen.

Generally, I feel like I bungled the whole affair, which was only saved by my adroit friend speaking up. I did what every good bus driver does after bungling a situation; figure out a plan for what to do next time it happens. Because whatever it was, it will happen again.

Four years later, I'm once again driving the 49. Another entitled man, this time older, fifty-something with shades and big headphones, coasts into the bus with a dismissive air and settles into the rear lounge. As we service the Roy Street zone he yells up toward me, "Ey driver, hold up! I wanna get some snaps o' this!"

He's eyeing a classic car across the street. I'm hardly enthusiastic to indulge such whims, but the light is turning red, and I remain stopped. Like all self-absorbed souls, he imagines I acted just for him, and hollers a thank you, letting me know I can drive again. The light turns green and I do so.

Operators know that in our new landscape of all-door boarding, most problem passengers enter the bus by sneaking in through the rear doors. Psychologically this is unsurprising but try convincing policymakers that rear-door boarding exacerbates safety issues. Another man has entered, this time through the rear, and I know to pay attention. He is big-boned, dressed in starchy clean, oversized, all-black denim, with spectacles and a fresh, flat-billed baseball cap.

Sure enough, he begins stalking up and down the aisle, sniffing at the female passengers, sitting down next to this one, now that one, forcing them to squeeze closer to the window. He speaks in low tones; I can't make out words. Nothing backfires worse than a false accusation, so I hold off for now. What is he saying to them? Would he even respond to anything I ask? Sometimes people are too far gone to hear you.

On the 7, passengers often have the street smarts to deal with such matters themselves. Less so on the 49. But here is a female college student, quiet and demure, clearly uncomfortable, standing up and moving away from the man's advances—remember how hard this is to do—standing up and moving toward the middle door, while he looks on dumbly. She makes eye contact with me. Her expression says everything. *Let me out of here.*

Some rules are made to be broken. We're not at a stop but I open the doors. She thanks me with her eyes and is gone.

Now the man in black stares at me dumbly. He says, "Why'd you let her escape?"

Once again, I freeze. His sentence confounds me. *Escape?* My starting frame of reference for what constitutes acceptable behavior is so galactically far from his that I don't know where to begin.

One stop later, two other passengers from the back walk up to me, a man and a woman. They couldn't be an odder couple—another demure college student, short and bookish in appearance . . . and the middle-aged man from earlier with headphones and shades, the classic car aficionado whom I'd written off as entitled.

We are always more than one thing.

What they have in common now is their urgency, a shared sense of mission. Both begin speaking at once.

"Hi um there's a guy who's being horrible—"

"Listen that dude with the hat, all in black—"

"He's harassing the women, saying stuff—"

"He actin' way outta line, jus' like she say, botherin' everybody. You got to say someth—"

"Please say something!"

"—tell that fool to stop."

"I'm on it," I say. "Thank you for telling me."

They hurry off (still discussing it together on the sidewalk, in a flash of beautiful bonding), but they've done enough to burst me out of my frozen state. I love when passengers tell me. Only then am I sure my suspicions are correct, and only then am I sure others are on my side. Our side. I get on the mic.

"Okay everyone, special announcement. *SEXUAL harassment*"—instantly I have everyone's attention—"*is not cool. That's not okay.* We can't be botherin' people like that, it ain't right. Gotta give the female passengers a lil' bit a personal space, let 'em do their thing. *I'm really only talking to one guy, all the rest a you guys are cool.* But let's try to look out for each other, try to show some respect for everyone. Thank you all for lookin' out."

The effect I was hoping for happened: others intervened. I wanted to suggest community, standing up for the right thing, often dangerous when alone but easier in a group. I wanted everyone to know they had my respect—and, crucially, my implicit encouragement. In speaking up I was the first vocal bystander, but the critical ingredient which gets everyone involved is not the first bystander but the *second* bystander who takes action. The two men, and then a woman, who began standing up, moving hesitantly but firmly toward the offender (remember how hard that is to do), were the real heroes. A verbal tussle ensued, becoming physical; one departed, then the offender himself. We all sighed collectively, me most of all.

I'd been practicing four years for that.

We fail so we can learn. Regret is good, because it's proof we've grown. It is the purest evidence of personal progress. I say, own the sensation. Failure comes for all of us, a silent proposition, the universe waiting to see if we'll bite at the chance to improve ourselves, the chance to exercise grace, mercy, empathy. When people say experience is the best teacher, they're being euphemistic. They mean failure. We go through our trials so we know just what to say, do (or not do) next time.

So we can ace it.

Don't beat yourself up for bungling things. Aspire instead, as much as possible, for that awesome, nigh-superhuman feat:

To make each of your life's biggest mistakes only once.

AJ

6/3/20

Who was he?

I was sitting on the sidewalk cement, leaning against a brick wall waiting for my bus to show. He walked toward me, calling out "Nathan," arms outstretched in victory. He told me I probably wouldn't remember him, and I looked on in pleasant bewilderment. But the first echoes of recognition were starting to pulse though:

"Your hair is different," I said.

"Yeah, I was way different back then," he said. "I'm sober now, I got a job working down at the market."

I pointed at his guitar. "Still playing music, that's great!"

"What it took was the job. Someone told me if you don't change what's going on, who's around you—"

"The environment—"

"Your environment exactly, then it's never gonna happen. I was relapsing and relapsing again but then the job got me out of it. Someone giving me a chance, that's all it took."

You've heard such words before, I imagine, but hear the spirited verve in which he spoke them! Sure, everything we experience has been felt by someone else, and there's a book already written about everything we find and feel . . . but that doesn't mean it isn't new for you and me. We are, each of us, living life for the very first time.

And for him, this new ascension to a healthier state was massive. I agreed. How could it not be? He was a man on 2nd Avenue with the hopeful resilience of youth that's been scarred but not broken. Picture River Phoenix from *My Own Private Idaho*, reborn.

He said, "I used to wake up play music go to bed with nothing.

Wake up with nothing, play music, spend it all, go to bed, and get my phone stolen like once a week and have to go through all the trouble on top of everything else. And now if I get my stuff stolen or something happens, I've got a base. I live on Queen Anne."

"Wow!"

"I work down at the Market. I make $125 a day."

I congratulated him on conquering addiction, and that he's still playing music. "Still creating, that's important."

"Yeah, I'm never gonna run out of material. People say you can only make art when you're going through awful stuff, that creativity fizzles out when you get your life together but *man*, I can always go back there mentally and get creative. It's not like I'm gonna run out of things to say. And you too, I remember you let me sleep on the bus a bunch of times and the conversations we would have . . . you have no idea how that type of thing can help."

It clicked. This was the guy my colleague Robert was talking about. "Thanks man," I said. "It was good to have you there. It's crazy actually, because I remember us talking about how years from now one day we're gonna laugh about all this."

I could recall the exact moment: on a southbound 4 on 5th Avenue crossing Mercer, and the sun setting behind him. That would have been over six years ago. The discussion had brought him up at the time, but only just; you hope, but you don't know. You don't know a circle is a circle until you're nearly at the end of it. Now we knew.

"Ha," he laughed. "I remember that too, and I remember being kind of pissed in the moment because it's like, *years* from now!?"

"Yeah it sucks in the moment, but here we are, it happened! Dude, this makes my month!"

"I don't know if you remember but my name's AJ."

"AJ, Nathan." We shook hands. "You're the man."

"If you ever wanna come by, stop by the market if you ever wanna see me. I'm down there. Selling fruit!"

He gave a self-aware smile. I gave an unadulterated one, and he grinned wider, walking off into the sunlight.

Six years ago, I thought. I watched his form grow smaller in the busy distance.

He remembered my name.

THE CHILD: II

8/31/17

A figure under streetlights, his gesticulating arms spread wide as he stood in front of his companion.

The high-pressure sodium-vapor lamps of yore have a way of collapsing the color spectrum just so; the deep shade of his skin made less of an impression, and I couldn't discern what color his open denim jacket was, nor his baggy jeans, layered undergarments and assorted street jewelry, contrasty basketball shoes which could as easily be blue as red. Tonight he was just a forty-something figure cloaked in monochromatic orange. I called out to him.

"Hey, there he is!"

"Hey, iss muh boy!"

"What's happening?"

"This damn cigarette." He didn't need the bus but wanted the camaraderie. He leaned in for a handshake—no fist pound tonight, just the classic "gentleman's agreement" approach. In his other hand was an unlit cigarette.

"Say my Daddy *cracked*," he said, raspy voice rising. "Said he *over*."

What did he mean? He sounded unhappy about it, and if it was an accusation I wanted him to know I'd said no such thing.

"Who said that?"

"Cancer, man. Cigarette smoke."

"Aaaoouuh," I said. "I'm so sorry. I am so sorry."

Sometimes tears come very quickly.

"*Cancer*," he said again. His eyes crinkled over; his lips tore downward. His body pitched forward in helpless rage and love.

He saw his father then, and he saw the size of death, the savage indifference of unearned punishment come too soon. I didn't know what to say. I stammered in sympathy. We all have a Paris of our own, some trauma we carry close to the vest, like Little Leon and his mother, like COVID and the rest of us; shadows we think we have to nurse alone.

He screamed. He screamed his pain with primal force, wordless, body scrunched up with effort, a vowel of catastrophe roared so mightily I thought he would break glass.

People looked up. They turned around. A just-deboarded friend of mine was on the sidewalk. She paused, perhaps fearing the worst. A companionable freeloader skulked up to me on the pretext of checking the time, but more likely to ensure my safety.

There was no cause for fear. Our man was just in lamentation, struck low on an elemental level.

"I'll see you fuckin' *later*!!" he yelled between gritted teeth, caught between cosmic frustration and the decorum of acquaintanceship. Still the tears, bending his face toward a delicate ugly, painfully beautiful in its truthfulness.

We grow, but do we ever change? In moments of joy and extreme sorrow, you sense the boy in every grown man, no matter how dense an alpha-dog outfit they muster. I saw him as outside of time, never mind all the tough swagger and accoutrements; there's a hurting child in there, confused from day one as we all are, as to why there can be no life without suffering. Beneath all the attainment and attunement of age . . .

Deep down, always, the child is the father of the man.

I didn't have the answers; I let him speak. I hugged him with my eyes, and we shook hands again, nothing fancy tonight. Just the connected human touch.

Why did I live?

CLEAN-SHAVEN REVELATION

3/31/20

"Hi, Mister Nathan!"

"Heyy! Abdirahim, how are you?"

"I am good, Mister Nathan, how are you?"

"Great! It's good to see you!"

"What bus you driving now?"

"Same as before, number 7!"

Not the most shocking of exchanges, you're thinking. But let us recall the state he used to be in, constantly, year after year . . . Abdirahim was usually so drunk he couldn't keep balance, and whether it was spilling popcorn all over the front half of the bus floor, or collapsing in the doorway and needing to be carried off by Lukas and myself, passing out in various states of unconsciousness untold numbers of times—Abdirahim was a handful and a half. You sighed when he got on your bus, because it meant you'd be on the radio with the coordinator and filling out paperwork later tonight, as sure as the wheels on the bus go round.

But I found it impossible to dislike him. I've never seen a happier drunk, and I mean *truly* happy—not the happy drunk who can tip into anger at one wrongly interpreted word, but a happy man genuinely pleased to see you, who always remembered my name no matter how slosh-tanked he was, who never bothered the other passengers, female or otherwise. I like to think we were both resourceful, even if we couldn't be more opposed on personal health. Because although Abdirahim's method for surviving may have been annoying, selfish, and shortsighted, it was nothing if not clever. Here's what he would do.

Step One: get plastered. There's an art to this and he knew it. You have to get *so* plastered that Detox has to come, or Medical has to be called. Other homeless people try to do this, but their own attitudes get in the way. Abdirahim has the self-possession to avoid making hurtful decisions during Step One. No one would accuse him of actually being good at holding his liquor, but somehow he always managed to avoid causing disasters. He knew the system: if you request medical assistance from an operator, they are required to call for that assistance, even with no reason given.

Which brings us to Step Two. Step Two is when Medical shows up. I knew who Abdirahim was; the coordinator on the radio knew by the description whom I was referring to; if police were called, they knew him also; the gents at the fire department and the guys in the Detox van and the folks driving the AMR—we all knew him by name. Every person in the chain was familiar with the drill by now.

It's Abdirahim hour.

I remember more than one occasion of a medical response team stepping onto my bus with weary bemusement: "Oh, it's Abdi. Here we go again. What's up, man?" Once I was shown a call sheet. "We've admitted this guy to Harborview 32 times in the last two months," the aid responder chuckled ruefully. You'd overhear the fire department, cops, and ambulance drivers working it out amongst each other: "Can you guys take him to a different hospital tonight? Please? Somewhere way out in the South End? We don't wanna do this again tomorrow, and it's not like we have room . . ."

They didn't want another situation where somebody's grandmother was dying, or somebody's kid was getting shot, and resources weren't available because of this. But what can you do? All you can do is Step Three, which is drive Abdirahim to a nice, warm hospital bed, where he can sleep off the alcohol away from the elements, get a free meal and a fresh change of clothes before being sent on his way to do it all over again. It didn't matter what hospital they took him to. He'd be back in Chinatown in eighteen hours.

Admit it. The man's got this game figured out. While others in his condition are drinking themselves stiff to avoid feeling cold, or killing themselves with drugs they thought would only numb the pain, Abdirahim's on another level. He's in a climate-controlled room with free care, food, clothes, and attention. He's way past them in enterprising ingenuity.

Yes, he may be the most expensive person in King County, and yes, it would *actually* be cheaper to set him up in a one-bedroom apartment and pay market rates for his rent, instead of what we all chip in for his Three-Step method . . . but ethics are a privilege of those who are doing well. His mandate is to survive, and he prefers sleeping inside to sleeping outside. He prefers hot food to scraps, clean clothes to dirty ones, friendly nurses to angry strangers, being chauffeured to struggling . . . and don't you? *Wouldn't you*? Survival is necessarily a selfish act. Abdirahim found the paradox of generosity, the loophole of our flawed systems, and he *milked* it. Someone had to. May as well have been the friendliest drunk on the West Coast.

He married his childhood sweetheart at the age of seventeen. He's a US citizen and proud of it. He's a sweetheart himself, and never once got angry on my watch, which I find staggering when I consider how much frustration must daily be thrown his way. He's gone through hardships worse than this. I think of other men I know, ex-child soldiers from Central Africa who now don't have to kill people, who can instead while away their days drinking with friends who understand them; no money, sure, but no responsibility, no more evil. If that's not an upgrade, I don't know what is.

You never know the full story.

Abdirahim started life over on the other side of the planet, in a strange land that works to keep Black people uneducated, unemployed, angry, and imprisoned. I once read five personal essays by adult immigrant students at Shoreline College. They were from various countries in Asia, East Africa, and Northern Europe. By coincidence, all five separately mentioned an identical observation in each of their essays. The wording varied, but the meaning was the same: *I never thought about my race much, nor had it impacted my life to any meaningful degree . . . until I moved to the US.* We are the land of unspoken mysteries, and our unsolved problems are cover-ups for other problems. In a place like this, you tread water because it works.

All systems are taken advantage of by a percentage of their users, and that percentage is always going to be smaller than the benefit that system reaps for those who really need it. Do we abolish voting because it is sometimes fraudulent? Do we suppress compassion because it is sometimes abused?

I don't. The only valuable thing I have to give at the end of the day . . . is, well, love. I get more out of trying to be good than the opposite. It's gotten me in trouble before, believe me, and it'll likely happen again; but I am all I can offer.

And Abdirahim is more than he let on during his Three-Step years. He's clever, and clever people eventually need more. Should I have been surprised when, after a long absence, he reappeared on my 120 *and got off partway through the route*? You have to understand: non-destination passengers always ride to the end of the line, because they're not going anywhere. If you get off somewhere along the line, it means you have an actual plan. He got off *like he was going someplace*, with paperwork in hand that looked important, wearing clothes that weren't soiled, torn, or stained. He wasn't drooling any more than I was. And he now had two perfectly functioning eyes.

It was a revelation.

That was a year ago. He's the very same now—sober, neatly groomed, gradually fading from the memories of an ocean of public service responders. I hope they discover how well he's turned out, because Abdirahim's rehabilitation represents one of the most genuinely shocking reversals I've seen on the street. I do see people turn their lives around, but I never would've guessed him. Abdi? The guy whom I (with his consent) once bodily dragged from the bus onto the sidewalk and into some bushes while wearing dishwashing gloves, who was once so plastered he stood a foot away from my face and innocently yelled, “Do you have eyes?”

Perhaps I should’ve known from that smile of his, and the razor-sharp memory that could always slur my name correctly. *Mister Nathan,* he’d say, with a twinkle in his eye. Maybe that twinkle knew what beauty the future held.

We look for miracles because we would like to believe in goodness. We would enjoy learning of proofs that render our hopes valid, make worthy our faith. I can think of no greater miraculous validation of the possibility of human growth, progression of the soul and body, persistent resilience, and rebirth of the best in ourselves . . . than Abdirahim, Version 2020, chatting me up on Jackson Street, the two of us the most sober people on the block right now.

Miracles do happen. Sometimes they are absolutely and unimaginably massive. This is what they look like.

A man walking up the sidewalk with clean clothes and a smile.

THE VETERINARIAN

Summer 2019

He started, quietly. A grizzled look about this fellow; he had the air you carry after you've been traveling.

"I just wanna say I appreciate your attitude."

"Aw thanks, man!"

"We need more of that, you know?"

"Thank you," I said. "One person at a time, right? I feel like my arms reach this far, and it's within here that I can effect change."

Agreeably: "Well, I think it's a little bigger than that."

"Yeah, you're right. Paying it forward. How was your day?"

"Mostly fine."

"Cool! Same."

He said, "I've been trying to be more mindful of when I say good and bad, basically trying to cut those out of my vocabulary. Dualities."

"That's smart. You know—okay. So I grew up in a Korean household, and my parents both speak Korean. But for the longest time I never knew the Korean word for 'no,' and the reason is because usually you never need to say that word. You don't have to directly contradict people."

"Wow," he replied, taking it in. "I like that."

"Yeah. 'Cause if they say something that's obviously wrong, like 'the sky is red,' you can say something like, 'sometimes it looks red.' Or, 'I think it looks blue.' You don't have to, like, bulldoze them, you know what I mean?"

"Do you have any philosophy or faith system you subscribe to?"

"You know . . . I don't know. That's the most truthful answer I can give. The longer I'm alive, I feel like the less I know how the world works, so mostly these days I just try to listen."

"That's cool," he said. "Listening is better anyways. Faith systems . . . that's just what we resort to when we don't understand something."

"Okay fascinating! I'm gonna have to write that down!"

It was a pleasant exchange and unexpectedly candid, born out of the years of who we were. It brought me up. But.

I had no idea how differently this conversation would sit in my memory five minutes from now. Because right now everything was still okay. We were another Tuesday evening rush hour, coursing down 35th passing Edmunds, no big deal. It was the gentle cluelessness of life before tragedy, when everything was still possible, when you could chuckle about topics like this without your heart collapsing.

That morning, I had woken up with the line. The sentence came to my mind as I lay there, unbidden, and again in the morning shower. I don't sing in the shower; I think. But today I felt as though the line was thinking *me*, a slow dance to and fro, and I tried to touch it, testing out different tones, ways of saying it and how, all in silence. It was a simple line, but it managed to be a sequence of words I'd not heard before. Even alone it was slightly too powerful to say out loud.

What did it refer to?

I wrapped it up in my pocket and kept it to myself, venturing about my duties. These are the tiny thoughts that compose most of human existence, the diamond slivers of contemplation we don't realize form who we are.

As the hours wore on the day relaxed into itself, and I forgot the sentence. I headed into the evening, into West Seattle, driving an uneventful 21. The 21 is always uneventful. I picked up commuters and dropped off commuters, not minding the pleasant reverie brought on by such repetition.

Sort of meditative, this.

I was lifted from my dream state into pleasant wakefulness by an old route 7 passenger: short guy, mixed-race fifties with a killer singing soprano, respected by the street hoods who hang outside Franklin, but always a little less drunk, a little less high, a little more put together than my other buddies there. Isaac. He had recently moved to West Seattle to "get away from all that mess" on Rainier. I felt comforted seeing a familiar face here in the wilds of High Point and intimated so by way of greeting.

"Hey, my guy!! What's been up?"

Isaac mumbled. " . . . my daughter this morning."

"Wait," I said, indicating I hadn't understood.

"I left my daughter this morning."

"You *left* her?"

"I *lost* her," he said again, and this time I followed. "She died."

We take a moment so we can feel things. I paused.

He is so small right now. All the world and its people leave me for a moment, vanish from my psyche. There is just Isaac and I, privately, broken men speaking in quiet voices. I reach my hand out to his, shaking it, firm. Then his earlier sentence hits me, in combination with his most recent words: *this morning*.

Must feel like years ago.

I pulled him in for a hug. We held each other for a while, standing there on a city bus at southbound 35th and Morgan, with a crowd of people onboard. I didn't care.

Why do terrible things happen to you, who are good?

So that when they happen to others, you can be there, and they can feel you being there.

"God, I am so sorry. I am so . . . God," I said, with primal disappointment. "Oh, my God. This *morning*?"

"She was fifteen years old." Isaac continued as we drove away. "She's walkin' down the street this AM, when somebody rode up shooting, she got caught in the crossfire . . ."

"God," I said again, surprising myself. I'm used to saying "gosh," out of respect for my believing friends. Is it really blasphemy, though, when your lot feels this cosmically vacant? Some days I believe in God, and some days I don't. But friend, have you been to that third place, not in between those two perspectives but beyond them? Where you're so devastated that neither is a comfort? Some of us have been thrust there, and it's never by choice. That's where he and I stood now.

"Man. I am so sorry. Stuff like that I just keep askin' why."

"Exactly," he murmured.

"'Cause there's no explanation, there's literally no reasonable expl—"

"Yeah. She's . . . I'm *good* to people. I don't never mistreat none of the guys."

"You're *great* people, man, I know!" I exclaimed. "I seen you around, you're always great. People love you, they respect you."

"Ah just can't even understand a thing like this."

"Fifteen years old."

He answered with silence. I agreed, saying, "This world, sometimes."

"Right now I jus' don't know what to think, or how. I don't know if ah wanna . . ." Isaac stopped short, even in his hardship now, he stopped just short of saying it. *Continue*. At his weakest, he was still strong enough to stay away from there. Revising his thought: "Well, ah just don't know."

In the space where there are no solutions, I decided to ask him about what really mattered. "Well. I'ma be thinkin' about you. Hey, what was the last conversation you and her had? What d'you guys talk about?"

"We were, we were." Thinking back. "She's thinkin' about, she's gonna become a veterinarian."

"Brother, you're gonna make me cry." I felt a tickle in the back of my brain and reached out for his hand again. A woman getting off, and he moved aside— "Excuse me, ma'am—"

"You coming home?" she asked. They must be neighbors. It was his stop too.

"Hey," I said. "I'm glad I got to see you today."

"It's an honor to see you today, man."

"I'm a be thinking about you."

"Say some prayers for me."

"You know I will."

He crossed, heading over to the gas station. Lonely on the parking lot, the kind of place you don't recall even as it's happening. Especially now.

What will I remember of my thirties? I will remember holding him amidst an impatient crowd and indifferent traffic, us two strangers united in pain. I will remember him walking up to that Chevron, nerve-naked and abandoned. I should've told him to take care of himself. Don't drink yourself to oblivion, buddy. Not like some of these other guys. I should've asked if he has good people around him.

I realized then I had spoken the line I'd woken up with. *Brother, you're gonna make me cry*. It had come to me unbeknownst; I've never thought that sentence before. But because I did earlier today, because I'd turned it over in my mind, I knew *exactly* how to say it tonight. How to tense it into something that cut deep and true, that could touch his bone-bare soul softly, just right. The look in Isaac's eyes: *well, at least somebody cares. A lot.* I knew the moment before the present came to be.

What does that mean?

You have to let them talk about whatever they need to talk about. Especially when the last time you saw them the conversation went *there*. Sometimes the best way to address grief is to ponder something else for a spell; time is the preeminent healer, and while we wait around for it to give us some perspective, maybe chit-chatting about selling your record collection isn't the worst idea.

That's what was on Isaac's mind tonight, a week after the world ended. Some people cut their hair off. Others wear black for a year. For Isaac, music and cleaning house were the healthy distraction he needed. We rolled down a moonlit First Avenue together, approaching the rise toward West Seattle Bridge.

"My daddy though, he got more vinyl than me even, he got a

stack like from here to here. Original stuff like I got, too. Stevie Wonder—"

I interrupted. I'm a sentimentalist. "Man, you got Stevie Wonder? You sure you wanna sell those?"

Pragmatically: "Iss for my grandson's tuition."

"Okay, that's cool. Good cause."

"Yup yup. I got the Temptations, the Dramatics—"

"The Temptations! Oh I love that! Their sound, you know?"

"Lemme ask you somethin', check this. Is there any sound better than The Temptations?"

Somehow this led to us cresting the bridge's high rise with him singing. He was great. "I'm half Black half Italian," he reminded me, alluding to a musically inclined upbringing, but I didn't need the reminder. It was right there in his voice. I was listening to Pavarotti croon "Ain't Too Proud to Beg," and it would've been magical even without the unspoken knowledge of what we both knew: that this enthusiasm was but the feeble cover for an open wound, each moment a marathon hurdle of improvisation, the desperate search for a salve that never lasts more than a few minutes. He was doing the smartest thing available: taking on the challenge of fighting pain with joy. The harder thing and the right thing, as ever, are often the same.

I knew from Little Leon the value of song at times like this and let him ride the melody out. Our conversation drifted. He may have had the electric soul of Pavarotti's voice but rather a little less of the man's philandering habits; I was privy to a monologue wherein Isaac explained that sleeping with his ex, his son's mother, was "just too messy." It was Ibsen by way of Tarantino.

"Listen. I go over there and him and me play video games. We like to siddown and stay up late. And she be there. She leavin' the door open to her room, crossin' the hallway in her underwear. Lookin' sexy as hell. But I don't go there. I'm not trying to say she ain't sexy as hell. She is sexy as hell. She know she got it. But I'm tryna peep the long term. Iss about keeping it simple. Keeping it friends, respectful, easy, what I can go over there and kick it with my boy, kick it with her without no . . ."

"Soap opera drama?"

"Exactly. Without no soap opera drama. It just gets too messy that way!"

"Stayin' on good terms sounds all right, especially 'cause they're always gonna be part of your life, him and her."

"Yeah." *Yeeeeah.* He switched course suddenly. Maybe the future was too much to think about. Because thinking about the future usually means thinking about the past.

"I'm goin' to Brazil," he said.

"What?"

"Yeah man, I need a vacation. I'm cool though."

"I'm glad you're takin' care of yourself, some of these guys something like that happens they just fall apart out here. I been thinking about our last conversation, man, and my heart's still broke."

"I got love for everyone I meet," Isaac replied, without missing a beat. "I ain't mad at nobody. That's what I respect about you, Nate. Iss an honor. I love, I've always loved, and I ain't gon' stop now. I love hard. Listen." He leaned in, conspiratorially. "I done talked to the guy who did it. To mah daughter."

"Bro."

I slowed down. I needed to hear every word.

"He said, 'I apologize.' Ah said, 'I need you to look at my daughter. I need you to go look at my daughter. And I want you to take her some flowers. And I want you to put some money in those flowers.' And he said, 'okay.' And he did. He put a hunnerd fifty and a bunch of dark chocolates and everything else up in those flowers. The point is, he meant it. He came and looked at her. He said, 'I apologize.' He said 'Mr. Santoro, I heard you're full-blooded Italian.' I said, 'that don't matter. Iss the principle. I ain't no violent man. But if you come at my family sideways again, I'm gon' run up on your whole house and that ain't no joke. I ain't no violent man. But I need you to go look at my daughter's eyes, bruh.' And he did. I ain't mad at nobody. Ah got love, and I love hard."

This wasn't Ibsen, or Faulkner, or August Wilson, or anybody. It had no conscious design or intended moral. It was simply and crucially *existence*, and it was up to us to make it significant, to tie the present to our past as we choose, and thus give it meaning. This is the advantage life has over art. But it's also what's terrifying about life: you have to *decide* what it means. And all the while the clouds above keep rolling by, silently.

They will never tell you if you're right or wrong.

About four months passed. I was talking to someone I'd never seen before. She was like a river, the way her words tumbled out. In the same way that you never remember how a dream began, only that you're suddenly there, I have no recollection of how this all started.

She wasn't on the bus until at some point she was, and now she told me not what was on her mind, but what was on her heart. An officer outside had been hassling a Black man, and I'd made an observation; something about life being complicated and difficult.

"Well the police took my son, my nephew got shot, my second cousin she just got kilt, and two of my grandsons died before they time."

I sighed. "Wow. You're breakin' my heart in all kinds of places."

"But I got to be thankful," she replied, immediately, voicing it not as an unwelcome task, but as though it were the most obvious common sense in existence. She continued, breathless and optimistic: "I know I was born to die, but we're here for a short time and I know I gotta recognize all that's beautiful and count my blessings. I'm so blessed and so fortunate every day o' my born life. I could tell you got a beautiful kind soul too and that's good on you, what's your name, my name is Phyllis May Walker."

"Miz Walker, my name's Nathan, but lemme tell you, you got the most positive, beautiful, inspirational attitude of anyone I've met. I'm bein' serious now."

"I love you and your spirit. Lemme off right here, that's my cousin."

Totally unaffected, like isn't this how everyone goes through tragedy? She was eager and ebullient even in the toughest of times, as if the bounty of life was too good to be true and how could we possibly handle it, how could we possibly *process* how lucky we are. I was reminded of a child in a sandbox, or a naturalist in a greenhouse. But the difference was she could do this when things were *not* going well. Her chips were down hard, and some would never rise. And yet.

Wonder is a special thing. It's different from awe—surprise and admiration commingled with enthusiasm, not fear. It requires humility. You can't be world-weary, seen-it-all snobbish . . . *and* marvel at existence, because at the end of the day wonder is thankfulness, cloaked in the puzzled absorption of youthful discovery. Maybe the know-it-all route feels safer sometimes, but I say we wouldn't know what we were missing. I thought back to the traveler who started this story, and his question about faith systems.

Are joy and wonder among our seeds of belief? "If God did not exist, it would be necessary to invent him," Voltaire wrote. Maybe because doing so is such a natural response to the impossibly intricate, interconnected beauty of life and nature. You feel like a louse just sitting there calling it coincidence.

But all that is secondary, part of the human urge to get distracted by Why and How, diving into comprehension rather than experience. Phyllis embodied her perception with mystifying ease: despite her hardships, she could somehow still feel—generate—goodness all around.

Her cousin stepped toward the bus upon recognizing me, and she went over to hug him. Each knew me separately, and simultaneously tried to introduce me to the other.

"He a great guy, good driver."

"Yeah, he's a cool cat."

Her cousin was Isaac, the grieving, singing father, who loved hard. Things were falling into place.

Phyllis's attitude made her beautiful, and Isaac reflected that beauty now. She was the kind of woman people talk about. I'm not referring to appearance. I mean that she, by sheer force of genuine, charismatic personhood, made everyone around her believe they were having a good day. Some of us radiate energy; others are receptive, listening attentively. I could see that Phyllis was both. She and others like her make you ask yourself, *why seek greatness, when goodness is so much more?* She awakened your better angels without your even realizing, your belief in hope, and I saw him transform. Their hug was one of awareness and understanding and uncomplicated love. I needn't have worried, earlier; Isaac did indeed have good people around him. People who helped him know the best way to fight emotions . . . is with other emotions. With love. Because the antidote to despair is never reason.

It's gratitude.

ALONZO RISING

6/8/19

We've grown accustomed to requiring a certain dose of cynicism in our fictions in order to find them believable. "Few people have the imagination for reality," Goethe wrote. Truth is different from fiction in that fiction has to be plausible. Truth does not.

I begin with these thoughts because I want you to know it really did happen. We have become, perhaps, necessarily blasé in our reaction to endless depictions of extremes; but what about that which is *happy*? Doesn't that equally warrant our interest and respect?

Readers of my first book will recall Alonzo, he of the indefatigable attitude, whose welfare and appearance I watched gradually wane over a period of years. He worked at a library, then as a custodian, then selling *Real Change*, until all was reduced to the disappointed present, passed out in a bus shelter, a shadow of his earlier good days. I'd included the story partly as a dare to the reader—to what?

To believe. Half of us think things won't work out. And the other half . . . believe in magic.

A friend and I were walking to the neighborhood post office with a handful of packages. In each package was a signed copy of my book, and in each book was, of course, the Alonzo story. He came to mind because the guy outside the post office resembled him.

Wait a second.

Could it be? Was that him? Standing there by the main doors, the same but different, as ever with the big smile? But look how put-together he is now. Yes, he was still selling *Real Change*, but he was doing it looking *sharp*. The dreads clean and fresh, no debris therein nor on his clothing—a trademark collection of black beanie, black carpenters, black sweatshirt, hooded of course, with shoes I forgot to notice, so powerfully did his effervescent grin offset his outfit, which another man might wear without knowing the first thing about how to make it as approachable, personable, and downright endearing as Alonzo did. *Clean* was clearly the word of the day. Spotless. His pride of self and belief in life were palpable, risen back up to the best moments of my first knowing him, and beyond. Certainly his attitude must have played a role in his recovery? How could that not be, honestly? Makes you wonder sometimes, how much control we may have in tipping things into being . . .

The building was just opening for the day, and a small crowd had gathered, the early birds with letters and packages. I could see that he had put in the effort, like I try for, to be known and loved by the community. The friendly neighborhood stalwart. They knew him and they smiled, never mind that they were North Seattle White, and he was a poor Black man on the corner. I saw real enthusiasm in their interactions, and several knew him by name. I thought of Tyrell, being kind when he didn't have to be, helping a person he wasn't expecting to help. This is where we start, in the massive undertaking of correcting history's wrongs. By tending to the living.

"Alonzo," I called out sharply, mock-serious, and he turned. He turned, he saw, and he exploded. Pure joy, reader. This man on this corner, today. This was the face and name of jubilation. How did he *still know my name*, all these years later? I'm surprised enough when people recognize me out of uniform, let alone remember my name a half-decade on, and on the far side of town to boot.

Our small talk was the conversation to end all small talk. Our "how you been doin'" and "man it's good to see you" exchanges were overflowing with so much love, surprise, respect . . . it must have looked ridiculous from the outside. Comical. But you know the feeling. My shock had mostly to do with the fact that my hopes as written five years ago could *actually have come true*. That this world had room for him to rise again.

After a chat my friend and I went inside to mail our packages. No, I didn't tell him about my book, or how much his story means to me. Let me find the right time for that. *This* was more important, what was going on now—not depictions or documentations of life but Life, the burgeoning immediate present of *his* accomplishments, not mine.

I was struck by an air which seemed to be affecting everyone. Something magical about this place. When did you last see the staff *happy* at a post office? The spry older woman in charge, who steered our small talk into what she loved about her job, calling out to customers she knew, speaking of the day's hardships—being understaffed, mainly—with a voice that knew there's more to life than complaining. People chatted amongst each other, chuckling, even a pat on the shoulders here and there. Others walked out past Alonzo, wishing him well all over again. He eagerly waved them on with a grin that restarted the whole experience.

Was I asleep?

Had I been dreaming? If this was in a movie we wouldn't believe it. If Nathan dreamt of a post office, then yes, this is what it would look like. But it was no dream, no movie. Only in life could something as absurd as a happy post office wherein the customers standing in line, the overworked staff, and the street person out front are all having the time of their lives at 08:00 on a weekday. This was the post office as fairy tale, community big and bright as life.

A cynic might roll their eyes, insisting something has to be wrong here. But let us remember Lukas's words: realists are forever doomed to mediocrity, because they lack the necessary naïveté to believe in the possibility of great things. They lack the requisite capacity to imagine. A realist wouldn't even notice that this building was on fire, in the best way. A realist wouldn't notice, elsewhere in town and nine years after I talked with him about his partner's suicide—Marlow. Marlow, beaming as he boarded my bus in April

2024, introducing the woman at his side as his girlfriend, Sarah. I saw their glowing joy and especially his, knowing what he once suffered, as the heroic, towering achievement it was. He and Alonzo embodied what my parents taught me from day one: you have to generate your own happiness, from scratch, within.

Anything else is a setup for failure.

IT'S ABOUT WHO'S AROUND

10/10/20

"Is that mah boy?"

"Jooohn! What's goin' on! Been a long time!"

In the days of COVID, pleasantries had to be yelled. John had entered through the middle door and now stood by it, just behind the temporary Velcro strap encouraging passengers to keep distance from the operator.

We went on like that for a bit, catching up. But right in the middle of it he hit me with the news:

"Hey I just got outta th' hospital. I got cancer, man."

"Cancer, that's terrible! John!"

"Yeah, I got cancer." He said it as though he was trying out the truth of the phrase, seeing how it molded to his reality. Remember the early moments of your traumas, when there seemed a chance they might not be true?

"I got cancer. They said I drink too much."

He ducked under the Velcro strap, carefully, to come closer. The last time someone did that, as you recall, I got spat on. But we have to remember these lives out here have nothing to do with each other. One night someone will scare you, and the next night another man who looks the same, talks the same, dresses (and maybe even smells) the same—will help you when no one else will. I thought of the accident with Alicia, and reminded myself: *if someone saves your life, they will probably be a stranger.*

But back to John, the fifty-something Latino and fixture on Rainier whom readers of my first book will remember. From one angle, he was another alcoholic breaking the rules on a Wednesday night. For me, he was a friend with whom I shared a history, because of whom my life was richer.

"Yeah man," he said, "I weigh 140 pounds. I used to be 235."

"Oh, no. One forty? That's what I weigh! One forty, 145 . . ."

"Yeah, doctor said I only got two months to live."

"*What*? John, this is *heavy*! Two months?! That cancer's no joke."

"Yeah they said two months."

I was so glad he came up. He came closer because you can't be sensitive from far away. What do you say to two months left to live? I was taught to think before speaking and usually do, but in this moment my body led the charge. My soul cut in, interrupting with the only words that could work, with a verve I was surprised by.

"Two months? Man, you' be around longer than that."

It was a feeling more than a thought, and that subliminal part of me spoke now with enormous confidence, complete belief in itself. I, who knows cancer kills people, who knows the very concept of "beating cancer" is sometimes nothing but cruel advertising, that cancer often comes back, that trying to tear it up tears you up too—*that* me somehow believed itself when it said:

"You got this."

"I'm gonna beat it."

"You are gonna beat it."

I believe hope in the face of certain failure is still beautiful. I do not know why this is.

"I'm 'onna beat it. Doctor said two months, ah say no way. Fuck that."

"Two months, more like two decades!"

"I'm gonna beat that cancer."

"You been through tougher stuff than this."

"Tha's right."

"I'ma be pickin' you up ten years from now, just like I was ten years ago."

As soon as we had made our own glow, it dissipated. Reality set in, and I was thankful he could share its weight with me.

John the tough guy. Boisterous. Fighter. Comic. Friend. John stared into the middle distance, staring forward as only a passenger in a vehicle can. He said, "I'm sad, man. It's sad."

"It is sad."

"I was 235 pounds. Now I'm 140."

"That's crazy."

"They're givin' me liquid morphine. They give me a bottle a week."

"Man, I bet you can't feel anything."

"Nothin,' man. I only got two months left. They kicked me outta my apartment."

"Man, that's heavy. I'm sorry, dude. Now's the time to hang out with good people. See your family, you know? Maybe you'll beat it, but either way, you wanna have good people around you. You still see Valerie?" His longtime partner.

John was lost in thought. "I stay behind that church there. Hey listen Nate, I hate havin' to ask you like this, but could you spot me any change? Get somethin' to—"

"Aw man, you know I don't carry money when I'm workin'."

"I know, It's cool. Hey man, it's always good to see you. I'ma get out right here." He cracked a grin. "Don't cut your hair! And stop beatin' people up!"

There was an echo in his tone, the enthusiasm you expend with great effort in the final moments, covering up the realization that you might never see your listener again. That was how John spoke now. He'd decided humor was the note to end on.

Good man.

An hour later I would see him, though, with Valerie at his side. More than once during the ride she'd tell me it's always good to see me. Finality had crept into our interactions. It encourages sincerity, goodness, truth. She helped John as he moved, slowly, slurringly ("I'm not gon' lie, Nate, I'm drunk right now!"), down the aisle with a tender gait as never before. I thought of the sillier times: him coming up to the door of my bus one afternoon and stopping in mock fright, proclaiming, "Nathan! Who did that to your hair?!"

"I know, I know, I had to get it cut! It was gettin' outta control!"

"You tell me who did that and I'll send 'em straight to Jesus!!"

I laughed. He'd said, "You gotta get those curls back, bro, like mine. We're like twins. Oh hey, I saw you walkin' the other day. You know how to walk?!"

"Ha!"

Tonight he was moving slower, but he was still John. They sat in the middle of the bus and struck up a conversation with two friendly compatriots and a dog. I couldn't hear them, but their arms and smiles said it all—gestures of togetherness among strangers, dog stories, traveling stories, communion found in exchanging the breeze. I marveled at Valerie and John's stalwart presence in each other's lives, particularly now as they faced the finish line. A kindness in their camaraderie tonight.

In the last days things will not be perfect. There will be pain, shame, unfulfilled dreams. Your favorite people won't all be there. But that's okay. It's not about that.

It's about whoever happens to be around.

Have a good time with them. Let them bring you up. Wave your arms in the air like John is now, telling another story, listening and laughing, making the most of the in-between moments; a post-sunset bus ride on a forgotten weekday, spent in the company of strangers and friends.

That's what living is.

REFLECTIVE

12/31/18

You remember the Deca Hotel. It stood there for eighty-six years, at 45th and Brooklyn, northwest corner.

The appropriately named venue had a lobby that must've made many an interior designer pause; for though they may have traveled far and wide, no room has ever had a greater variety of Art Deco-themed chairs. High-backed affairs with an African inspiration. Seats that looked like a musician's snare drum. Gold-trimmed arthropodic monstrosities from the fashion school that tries hard to be uncomfortable. It all bordered on ridiculous but achieved a certain warmth in its inclusive chaos, a welcoming coherence born of balanced disparities.

Doesn't that describe my 7/49 route to an exact tee?

No wonder I felt at home. Look at this hodgepodge, charm and creativity all sourced from the same period—jazz, bookcases, fireplaces: America the modern, counting time between World Wars.

For nearly five uninterrupted years driving the nighttime 7/49, I took my breaks in the Deca Hotel lobby if there was time. It was a breather both from, and of a piece with, the inherent ridiculousness of that route. The storied airs of Broadway and Rainier, chaotic, colorful, often absurd . . . naturally ending in an immaculate art deco time warp with a warm fire. Of course. It was just outlandish enough to make perfect sense, and I loved it.

I'd stretch out with a book from their color-coordinated shelves, or more often sprawl out with an eye toward the high ceilings, neither reading much nor thinking, just *being*, drifting off the focused high of driving and public engagement. Taking in the dulcet Eurotrance tunes, a piped-in tinny melancholy you associate with all-night settings, airports and cleaning crews and vacant reception desks.

I loved the conflation of sensations I'd feel. Exhausted, but pleasant; the shoulder aches fading away, blood returning to my calves. Echoes of recent conversation floating in memory. The warm fire, just the homey anachronism I needed to compliment the jungled urban night. Often the timing had me in there for a brief spell only: ten minutes, frequently five. But here there was room to breathe, and I'd be remiss if I didn't heed the advice of an Eastern European novel about a maid I opened up in there one night, whose title and author I've long forgotten, but a line from which I hold close to my heart as a maxim:

"She took life as it came, and made the best of it."

My eyes would wander up and out over the lobby, living in the raised ceilings and top-to-bottom wall mirrors. I saw myself as if from above.

The question was never, *Why did I live*?

The question is, *What am I going to do about it*?

I'll be older someday. I'll be older, and I'll drift back to this moment, these nights. The cluttered high-flying days of youth, and the peace we here and there managed to grab hold of. I used to drive city buses in the middle of the night by choice, I'll think to myself. And I took my breaks in the lobby of the Deca Hotel.

I will look back on these fresh-faced days in all their strife and color, and know myself enough to know that I will name them as some of the happiest days of my life.

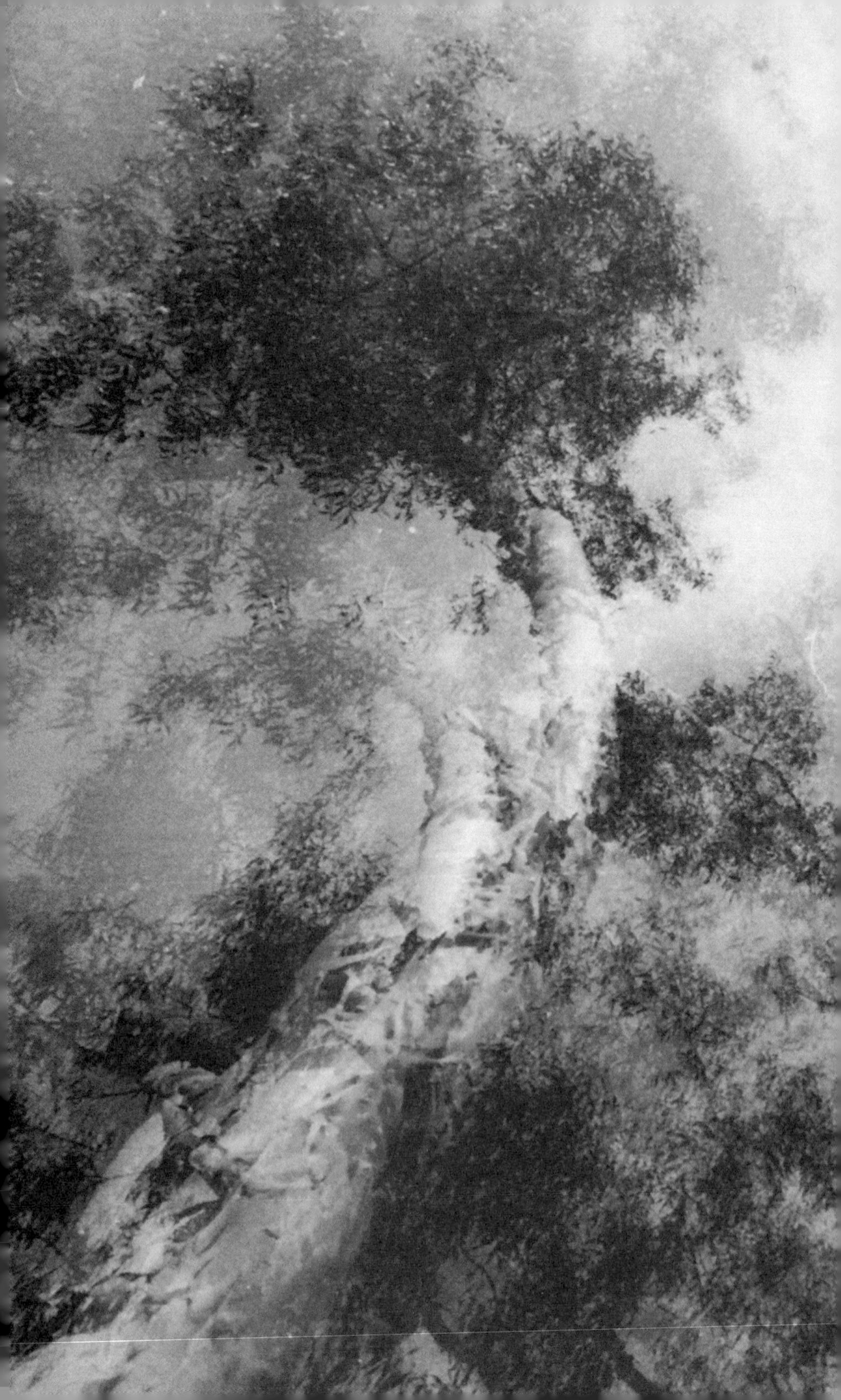

EPILOGUE: YVES KLEIN, COLOR OF THE HEAVENS

6/18/19

Ideas linger longer on summer nights, and so too do memories. They reach deeper, the gentle hothouse surge of our past coming forth, that much closer to touch.

As children we looked upward more. We saw objects and people as monuments, looming large. Is it any surprise that silhouettes still catch our eye, standing tall against the quiet blue dome? That's the child inside. Our default was wonder then, an attitude separate from fear and joy. Look at any infant's face. In their gaze is everything and nothing, the purest essence of how to see, frequently unlearned over life but never completely forgotten.

Tonight the 7 emptied out early, and I drove the Prentice Street neighborhood loop alone. Magic hour is always beautiful, but there's a specific moment within those golden minutes when everything comes together. It is less a visual highlight than an interior shift, an awakening.

Here was a smattering of companions in the neighborhood square, an extended family maybe, sitting outside post-dinner on stoops, lawn chairs, kids playing on grass and pavement. A little Vietnamese girl with a fluorescent green glowstick worn as a necklace around her chest: could she have known just such a glowstick lived in my memory, on an evening with these same colors, when I was her age? The park of my youth was lit similarly to this small plaza, with white fluorescents for the baseball fields, kind of eerie but kind of festive. I remember cracking into brightness the glowstick my parents gave me and gazing up at the stadium lights exactly as I now looked upon the streetlamps and telephone poles, noting the contrast between their uniform dark shade and the soft gradient of post-sunset light behind them.

I turned the corner from Prentice to 64th, high on a hill in the quiet suburbs of old Seattle, land falling away to the east-northeast, the panorama of Lake Washington and Bellevue sitting pink and blue in the vast evening air.

Look at those hues, a voice inside me said. I slowed to a stop. The sky was the color of childhood, yellow fading upward into evening indigo, the golden yellow orange that shifts imperceptibly into Yves Klein blue without a hint of green, as only sky can do. Look at that pink wisp of a cotton ball cloud with the light blue contrasting behind it. Lower down, the telephone poles again, silhouetted by pale gold.

The only thing more exquisite than a sunset is the period after a sunset. It is in those moments, when light is becoming a shared memory, that the aforementioned moment of clarity takes place. It doesn't happen every night, and it's unrelated to how beautiful the sunset is. But deep inside a certain sometime, you'll feel a silent whisper coursing through your soul, warmly. It is made up of two things:

That part after a sunset which feels oddly like a predawn sunrise, the time before the world starts, when every aspect of existence is drenched with possibility . . .

And the pathos of fading twilight, a comforting darkness, but tinged with death and endings and the enveloping finality of all things.

There is a moment when it makes sense to mix these moods, to feel that they might in some strange way be the same. That the concept of growth, trajectory, sequence—*time*—requires both of the above; the first to give it shape, the second to give it dimension. In the quiet flash of occasional evenings, when twilight becomes dawn and no other time seems ever to have existed, for that brief glimpse of a moment . . . we understand, and a well-being courses through us like never before. It is, all of it, valuable. They are glorious and terrible, these two halves, and they are equally worthy and necessary and part of life. They add up to goodness.

We have all we need.

THE END